Adobe Photoshop
Creative Cloud 2017

Munishwar Gulati
B.E. (IIT Roorkee), A.M.I.E.,
CTO, ABES Engineering College
CEO, Siliconmedia Infocomm

Mini Gulati
B.E. (NIT, Bhopal)
CTO, Siliconmedia Infocomm

SILICON MEDIA PRESS
New Delhi

Contents

BASICS OF PHOTOSHOP

An electronic image can take almost any form such as a photograph, drawing, painting, etc. that has either been created using a computer or digitally "imaged" and stored in one of a number of popular graphic file formats.

There are many ways for you to get your photos onto the computer. You can retrieve photos from your hard disk, floppy diskette, digital camera, scanner, CD-Rom, or directly from the Internet. If necessary you can transfer them to digital format by scanning them. Select the photo that you want to use and follow the instructions provided with your scanner to scan them and save the photo to your hard drive or a floppy diskette.

An image can be represented in many forms, such as a painting, or a picture. In the computer world, an image is a collection of dots called "pixels" arranged in a rectangular grid of rows and columns. Each pixel is a specific colour. The number of possible colours in an image can vary from two to 16.7 million. The simplest type of image has only black and white pixels and is referred to as a "monochrome" image. "True colour" images can contain any of 16.7 million colours. In between you have images of 256 colours and 65,000 colours (High colour). The more about colours has been discussed in next section of this chapter.

FILE FORMATS

Images are stored in a variety of file formats. Many different image file formats have been developed over the years for specific applications and hardware. These include:

Windows Bitmap (BMP)

The Windows Bitmap file format is the standard file format used by Microsoft Windows. Bitmap files can contain either 2 (black and white), 16, 256, 65,000 or 16.7 million colours. Most Windows bitmap files are not compressed. It is possible to save 16 and 256 colour images in a compressed format but some applications (like Windows Paintbrush) are not able to read the compressed files.

The default file extension for Windows Bitmap files is ".BMP". Occasionally you may see bitmap files with the extension ".DIB".

Windows Run-Length Encoded (RLE)

The RLE format is a variation of the Windows BMP format that offers a modest degree of image compression. It can be used to create compressed wallpaper files and it can be used to replace the opening Windows logo screen with a file of your own choosing. RLE files are always either 16 or 256 colour image files.

The default file extension, for Windows RLE Bitmap files, is ".RLE".

CompuServe Graphics Interchange Format (GIF)

The GIF file format was developed by CompuServe Inc. for use on their on-line service. GIF files are colour-mapped files that can have anywhere from 2 to 256 colours. There are two versions named 87a and 89a of GIF standard. GIF files are always compressed and offer an efficient way to store large images.

The default file extension, for CompuServe Graphics Interchange Format files, is ".GIF".

Joint Photographic Experts Group (JPG)

The JPEG format uses a method of compression that reduces image file size by selectively reducing the amount of detail contained in the image and by transforming the image data into a format that is better suited for compression. Images with fewer details compress extremely well, while pictures with a high degree of random detail do not compress as well, or suffer some degree of image degradation.

At lower values you will experience better compression, but with a marked loss of image quality. JPEG images are either true colour or grayscale (256 shades of gray).

The default file extension, for JPEG files, is ".JPG".

Photoshop Format

Photoshop format (PSD) is the default file format and the only format, besides the Large Document Format (PSB), that supports all Photoshop features. All the Adobe products such as Adobe Illustrator, Adobe InDesign, Adobe Premiere, Adobe After Effects, and Adobe GoLive are tightly integerated and can directly import PSD files while preserving many Photoshop features.

You can save 16-bits-per-channel and high dynamic range (HDR) 32-bits-per-channel images as PSD files.

FlashPix (FPX)

A FlashPix file contains the complete image plus several smaller copies, all within the same file. This has the advantage of producing high-quality printouts using the higher resolutions, along with fast image manipulation by using the smaller resolutions for screen display. Images at each resolution are also divided into tiles, which enables the application to minimize the amount of data processed while accessing, displaying or printing a portion of the screen content.

Truevision Targa (TGA)

The Truevision Targa format was originally developed by Truevision Inc. for use with their line of graphic display cards. The Targa format is used by several high-end paint and CAD programs. colour resolutions range from 256 colour, 32768 (16-bit) colour, 24-bit true colour and 32-bit true colour formats. The 32-bit Targa format contains 24 bits of colour data as well as 8 bits of transparency (overlay) data. Targa images exist in both compressed and uncompressed formats.

The default file extension, for Targa files, is ".TGA".

PC Paintbrush (PCX)

PCX files were originally developed for Z-Soft's PC Paintbrush package. These files come in monochrome, 16 colour, 256 colour and true colour (24-bit) varieties. PCX files are compressed using a method that offers a modest degree of compression compared to other compression formats. The default file extension, for PC Paintbrush files, is ".PCX".

Tagged Image File Format (TIF)

The TIFF format was developed by Microsoft and Aldus Corporations as a portable method of storing bitmap images. TIFF files come in monochrome, 16-colour, 256-colour, 16-colour grayscale, 256-colour grayscale and true colour (24-bit) varieties.

TIFF files exist in both compressed and uncompressed formats. The compression format offers a high degree of compression. However, certain older paint programs that use an early version of the TIFF format may have difficulty reading compressed TIFF files. The default file extension, for TIFF files, is ".TIF".

Pegasus Image Corporation (PIC)

Pegasus Imaging Corporation's compression provides better standard JPEG image compression. PIC is a compressed image format that provides faster decompression, better colour handling and colour reduction.

Desktop Colour Separations (DCS)

Desktop colour Separations (DCS), developed by Quark, is a version of the standard EPS format. It lets you save color separations of CMYK images.

Photoshop EPS

The Encapsulated PostScript (EPS) language file format can contain both vector and bitmap graphics and is supported by virtually all graphic, illustration, and page-layout programs. EPS format supports Lab, CMYK, RGB, Indexed Color, Duotone, Grayscale, and Bitmap color modes, and does not support alpha channels. EPS does support clipping paths. To print EPS files, you must use a PostScript printer.

Photoshop RAW format

The Photoshop Raw format is a flexible file format for transferring images between applications and computer platforms. This format supports CMYK, RGB, and grayscale images with alpha channels, and multichannel and Lab images without alpha channels. Documents saved in the Photoshop Raw format can be of any pixel or file size, but they cannot contain layers.

The Photoshop Raw format consists of a stream of bytes describing the color information in the image. Each pixel is described in binary format, with 0 representing black and 255 white (for images with 16?bit channels, the white value is 65535). Photoshop designates the number of channels needed to describe the image, plus any additional channels in the image.

Radiance Format

Radiance (HDR) is a 32-bits-per-channel file format used for HDR images, often used in 3D modeling. This original format was developed for the Radiance system, a professional tool for visualizing lighting in virtual 3D environments. The file format stores the quantity of light per pixel instead of just the colors to be displayed onscreen. The levels of luminosity accommodated by the Radiance format are far higher than the 256 levels in 8-bits-per-channel image file formats.

Digital Negative Format

Digital Negative (DNG) is a file format that contains the raw image data from a digital camera and metadata that defines what the data means. DNG, Adobe's publicly available, archival format for camera raw files, is designed to provide compatibility and decrease the current proliferation of camera raw file formats.

EPS TIFF or EPS PICT Preview

These formats, which appear as options in the Open and Open As dialog boxes, let you open files saved in file formats that create previews but are not supported by Adobe Photoshop.

Filmstrip

The Filmstrip format is used for RGB animation or movie files created by Adobe Premiere®.

IFF

The Amiga™ Interchange File Format (IFF) is used for working with Video Toaster and transferring files to and from the Commodore Amiga system.

PDF

Portable Document Format (PDF) is used by Adobe Acrobat, Adobe's electronic publishing software for Windows, Mac OS, UNIX®, and DOS.

PICT File

The PICT format is widely used among Macintosh graphics and page-layout applications as an intermediary file format for transferring files between applications.

7

PIXAR

The PIXAR format is designed specifically for exchanging files with PIXAR image computers.

PNG

Developed as a patent-free alternative to GIF, the Portable Network Graphics (PNG) format is used for losslessly compressing and displaying images on the World Wide Web.

Scitex CT

The Scitex Continuous Tone (CT) format is used for high-end image processing on Scitex computers.

COLOURS

We all see colour and see it differently. colour is subjective to the human eye. Each device that interacts with your project's file: the scanner, monitor, and printer may have a different colour space. For example, a colour that is visible to the human eye may not be reproducible by your printer. Therefore we require a precise method for defining each colour. A colour model is a system used to organize and define colours according to a set of basic properties which are reproducible.

COLOUR MODEL

Various colour models are used to display and print documents. The established models for describing and reproducing colour include HSB (for hue, saturation, brightness); RGB (for red, green, blue); CMYK (for cyan, magenta, yellow, black); and CIE L*a*b*.

HSB Model

Based on the human perception of colour, the HSB model describes three fundamental characteristics of colour:

- Every object reflect few colour while transmit other colours. Hue is the colour reflected from or transmitted through an object. It is measured as a location on the standard colour wheel, expressed as a degree between 0° and 360°. In common use, hue is identified by the name of the colour such as red, orange, or green.

  To give each colour its proper position, the 360° is subdivided into six equal sectors, alternating primaries and secondaries: this is called the **"colour circle"**.

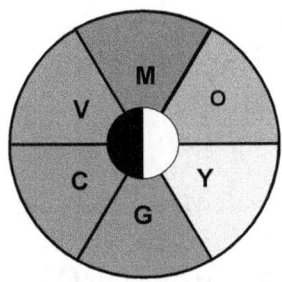

Fig 1.1 colour Circle :The hues represented are magenta, orange, yellow, green, cyan & violet

- Saturation, also called chroma, is the purity of the colour. It is used to describe the state of absolute purity of a colour. The saturation is the measure of the true and proper content of a colour in a given instance. When we see one red that is redder than another (which thus appears more gray), we experience a particular sensory quality that is manifested in greater or lesser purity, rendering colours more or less rich and full. Saturation represents the amount of gray in proportion to the hue, measured as a percentage from 0% (gray) to 100% (fully saturated). On the standard colour wheel, saturation increases from the center to the edge.

- Brightness is the relative lightness or darkness of the colour. It is usually measured as a percentage from 0% (black) to 100% (white).

9

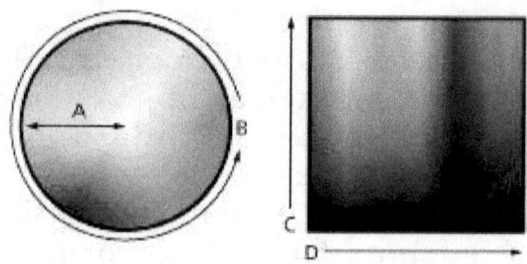

Fig 1.2 A. Saturation B. Hue C. Brightness D. All hues

RGB Model

The millions of colours you see on your monitor can all be described as mixture of red, green, and blue in various proportions and intensities. These three colour components form the basis for the RGB (Red, Green, and Blue) colour model. Where the colours overlap, they create cyan, magenta, and yellow.

Each of the three colours is assigned a numeric value between 0 and 255. The RGB model is based on colours of light, and higher RGB values correspond to the presence of greater quantities of white light. Consequently, higher RGB values result in lighter colours. When all three colour components are at the maximum value, the resulting colour is white light.

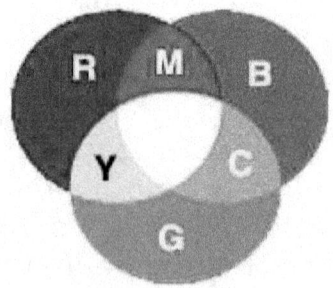

Fig 1.3 Additive colours (RGB)

Because the RGB model creates colours by adding light, it is called an additive colour model. Video, monitors and scanners employ the additive colour model because they emit light. They emit particles of red, green, and blue light and create the illusion of millions of different colours.

CMYK Model

The most common method of reproducing colour images on paper is by combining cyan, magenta, yellow, and black pigments. These four colours are the colour components of the CMYK (Cyan, Magenta, Yellow, and black) colour model. Each colour of the CMYK colour model is described as a percentage (from 0 to 100). Because the CMYK colour model is based on pigment colours, higher percentages of pigment result in darker colours.

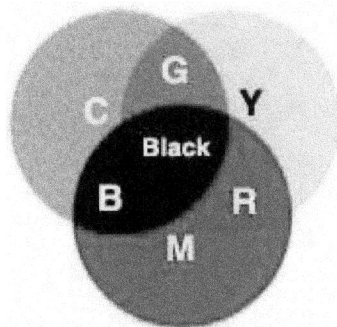

Fig 1.4 Subtractive colours (CMYK)

Theoretically, pure cyan (C), magenta (M), and yellow (Y) pigments, when combined, absorb all colour and produce black. But all printing inks contain some impurities, therefore these three inks actually produce a muddy brown and must be combined with black (K) ink to produce a true black. The CMYK colour model is called a subtractive colour model because it creates colours by absorbing light. Combining these inks to reproduce colour is called four-colour process printing. All the offset process of printing uses the four colour printing.

L*a*b Model

In 1931 La Commission International de L'Eclairage (CIE) defined a device-independent colour model, based on how the human eye perceives colour. The CIE Lab model incorporates the theory that a colour cannot be both green and red at the same time nor can it be yellow and blue at the same time. As such, single values are used to describe the green/red and blue/yellow components of any colour. In 1976, this model was refined and named CIE L*a*b.

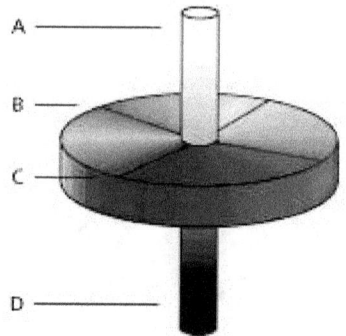

Fig 1.5 A. Luminance =100 (white) B. Green to red component C. Blue to yellow component D. Luminance = 0 (black) to red component

Lab stands for the three values this model uses to define colour lightness value (L) which can range from 0 to 100 and two chromaticity ranges: green to red (a) and blue to yellow (b). The two chromaticity values can range from +120 to -120.

COLOUR DEPTH

"colour Depth", also called bit depth or pixel depth, is a term that is used to specify the maximum number of colours available or number of colours that a file can support. The simplest could be a 1-bit file supporting two colours (usually black and white). Since each pixel can have only two different states, only one "bit" of information is required to store each image.

Similarly a 2-bit file supports four colours (two bit can store four colour, 2 to the power of 2), a 4-bit file supports 16 colours, an 8-bit file supports 256 colours, and a 24-bit file supports 16 million colours. A grayscale image is an 8-bit file, with 256 increments, ranging from black to white. The higher the colour depth supported by a file, the more space the file takes up on disk. The actual number of colours you will see on your monitor depends on the type of video hardware and video drivers you are using.

Monochrome

One-bit data type. Each pixel can be either black or white.

Grayscale

Grayscale images can contain black, white and a range of grays. 16-colour (4 bits per pixel) grayscale images contain 16 shades of gray ranging from pure white to pure black. 256-colour (8 bits per pixel) grayscale images contain 256 shades of gray ranging evenly from pure white to pure black.

Indexed 16 and 256-Colour

Indexed, or colour-mapped, images contain colours specified by a table of colour values. The colour values may be chosen from a larger range of available colours, but only the colours actually in the table are displayed in the image. For example, your system may be able to display 256 colours simultaneously, but if you load a 16-colour image, you can only draw in the image using the 16 colours contained in the colour table for that image.

Indexed 16-colour images use 4 bits per pixel to represent the image while indexed 256-colour images use 8 bits per pixel.

True Colour (16.7 Million)

True colour images use values of red, green and blue to represent colours. Each pixel can contain 256 different intensities of red, green and blue which are combined to obtain the final colour. For example, if red, green and blue all have a value of zero, the final colour is pure black. If red, green and blue all have a value of 255 (the maximum intensity), the final colour is pure white. If red and green have a value of 255 but blue is zero, then the final colour is pure yellow, since red and green combine to produce yellow when displayed on a computer monitor.

True colour images use 24 bits per pixel to represent the image, divided into 8 bits for each primary colour (red, green and blue). Certain file formats store true colour images as 32-bit images, which have an extra 8 bits to store transparency or overlay information.

STARTING ADOBE PHOTOSHOP

Adobe Photoshop is a powerful application for colour painting, photo retouching and image editing.

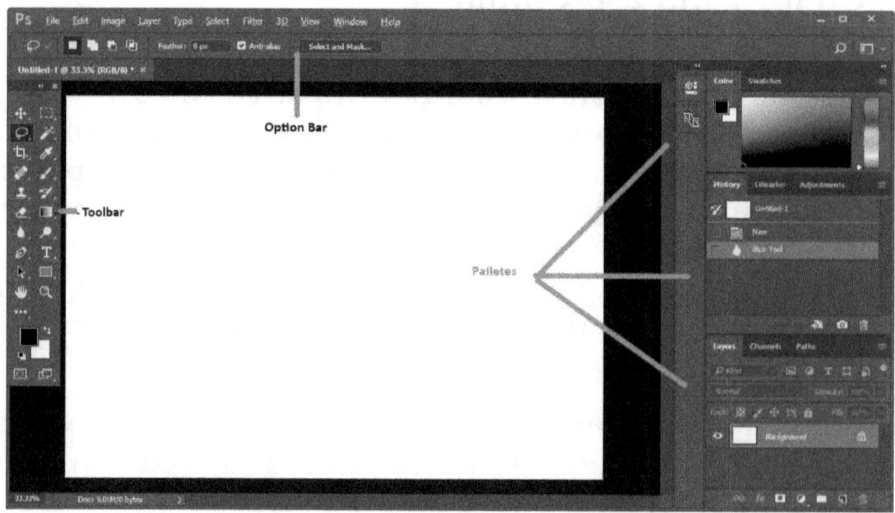

Fig 1.6 - Adobe Photoshop CC Window

You'll find that Photoshop excels as an art production tool, whether you are a graphics producer who needs to merge and edit colour images, a photographer who wants to retouch proofs, or a graphic designer who is creating original or composite artwork, collages, or photo montages for print or on the Web.

Adobe Photoshop allows you to cut and paste images between popular applications in seconds. For example, Adobe Photoshop supports a wide range of industry-standard file formats as discussed above, which makes it ideal for copying, modifying and pasting images from Adobe Photoshop into any word processing document. You can also enhance a photo using Adobe Photoshop's built-in special effects and image editing tools. Adobe Photoshop lets you change colours, zoom in on the smallest detail, insert text, add and delete objects, apply special effects, rotate and stretch images, create posters and preview your changes - you can do just about anything you can imagine. It's fast and it's fun. And don't worry, you can use the Undo/Redo feature of the program at any time.

To start Photoshop, select Start ➤ Adobe Photoshop CC.

PHOTOSHOP WINDOW

USING THE TOOLBOX

The tools in the toolbox let you select, paint, edit, and view images. Other controls choose foreground and background colours, create quick masks, and change the screen display mode. Most tools have associated Brushes and Options palettes, which let you define the tools' painting and editing effects. To display the toolbox, choose Window ➤ Tools. To move the toolbox, drag the toolbox by its title bar.

SELECTING TOOLS

You select a tool by clicking its icon in the toolbox. A small triangle to the right of a tool icon indicates a pull-out menu of hidden tools.

Move Tool — Marquee Tool
Lasso Tool — Magic Wind Tool
Crop Tool — Eyedropper Tool
Spot Healing Brush Tool — Pencil Tool
Clone Stamp Tool — History Brush Tool
Eraser Tool — Gradient Tool
Blur Tool — Dodge Tool
Pen Tool — Type Tool
Path Selection Tool — Rectangle Tool
Hand Tool — Zoom Tool
Edit Toolbar
Foreground Colour
Background Colour
Quick Mask Mode — Change Screen Mode

Fig.1.7 Adobe Photoshop Toolbox

To select a tool, do one of the following:

● To select a visible tool, click its icon.

● To select a hidden tool, position the pointer on the visible tool, and drag to highlight the tool you want.

Use these shortcuts to select tools:

● To select a tool quickly, press its shortcut key on the keyboard.

- To cycle through a set of hidden tools, press Alt and click the visible tool; or hold down Shift and press the visible tool's shortcut key.

To display the active tool name:

- Position the pointer over the triangle in the bottom border of the program window, hold down the mouse button, and choose Current Tool from the menu.
- The name of the currently selected tool appears in the lower left of the window.

USING THE STATUS BAR

The status bar at the bottom of the program window displays useful information-such as the current magnification and file size of the active image, and brief instructions for using the active tool.

USING PALETTES

Palettes let you monitor and modify images. You can display or hide them as you work. By default, they appear in stacked groups. To show or hide a palette:

- Select the appropriate Window ➤ Palette name.
- To hide the pallete, simply unselect.

CHANGING THE PALETTE DISPLAY

You can reorganize your work space using the following techniques:

- Click on the palette's tab to make a palette appear at the front of its group.
- To move an entire palette group, drag its title bar. To rearrange or separate a palette group, drag the palette's tab outside of an existing group.
- To move a palette to another group, drag the palette's tab to that group.

- Click on the triangle (▣) to display a palette menu.

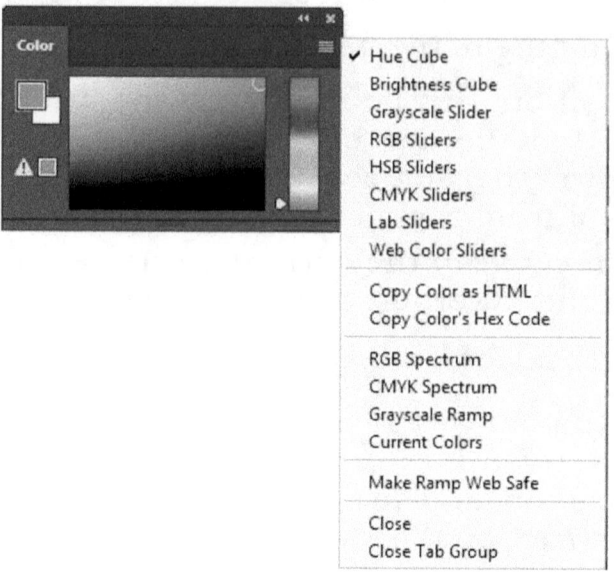

Fig 1.8 Selecting options from Palette's menu

- You can also change the height of the palette by dragging its lower right corner. This, however, is not applicable to the colour, Options, or Info palette. To return the palette to default size, click the minimize/maximize box in the right of the title bar.

RESETTING THE PALETTES

The positions of all open palettes and moveable dialog boxes are saved by default when you exit the program. Alternatively, you can always start with default palette positions or restore default positions at any time.

To reset palettes and warnings to the default positions:

- Choose Windows ➤ Workspace ➤ Reset Essentials.

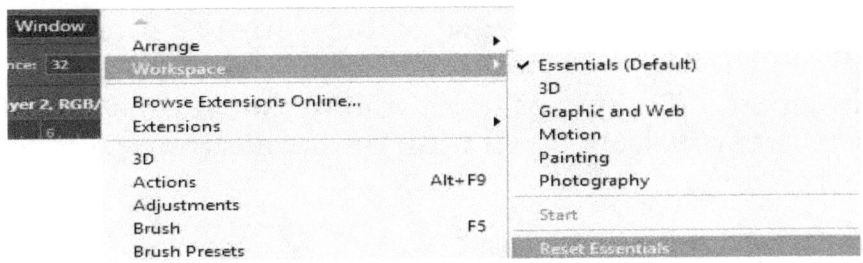

Fig 1.9 Resetting the Essentials

USING THE OPTIONS BAR

The Photoshop CC has Option bar. Depending on the tool selected, the option bar displays the various properties of the tool.

Some settings in the Options Bar are common to several tools (such as painting modes and opacity), some specific to one tool (such as the Auto Erase setting for the pencil tool).

To display the Options Bar, you can choose Window ➤ Options or double-click a tool in the toolbox (except the zoom or hand tool).

Using Popup Sliders

Various properties in palettes and dialog boxes vary from one value to another value. The Photoshop provides pop-up slider to change these properties. (for example, the Opacity option in the Paintbrush palette).

Fig 1.10 Using Pop-up Slider

To use a pop-up slider, click the triangle next to the setting to open the pop-up slider box, and drag the slider or angle radius to the desired value. Now, click outside the slider box or press Enter to close the slider box. (To cancel changes, press Esc.)

To increase or decrease values in 1% increments, press the Up or Down arrow key, while pop-up slider is open. To increase or decrease values in 10% increments, hold down Shift and press the Up or Down arrow key.

Resetting Default Value

To return to a tool's default settings, click the tool in the option bar, and choose Reset Tool from the Options bar menu. To return all the tools to their default settings, choose Reset All Tools from the Options palette menu.

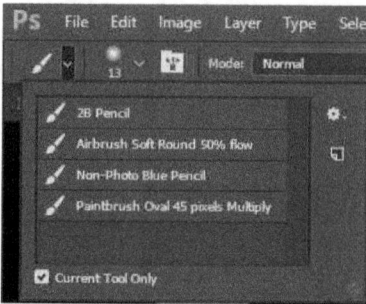

Fig 1.11 Resetting Tool

USING CONTEXT MENU

In addition to the menus at the top of your screen, context-sensitive menus display commands relevant to the active tool, selection, or palette.

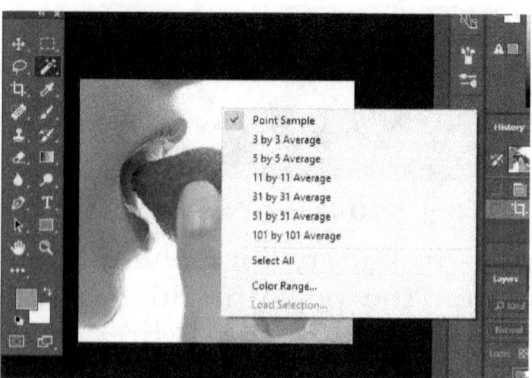

Fig 1.12 Using Context Menu

To display context menus:

- Position the pointer over the image or over an item in a palette list (for example, a thumbnail in the Layers palette).

- Click with the right mouse button.

USING ADOBE ON-LINE SERVICES

If you have an Internet connection and a Web browser installed on your system, you can access the Adobe Systems Home Page on the World Wide Web (at https://helpx.adobe.com/support/photoshop.html) for information on services, products, and tips pertaining to Photoshop.

Fig 1.13 Using Adobe Online Services

To use Adobe Online, choose Help ➤ Photoshop Online Help. Click a topic to open the Adobe Home Page.

USING PHOTOSHOP HELP

Photoshop CC provides complete help documentation in an HTML based help system. The help of Photoshop CC provides you varoius options to use the help documentation. These are Contents and Search.

- To browse through topics by category, Select the Begineers Guide and then select Learn and Support. Select the Photoshop manual to display the contents of the chapter on the top of browser. Click on the topic to display the help information. (Fig 1.14)

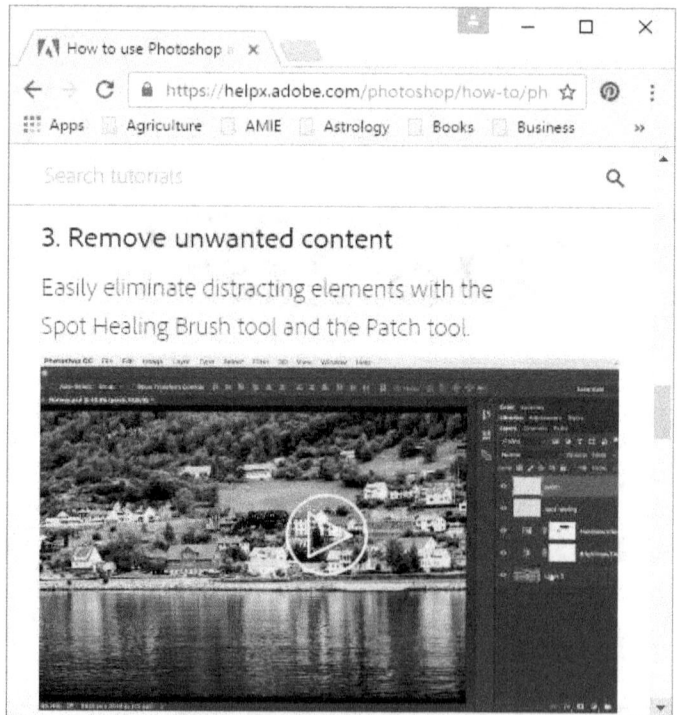

Fig 1.14 Using Adobe Help

- To download the previous versions of Photoshop in PDF, select Photoshop (previous versions).
- To get help on a particular topic, type the topic name in the search option on the left side.

USING PLUGIN MODULES

Plug-in modules are the applications which are used to give special-effects to your images. These are either developed by Adobe Systems or by other software developers in conjunction with Adobe Systems. By default, a large number of plug-ins are automatically installed in Plug-Ins folder. If you want to use a plug-in which is installed in another folder, you must change the preference settings so that Photoshop uses the other plug-ins location.

To set plug-ins preferences:

- Choose Edit ≻ Preferences ≻ Plug-Ins & Scratch Disk. (Fig 1.15)

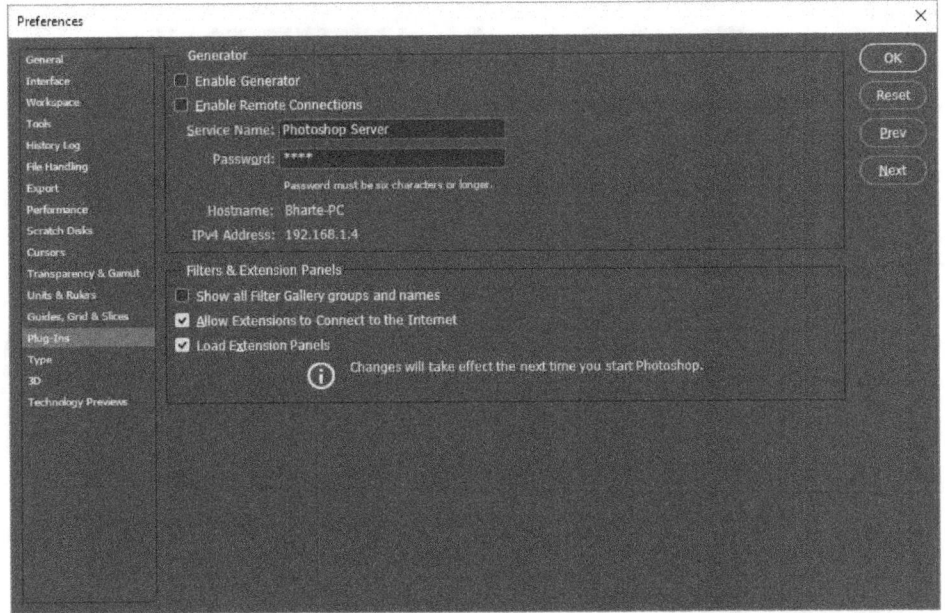

Fig 1.15 Preference Dialog box

- Select the additional Plug in in Filters and Extension Panel.
- When you have highlighted the new plug-ins folder, click OK and restart Adobe Photoshop for plug-ins to take effect.

SETTING PREFERENCES

Various settings for Photoshop CC are stored in preference files Prefs.psp, located in the Adobe Photoshop Settings folder. These settings include general display options, separation setup information, calibration options, display options, tool options, ruler units, and options for exporting information from the Clipboard etc. You can set these options as per your requirements through the Preferences submenus in the Edit menu. Preference settings are saved each time you exit Adobe Photoshop.

To open a preferences dialog box, choose the desired preference dialog box from the Edit ➢ Preferences submenu.

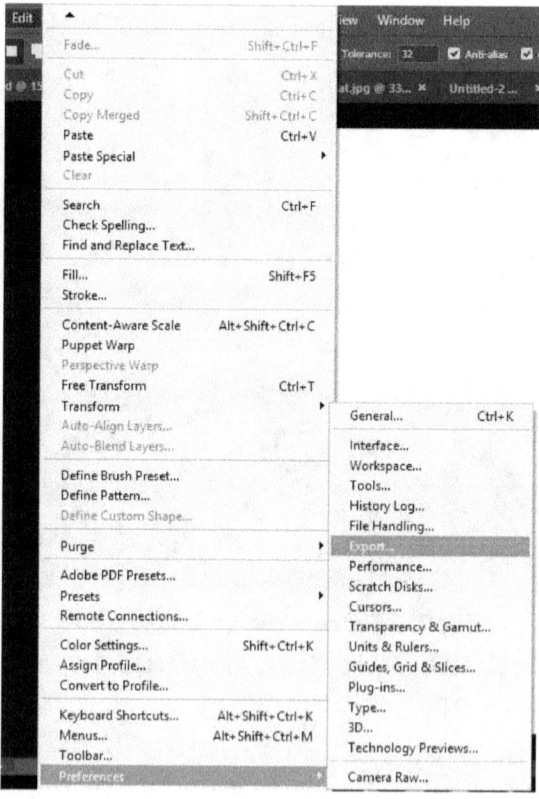

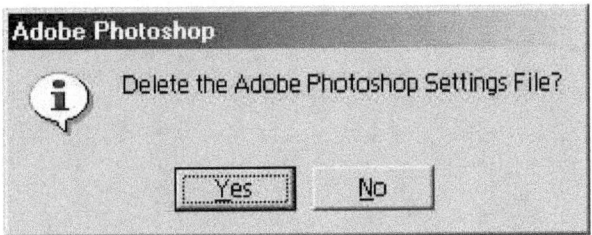

Fig 1.16 Restoring the default settings

To switch to a different preference dialog box, select another option from the options in the left side of the dialog box or click Next to display the next preference dialog box in the menu list or click Prev to display the previous preference dialog box.

WORKING WITH IMAGES

GRAPHICS

Computer graphics fall into two main categories-bitmap images and vector graphics. Understanding the difference, between the two graphics type, will help as you create and edit digital images.

BITMAP IMAGES

Photoshop and other paint and image-editing programs generate bitmap images, also called raster images. Bitmap images use a grid (the bitmap or raster) of small squares known as pixels to represent images. Each pixel is assigned a specific location and colour value. When working with bitmap images, you edit pixels rather than objects or shapes.

A bitmap image is resolution-dependent-that is, it contains a fixed number of pixels to represent its image data. Therefore, when it is enlarged or viewed at high magnification on-screen, it appears jagged as it looses details. However, the colour and shape of a bitmap image appear continuous when viewed from a greater distance. Because each pixel is coloured individually, you can create photorealistic effects, such as shadowing and intensifying colour.

Fig 2.1 Bitmap Image

VECTOR GRAPHICS

Drawing programs such as Adobe Illustrator® or CorelDRAW create vector graphics, made of lines and curves defined by mathematical objects called vectors. Vectors describe graphics according to their geometric characteristics. Each object is a self-contained entity, with properties such as colour, shape, outline, size, and position on the screen included in its definition.

Vector-based drawings are resolution independent. This means that they appear at the maximum resolution of the output device, such as your printer or monitor. As a result, the image quality of your drawing is a higher quality resolution if you print from a 600 dots per inch (dpi) printer than from a 300-dpi printer.

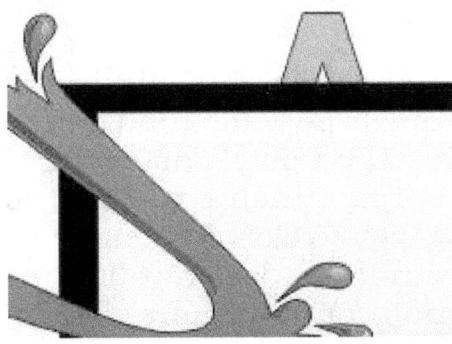

Fig 2.2 Vector Image

IMAGE SIZE AND RESOLUTION

PhotoShop lets you produce high-quality or low-quality images which can be used for various purpose, but to understand the concept of image quality it is important to understand how the pixel of bitmap images is measured and displayed.

PIXEL DIMENSIONS

Pixel Dimension of an image is defined as the number of pixels along the height and width of a bitmap image. The display size of the image on-screen varies with different monitor settings. On a typical 640X480 resolution of monitor, the image would appear bigger as compared to 800X600 resolution.

The On-screen size of the image depends on a combination of factors - the pixel dimensions of the image, the monitor size, and the monitor resolution setting.

RESOLUTION

The amount of detail information that an image file contains, as well as the level of detail that an input, output or display device is capable of producing is called resolution. When you work with bitmaps, resolution affects the quality of your final output and the file size.

Image resolution

Refers to the spacing of pixels in the image and is measured in pixels per inch (ppi) or dots per inch (dpi). You can understand pixels as small circles filling the images. At 72 dpi, 1 inch by 1 inch area will consist of 72 x 72 = 5184 circles. The same area will contain 600 x 600 = 3,60,000 dots at 600 dpi. An image with a high resolution contains more, and therefore smaller, pixels than an image of the same printed dimensions with a low resolution.

Thus higher resolution images gives more detailed output as compared to low resolution images when printed. It is so because they use more pixels to represent each unit of area.

However, if an image has been scanned or created at lower resolution, increasing its resolution will hardly improve the quality of the image. Assume that you scan a photograph at 72 dpi. It is commonly said that this photograph was sampled at 72 dpi. By scanning, its continuous information was broken into 72 samples per inch, and in doing so, some of the richness of the original photograph was lost. If the scan is resampled down to 50 dpi, even more visual information is removed. Now, if you increase the resolution of the photograph, it will not help to restore the lost visual information.

Monitor Resolution

A computer monitor is comprised of rows and columns of dots called pixels. Just like cylinders in a car engine, the more you have, the more powerful you feel. All monitors are not created equal. Some monitors display a fixed size, usually 640 pixels wide by 480 pixels high. Others are capable of up to 1280x1024 or more. The standard is 640 pixels horizontal and 480 pixels vertical. Monitor resolution depends on the size of the monitor plus its pixel setting.

In Photoshop, image pixels are translated directly into monitor pixels i.e. a pixel of image occupies a pixel on screen. Thus if your image resolution is higher (say double) than the monitor resolution, the size of the image that will be displayed on the screen will be double the actual print size. E.g an image of 1X1 actual size at 216 ppi will be displayed in 3X3 area on screen on a 72 dpi monitor as the monitor can display only 72 pixels per inch, it needs 3 inches to display the 216 pixels that make up one edge of the image.

Output Resolution

Refers to the number of dots per inch (dpi) that an output device, such as an imagesetter or laser printer, produces. Normally, an image resolution is used, which is proportional, but not same as printer resolution. Most laser printers have output resolutions of 300 dpi to 1200 dpi and produce good results with images from 72 ppi to 300 ppi.

High-end imagesetters can print at 2400 dpi or higher and produce good results with images from 200 ppi to 300 ppi.

FILE SIZE

The size of a computer file is measured in kilobytes (K), megabytes (MB), or gigabytes (GB). The size of an image is the size of the file in which it is stored. The higher the number of pixels in an image, the more space it will take on the disk.

The maximum file size, which PhotoShop supports is 2 GB. The maximum number of pixels supported in the image is 30,000 by 30,000 pixels per image. Thus, you can have a 3 inch by 3 inch file with 10000 pixels per inch or 100 inch by 100 inch file with a maximum resolution of 300 dpi.

CREATING NEW IMAGES

The New command lets you create a blank, untitled Photoshop image. You can also use this command to create a new image with the exact same pixel dimensions as an image or selection that has been copied to the Clipboard.

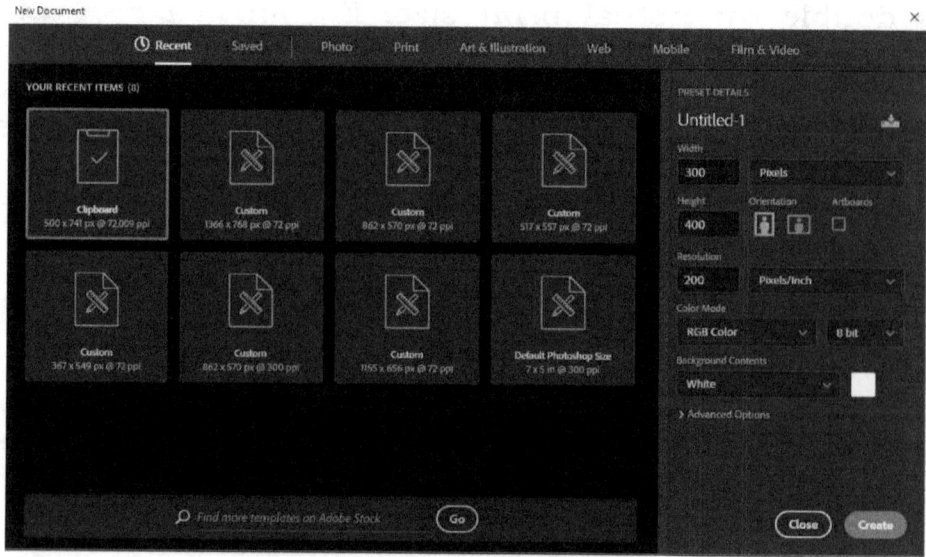

Fig 2.3 Selecting a New Image

Select File ➢ New to bring up the New dialog box. Here in this dialog box, define the size of the image in the required dimension and select the resolution and mode of the image.

If you want to open a new image, whose dimensions should be equal to an already opened image, select it from the options given under your Recent Items. If you want to open an image with the last entered settings, that also is listed in the Recent Items.

The New dialog box lets you choose the Background contents of the file also. Select White to fill the background with white, the default background colour, Black to fill the background with black. You can also select the Background colour to fill the image with the current background colour.

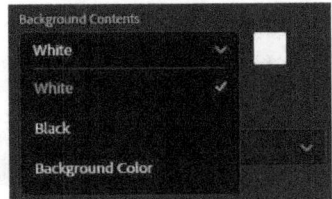

Fig 2.4 Selecting Background of the New Image

OPENING IMAGES

In Adobe Photoshop, you can open already existing images in various file formats and have multiple images open at one time. If a file format does not appear in the Open dialog box, install the format's plug-in module

OPENING FILES

To open a file in Windows,

- Choose File ➢ Open.

- Specify a file format. In Windows, for Files of Type, choose All Formats to display all the files in the selected directory. Choose an individual format to display only files saved in that format.

- Select the file. Click Open. In some cases, a dialog box appears, letting you set the open options. The formats requiring an open dialog box are described in the following sections.

In some cases a status bar appears indicating the file is being converted to a specified colour space.

To specify the file format in which to open a file, choose File ➢ Open As, select the desired format, and click Open.

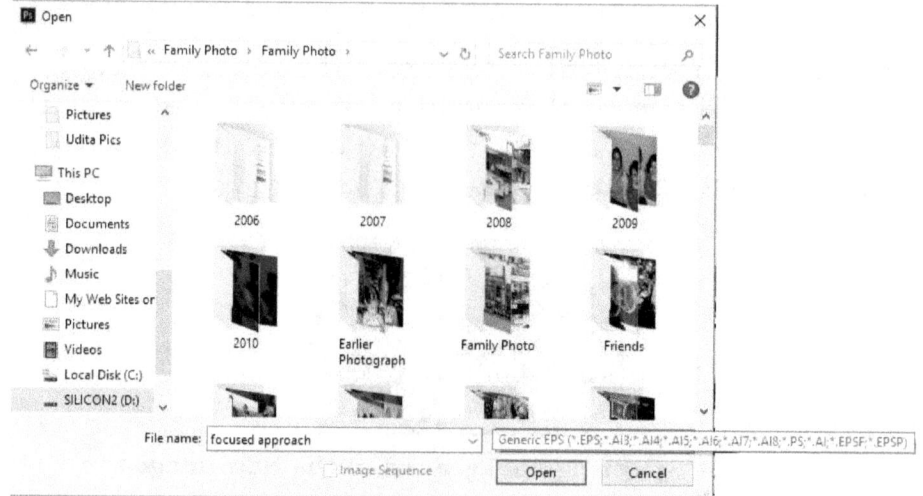

Fig 2.5 Open As dialog box

OPENING PHOTO CD FILES

Photoshop lets you open the Kodak Photo CD files, including high-resolution files from Pro Photo CD discs but doesn't provides the option of saving the files in PCD format. To open a Photo CD file:

- Choose File ➢ Open.
- Select the file you want to open, and click Open. If the file does not appear, for Files of Type, choose All Formats.
- Click Source. Choose a device and a profile description, pixel size for the image.

- Click Destination, choose a profile for the output device, resolution and click OK.

OPENING RAW FILES

The Raw format is designed to accommodate images saved in undocumented formats, such as those created by scientific applications. This format supports CMYK, RGB, and grayscale images with alpha channels, and multichannel and Lab images without alpha channels. Compressed files, such as PICT, and GIF, cannot be opened using this format.

To open a file using the Raw format:

- Choose File ➤ Open As.
- Choose Raw from the file format list, and click Open. It brings the Raw option dialog box.

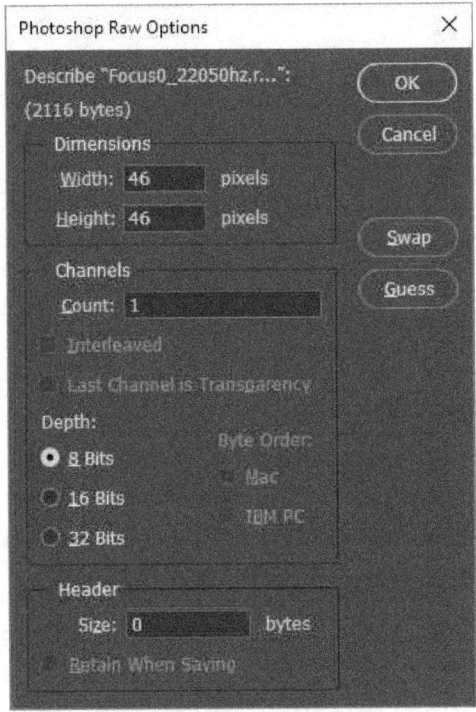

Fig 2.6 Raw Options

- Enter values for the dimensions of the file by specifying width and height.

- To reverse the order of the width and height, click Swap button.

- Enter the number of channels. Select interleaved, if the file was saved with an interlaced data option.

- Select a colour depth and, if necessary, a byte order and enter a value for Header. If you want Phototshop to do the Guess work for Header, click on the Guess button. Select the Retain When Saving option if you want to save the the header when you save the file. Click OK.

IMPORTING ADOBE ILLUSTRATOR, PDF, AND EPS FILES

You can import files created in Adobe Illustrator, PDF and EPS files containing vector art using following commands:

- The Open command to open an Illustrator, PDF, or EPS file as a new Photoshop image.

- The Place command to place an Illustrator, PDF, or EPS file as a new layer in an existing Photoshop image.

- The Paste commands to paste copied Illustrator artwork, into a Photoshop image either as pixels or as a path.

Opening PDF Files

To open PDF files, select File ➤ Open and select the PDF file you want to Open. This brings the Generic PDF Parser. Select the page you want to open.

When an Illustrator, PDF, or EPS image is opened or placed in Photoshop, it is rasterized i.e. the mathematically defined lines and curves of the vector image are converted into the pixels or bits of a bitmap image.

When you select the page, Photoshop displays the Rasterizing options, where you can define the desired dimensions, resolution, and mode. Select Anti-aliased to minimize the jagged appearance of the artwork's edges as it is rasterized. Click OK.

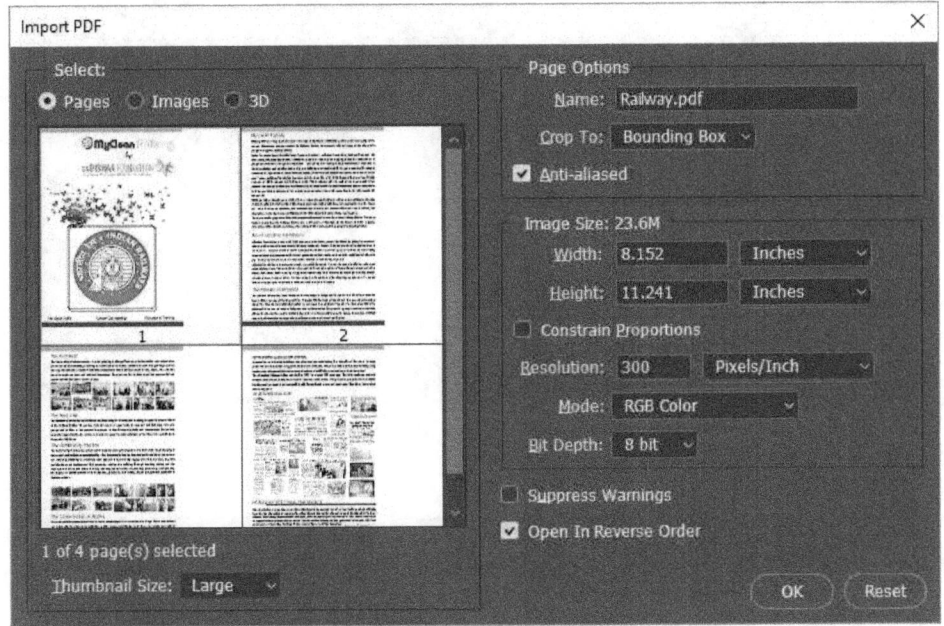

Fig 2.7 Opening PDF Files

Importing PDF Images

To import PDF images into Photoshop, select File ➢ Open. Select the appropriate file. This brings the PDF Import Images dialog box. Select the image or click on Import All Images to import all the images.

Placing Files

To place Adobe Illustrator, PDF, or EPS artwork into an Adobe Photoshop image:

- Open the Adobe Photoshop image in which you want to place the artwork and choose File ➢ Place Embeded, select the file you want to place, and click Place.

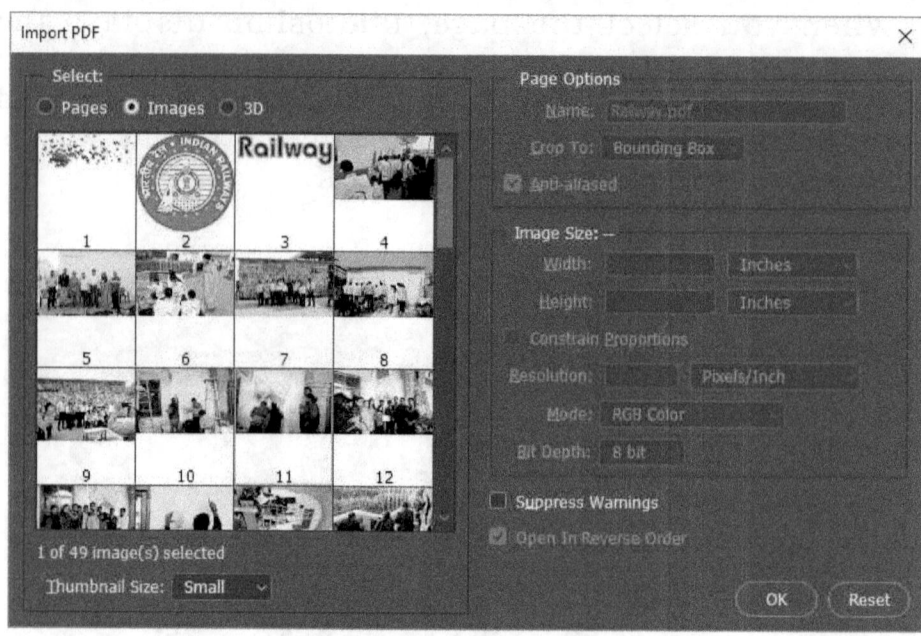

Fig 2.8 Importing PDF Images

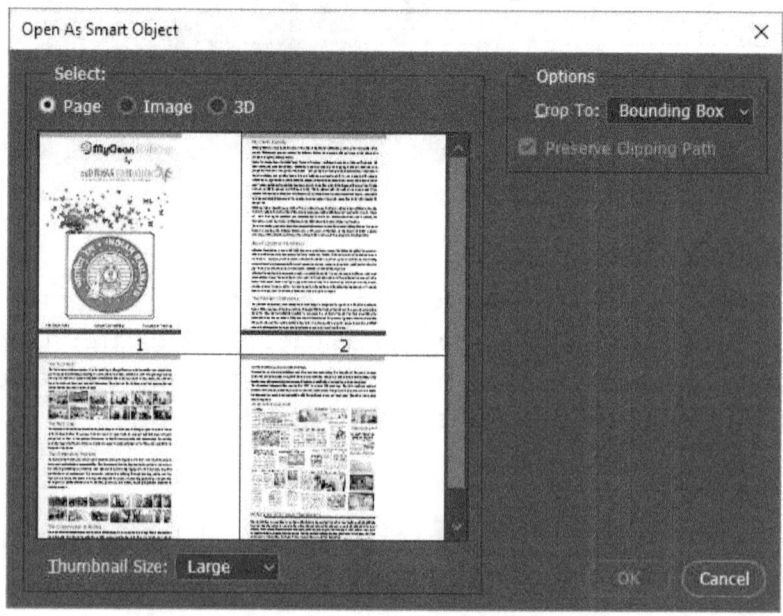

Fig 2.9 Selecting PDF pages tp Place

• If you are placing a PDF file that contains multiple pages, Generic PDF Parser dialog box, as shown in Fig 2.10 appears, select the page you want to place, and click OK.

• The placed artwork appears as a new layer inside a bounding box at the center of the Adobe Photoshop image. The artwork maintains its original aspect ratio. Now click on any tool in the toolbox. It brings the confirmation dialog box for placing the file. Select Place.

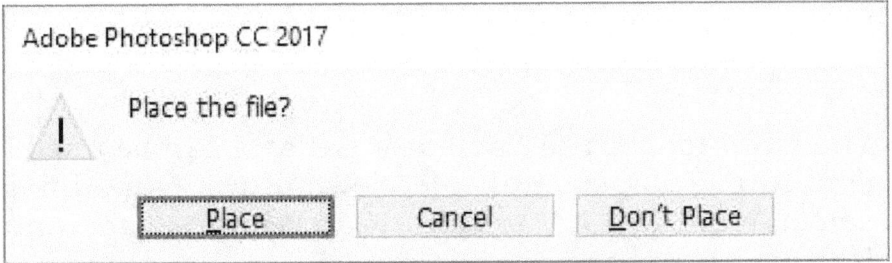

Fig 2.10 Placing the File

VIEWING IMAGES

The hand tool, the zoom tools, the Zoom commands and the Navigator palette let you view different areas of an image at different magnifications. You can open additional windows to display several views at once of an image.

A list of open windows appears in the Window menu. Available memory may limit the number of windows per image.

CHANGING VIEWING OPTIONS

To change the viewing mode of image windows, select one of the option in the Change Screen Mode in the toolbox:

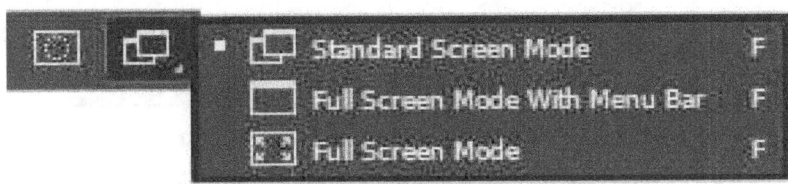

Fig 2.11 Changing Viewing options

- The Standard Screen Mode is to display the default window with a menu bar at the top and scroll bars on the sides.

- The Full Screen Mode with Menu Bar displays a full-screen window with a menu bar but no title bar or scroll bars.

- The Full Screen Mode displays a full-screen window with no title bar, menu bar, or scroll bars.

The hand tool or the Navigator pallatte can be used for scrolling. To open multiple views of the same image, select Windows ➤Arrange ➤New Window (Document Name)

To arrange multiple windows, do one of the following:

- Choose Window ➤ Arrange ➤ various options to display windows stacked, cascading or pre defined formats from the drop down.

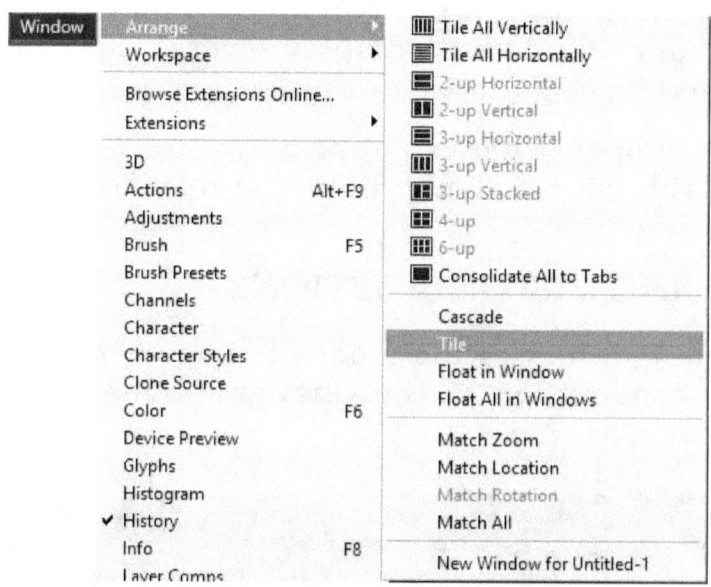

Fig 2.12 Arranging multiple windows

To close windows, choose a command:

- Choose File ➤ Close to close the active window.
- Choose File ➤ Close All to close all windows.

To view another part of an image, do one of the following:

- Use the window scroll bars.

- Select the hand tool, and drag in the image to move its view.

- Drag the hand tool to move the view.

- To use the hand tool while another tool is selected, hold down the spacebar as you drag in the image.

VIEWING IMAGES USING NAVIGATOR PALETTE

With a thumbnail, the Navigator palette lets you quickly change the view of an image.

To display the Navigator Palette, choose Window ➤ Navigator.

Fig 2.13 Navigator Palette

To move the view of an image using Navigator palette, do one of the following:

- Drag the view box, which represents the boundaries of the image window.

- Click in the thumbnail of the image. The new view includes the area you click.

To change the colour of the Navigator palette view box, do one of the following:

- Drag the view box, which represents the boundaries of the image window.
- Click in the thumbnail of the image. The new view includes the area you click.

MAGNIFYING AND REDUCING THE VIEW

You can magnify or reduce your view using various methods. The window's title bar displays the zoom percentage at all times.

The 100% view of an image displays an image based on the monitor resolution and the image resolution, not on the actual image dimensions.

To zoom in, do one of the following:

- Select the zoom tool, and click the area you want to magnify. Each click magnifies the image to the next preset percentage, centering the display around the point you click. At maximum magnification, the center of the zoom tool appears empty.
- Choose View ➤ Zoom In to magnify to the next preset percentage.

To zoom out, do one of the following:

- Select the zoom tool. Hold down Alt to activate the zoom-out tool, and click the area of the image you want to reduce. Each click reduces the view to the previous preset percentage.
- Choose View ➤ Zoom Out to reduce to the previous preset percentage.

Use these zoom shortcuts:

- To activate the zoom-in tool, press Alt+spacebar.
- To activate the zoom-out tool, press Ctrl+spacebar.
- To zoom in, press Ctrl+(=).
- To zoom out, press Ctrl+(-).

To magnify by dragging, do the following

- Select the zoom tool.
- Drag over the part of the image you want to magnify.
- Drag the zoom tool to magnify the view.
- The area inside the zoom marquee appears at the highest possible magnification.

To magnify or reduce to a specify percentage, enter a percentage value in the zoom percentage box at the lower left of the program window, and press Enter.

To display an image at 100%, do one of the following,

- Double-click the zoom tool.
- Choose View ➤ Actual Pixels.

To change the view to fit in the screen, do one of the following:

- Double-click the hand tool.
- Choose View ➤ Fit on Screen.

These options scale both the view and the window size to match the monitor size.

USING THE TOOL POINTERS

When you select most tools, the mouse pointer matches the tool's icon. This is the default standard tool pointer. The marquee, line, and gradient pointers appear by default as crosshairs.

Each default pointer has a different hot spot, where an effect or action begins. You can switch to precise pointers, which appear for most tools as cross hairs centered around the hot spot. For the magnetic lasso and magnetic pen tools, precise pointers appear as circles representing the lasso or pen width. With the painting tools, you can also display the pointer as a brush shape of a certain size.

To set the tool pointer appearance:

- Choose File ➤ Preferences ➤ Display & Cursors.

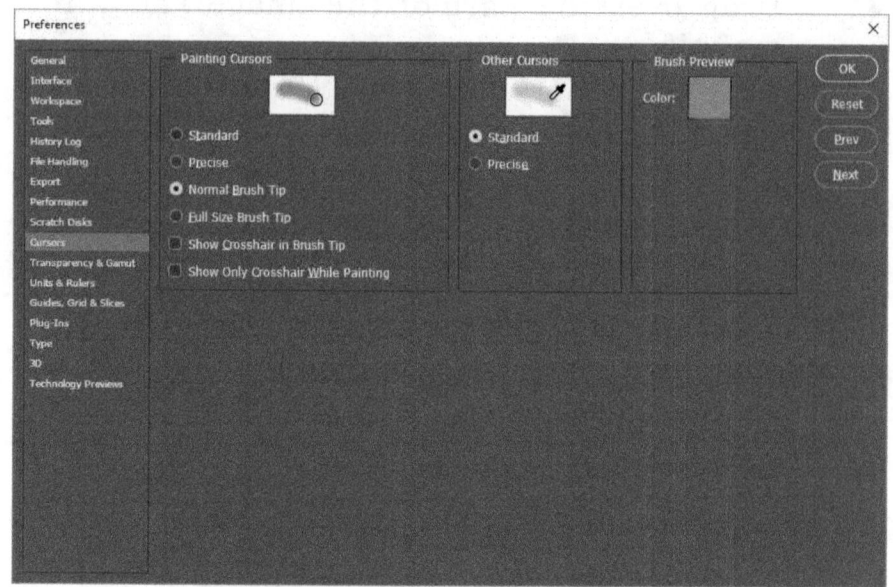

Fig 2.14 Display and Cursor options

- Select the tool pointer appearance:
    - Click Standard under Painting Cursors, Other Cursors, or both to display pointers as tool icons.
    - Click Precise under Painting Cursors, Other Cursors, or both to display pointers for most tools as crosshairs.
    - Click Brush Size under Painting Cursors to display the painting tool pointers as brush shapes representing the size of the current brush. Brush Size pointers may not display for very large brushes.
- Click OK.

With very small brushes, the brush shape is surrounded by four dots for finer accuracy. The Painting Cursors options control the pointers for the eraser, pencil, airbrush, paintbrush, rubber stamp, pattern stamp, smudge, blur, sharpen, dodge, burn, and sponge tools.

The Other Cursors options control the pointers for the marquee, lasso, polygon lasso, magic wand, crop, eyedropper, pen, gradient, line, paint bucket, magnetic lasso, magnetic pen, measure, and colour sampler tools.

To change the appearance of some tool pointers, press Caps Lock. Press Caps Lock again to return to your original setting. The pointers change in these ways:

- Standard to precise
- Precise to brush size
- Brush size to precise

USING RULERS, GUIDES AND GRIDS

The guidelines, grid, and rulers are designed to help you edit and arrange objects and selections with precision. Guidelines are non-printing lines used to align objects and selections. You can place guidelines anywhere in the Image Window by dragging them from the rulers or using the Horizontal and Vertical pages in the Options dialog box. The grid is a series of evenly-spaced horizontal and vertical lines that overlay your image so that you can accurately create and align image components. Rulers are displayed on the left side and along the top of the Image Window. They help you size and position the objects and selections in the image.

USING RULERS

The on-screen rulers appear along the top and left sides of the Image Window. The rulers provide a visual reference to help you determine the size and position of any image component. As you move the cursor around the image, marks on the ruler indicate its current position relative to the rulers' origin (the intersection of the rulers' 0 points.)

To display or hide rulers, choose View ➤ Show Rulers or Hide Rulers.

To change the rulers zero origin, position the pointer in the upper left corner, where the rulers intersect each other. Now click there and drag the mouse. As you drag the mouse, a cross hair moves with the mouse. Leave the mouse button where you want to place the new origin.

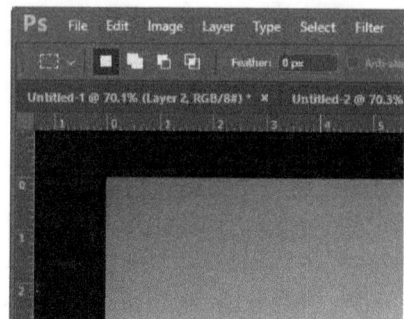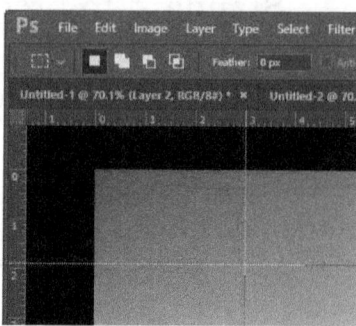

Fig 2.15 Dragging to create new ruler origin and result

To change the ruler's settings, either double click on any ruler or choose Edit ➤ Preferences ➤ Units & Rulers to bring the Preference dialog box.

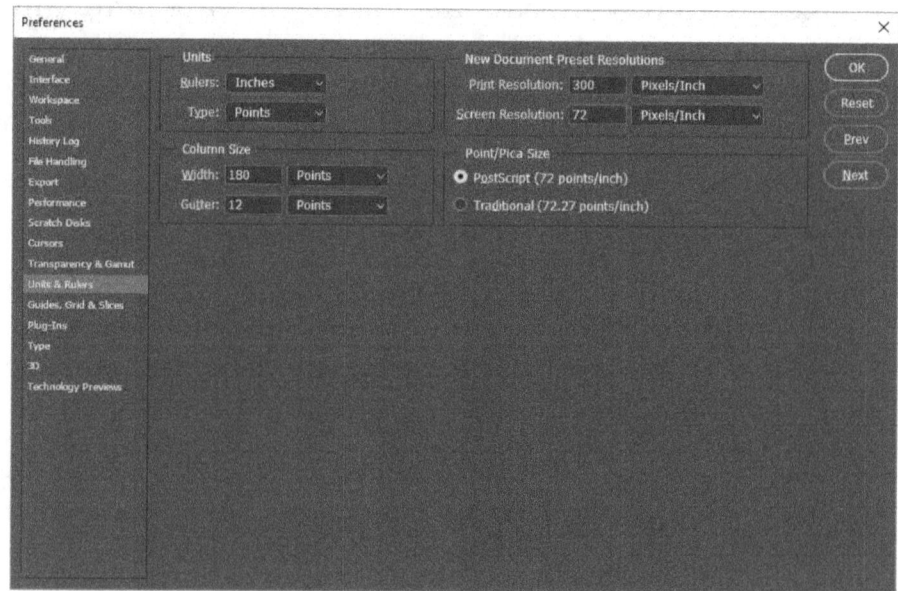

Fig 2.16 Setting Rulers and Guides Preference

- Select the units from the drop down menu. Also specify the width and gutter values.

- For Point/Pica Size, select PostScript (72 points per inch) if you are printing to a PostScript device else select Traditional.

USING GUIDES

Guides are vertical or horizontal lines, that you can place anywhere in the Image Window, to help you align and position image components. You can manually drag as many guides as you like from the ruler. Once created, you can select, move, and delete guides in the Image Window. Snapping objects and selections to guides, let you automatically align objects and selections with the guides.

To show or hide guides or the grids, choose View ➤ Show/Hide Guides. To add a guide, show rulers and then drag from horizontal or vertical ruler to create the respective guide. As you drag the pointer, it changes to a double-headed arrow. Leave the mouse button to add the guide.

To move a guide, select the move tool (►₊) and position the pointer over the guide, to convert into a double-headed arrow. Now drag the mouse and the guide is dragged along.

To lock all guides, choose View ➤ Lock Guides. You can remove a single guide by dragging it out of image. To clear all guides from the image, choose View ➤ Clear Guides.

USING GRIDS

The grid lets you align and position objects in the image accurately. By default, the grid is displayed as a series of intersecting lines that are superimposed on your image. You can customize the appearance of the grid by setting the distance between the grid lines and specifying its colour and style. Use the Snap To Grid command in the View menu to automatically line up image components with the grid.

To set guide and grid preferences, select Edit ➤ Preferences ➤ Guides & Grid to bring Preference dialog box.

- For The dialog box lets you select the colour of Guides and Grids. Also, it lets you control the distance between grid lines and type of grid lines. Click OK after selecting the required options..

CHANGING IMAGE SIZE AND RESOLUTION

Once you have scanned or imported an image into Photoshop, you may want to adjust its size or resolution. The Image Size command lets you adjust the pixel dimensions, print dimensions, and resolution of an image.

RESOLUTION FILE SIZE AND OUTPUT

The file size of an image refers to the total amount of pixel information in the image. For example, a 1-inch-by-2-inch high-resolution image has more pixels, and thus a larger file size, than a 1-inch-by-2-inch low-resolution image. In print, a high-resolution image has more detail than the same image at low resolution. On-screen, a high-resolution image appears larger. The enlarged on-screen display does not affect the dimensions of the printed image.

To display the file size, position the pointer over the triangle in the bottom border of the program window, hold down the mouse button, and choose Document Sizes from the menu. (Fig 2.18)

The file size appears at the lower left of the window. The first value indicates the size if saved as a flattened file with no layer data, the second value the size if saved with all layers and channels.

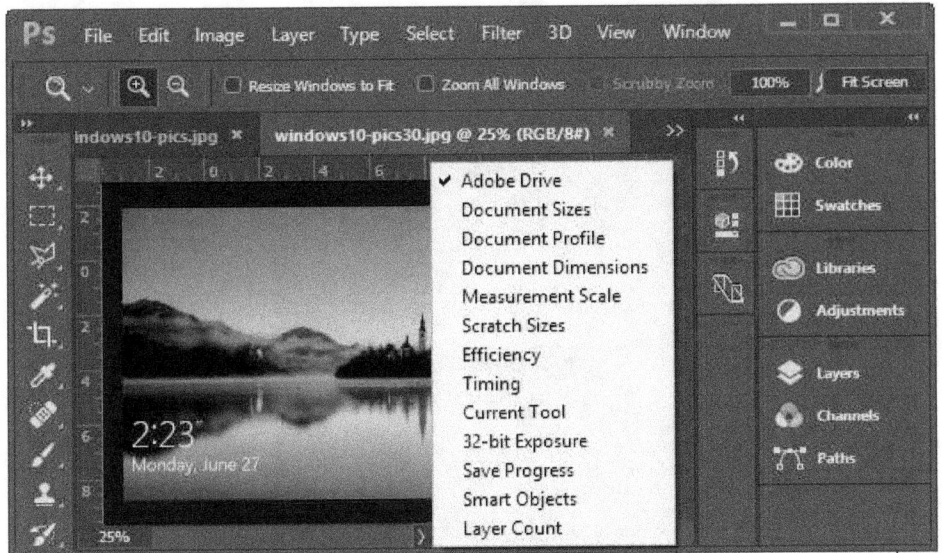

Fig 2.17 Displaying various options from Status line

To display dimensions, channel information and resolution information, press Alt, position the pointer over the box in the lower left of the window, and hold down the mouse button. The box displays the width and height of the image (both in pixels and in the unit of measurement currently selected for the rulers), the number of channels, and the image resolution.

To preview a page, position the pointer over the box where the file size is displayed, and hold down the mouse button. The dimensions of the page shown in the page preview box correspond to the page size specified with the Page Setup command. Other options selected appear as gray boxes.

To view the print size on screen, choose View ➢ Print Size. The magnification of the image is adjusted to display its approximate printed size, as specified in the Print Size section of the Image Size dialog box.

Fig 2.18 More information on Status Line

RESAMPLING

Resampling is changing the pixel dimensions which in turn changes the file size of an image. If you decrease the number of pixels, information is deleted from the image. Resampling adds new pixel into the image, based on colour values of existing pixels. To add new pixels or delete existing pixels, you can define the interpolation method.

To specify the interpolation method, select Edit ➢ Preferences ➢ General. Interpolation offers three options - Nearest Neighbour for fast but less precision, Bilinear for medium quality and Bicubic for precise result.

Fig 2.19 Interpolation Options

At times, resampling may result in poorer image quality, as the new pixels added to the image may make it blur or out of focus.

CHANGING PIXEL DIMENSION OF AN IMAGE

To change the pixel dimensions of an image:

- Select Image ➤ Image Size. (Fig 2.20)
- Select on the lock to Constrain Proportions or to maintain the current proportions of pixel width to pixel height. Both fields appears cnnected in front of width and height.
- Now you can specify the width and height of the image. You can also enter the width and height in percentage of the existing size. As you enter the new values, the corresponding file size appears along with the old file size in parentheses.
- Click OK to change the pixel dimensions and resample the image.

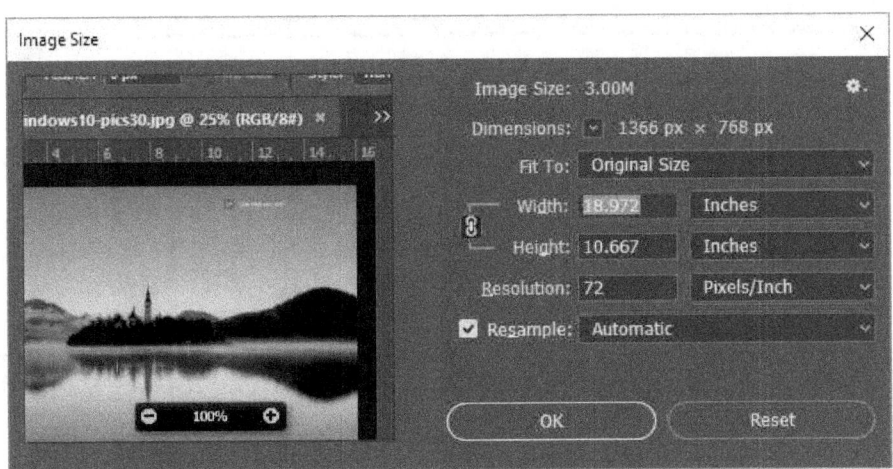

Fig 2.20 Specifying Image Size

CHANGING THE PRINT DIMENSION

To change the print dimensions and resolution of an image:

- Choose Image ➤ Image Size.

- Select on the lock to Constrain Proportions or to maintain the current proportions of pixel width to pixel height. Both fields appears cnnected in front of width and height.

- You can change the print dimensions or image resolution or both by defining values. Select the Resample Image option, if you want to change only one out of resolution or dimension and change the other accordingly while keeping the total number of pixels same for the image. Otherwise, you can deselect the Resample Image option.

- Now you can specify the width and height of the image. You can also enter the width and height in percentage of the existing size. As you enter the new values, the corresponding file size appears along with the old file size in parentheses.

- Click OK.

CROPPING AN IMAGE

Cropping an image reduces the visible area of the image. Photoshop provides two ways to crop an image - Using Crop command or using Crop tool. Using Crop tool, you can even rotate and resample the area as you crop.

To crop an image using the Crop command:

- Use the rectangle marquee tool to select the part of the image you want to keep. Make sure that the Feather option is set to 0 pixels.

- Choose Image ➤ Crop.

To use the crop tool

- Select the crop tool.

- Select the image you want to keep. When you release the mouse button, the crop marquee appears with handles at the corners and sides. When you use Crop tool, the area to be cropped appears as dark as compared to the image. You can change this by changing the opacity pop-up slider in the option bar.

Fig 2.21 Cropping Image

- Using these handles, you can adjust the area to be cropped.
  - Position the pointer inside the marquee and drag, to move the marquee to another position.
  - To scale the marquee, drag a handle. To constrain the proportions, hold down Shift as you drag a corner handle.
  - Position the pointer just outside the marquee to rotate the marquee. The pointer turns into a curved arrow. Drag the mouse to rotate the marquee.
- To crop the image, press Enter. To cancel the cropping operation, press Esc.

Cropping tool also lets you define the width, height and resolution of the cropped area. These values you can define in the option bar, as you select the cropping tool.

INCREASING CANVAS SIZE

Using Canvas Size command, you can add or remove work space around an existing image. You can crop an image by decreasing the canvas area. Added canvas appears in the same colour or transparency as the background.

To use the Canvas Size command:

- Choose Image ➢ Canvas Size.

- Choose the units of measurement you want. The Columns option measures width in terms of the columns specified in the Rulers & Units preferences. Enter the dimensions in the Width and Height boxes. A new file size appears.

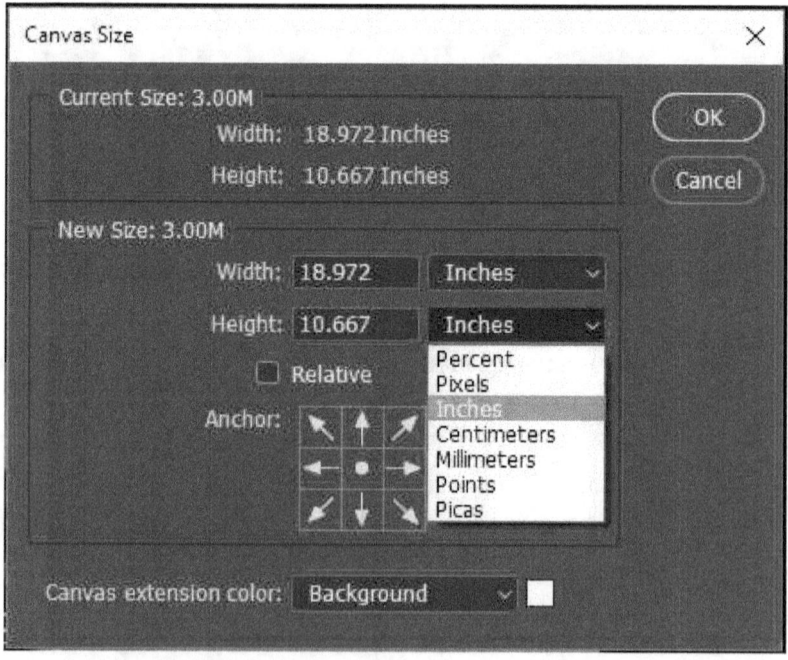

Fig 2.22 Making changes to Canvas Size

SCANNING IMAGES

Photoshop has no standard scanning module; different scanners come with different scanning software. Therefore, before you scan an image, make sure that the software necessary for your scanner has been installed. No matter what the size or dimensions of your original art, scan it at the highest optical resolution of your scanner to get the best output. "Optical resolution" refers to the number of pixels per inch that your scanner can capture mechanically, without digital enhancement.

If your original art is in colour, scan it in RGB (millions of colours) mode. Otherwise, scan it in Grayscale mode. Never scan an image in Line art mode, even if it's a black-and-white line drawing - you'll lose too much information.

IMPORTING SCANNED IMAGES

If scanner driver is installed on your system and is Adobe-PhotoShop compatible or supports TWAIN interface, you can directly import scanned images. To import the scan, choose the scanner name from the File ➤ Import submenu. If your scanner driver is not Adobe-PhotoShop compatible, you can use the manufacturer's software to scan your images and save images as TIFF, BMP, or PICT files. Then you can open the files in Adobe Photoshop.

To import an image using the TWAIN interface, select the device from the File ➤ Import submenu.

SAVING FILES

Adobe Photoshop provides several ways to save files:

- The Save command saves the file in its current file format.
- The Save As command lets you save an alternate version of the file in a different format, leaving the original file intact. You can optionally flatten the file copy and exclude non-image data or alpha channels, depending upon the format chosen.

- The Save for Web command lets you save a copy of the file for the internet. More about it will be discussed later in the book.

To save a file in its current format, choose File ➢ Save.

To save a file in a different file format:

- Choose File ➢ Save As.

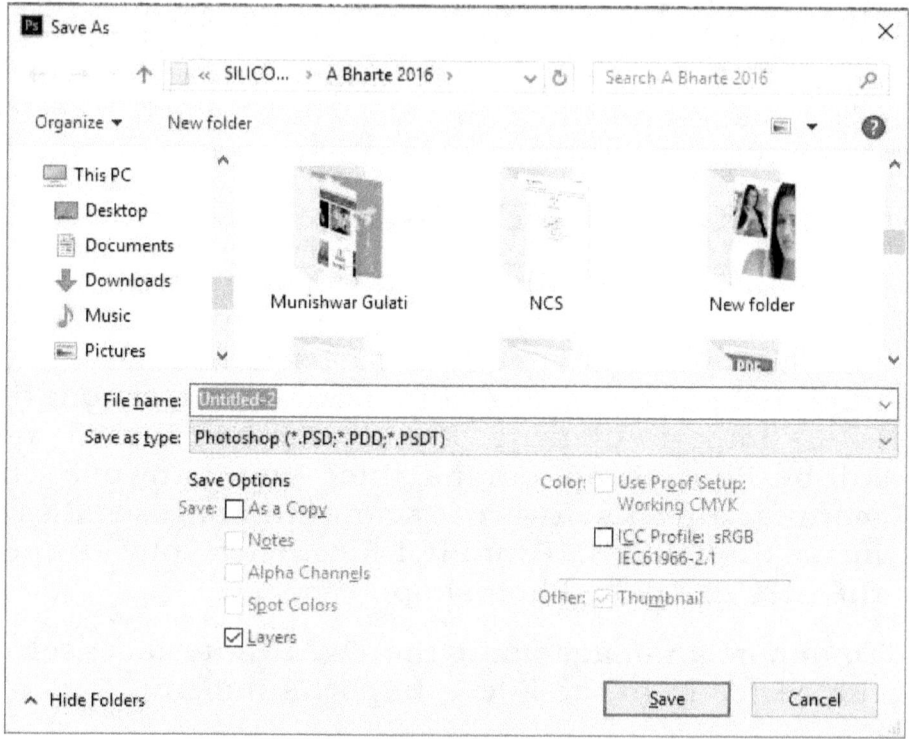

Fig 2.23 Saving Files in PhotoShop

- For Save As, choose a format. Unavailable formats are not visible. Type a filename, and choose a location for the file.

With some image formats, a dialog box appears. For example, if you want to save in PNG format, following option box appears.

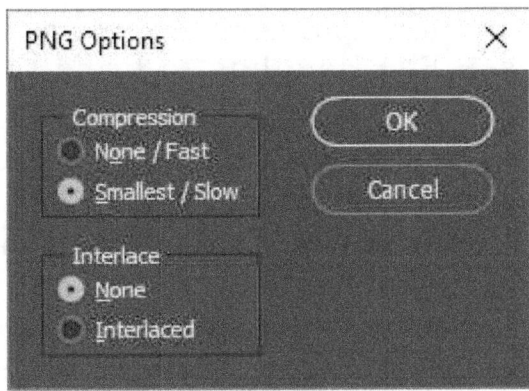

Fig 2.24 PNG options

To save as in JPEG format, following option box appears

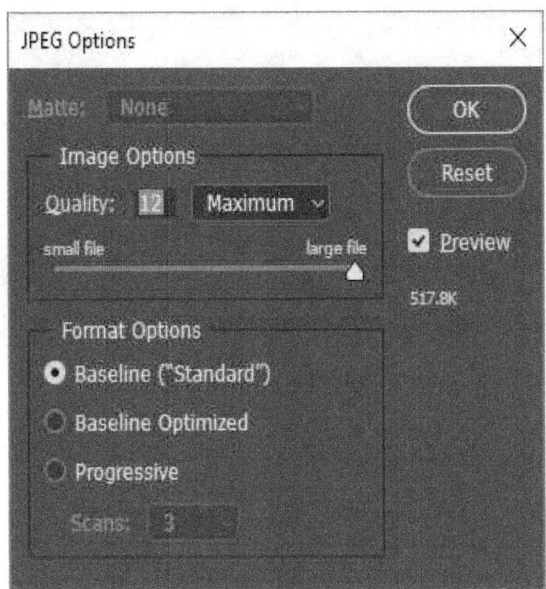

Fig 2.25 JPEG Options

To save a copy of a file, select the option Save As a copy.

- To remove alpha channels from the image, select Exclude Alpha Channels.
- Click Save.

To set saving preferences in Windows, select Edit ➢ Preferences ➢ File Handling to bring the Preference dialog box.

- For Image Previews, choose an option from the drop down menu:
  - Never Save to save files without previews.

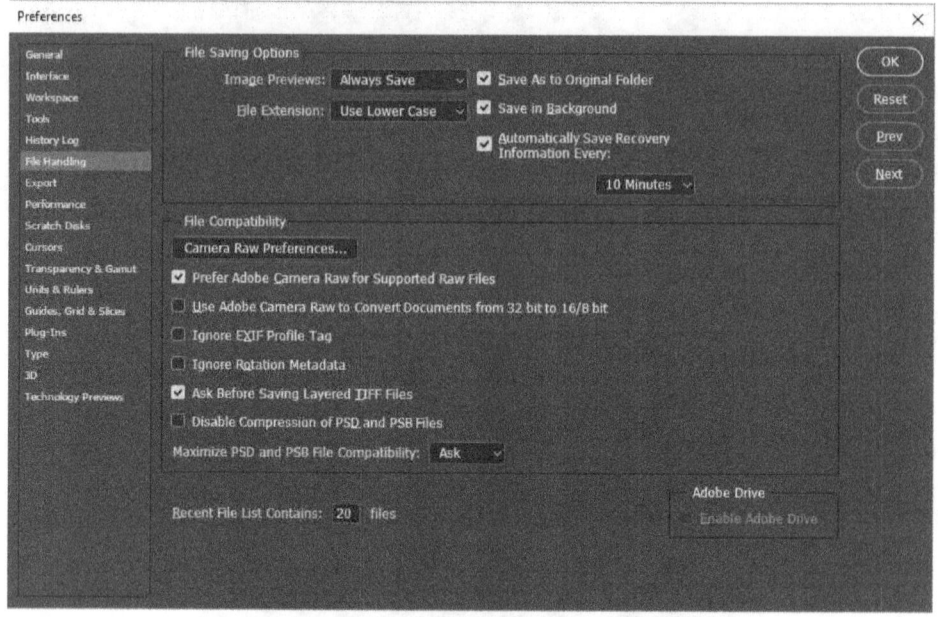

Fig 2.26 Specifying saving options

  - Always Save to save files with specified previews.
  - Ask When Saving to assign previews on a file-by-file basis.
- For File Extension, choose an option from the drop down menu:
  - Use Upper Case to append file extensions using uppercase characters.
  - Use Lower Case to append file extensions using lowercase characters.

WORKING WITH IMAGES

WORKING WITH COLOURS

COLOUR GAMUTS

A gamut is the range of colours that a device, such as a monitor or colour printer, can produce or detect. The spectrum of colours seen by the human eye is wider than the gamut available in any colour model, as is clear from the following figure.

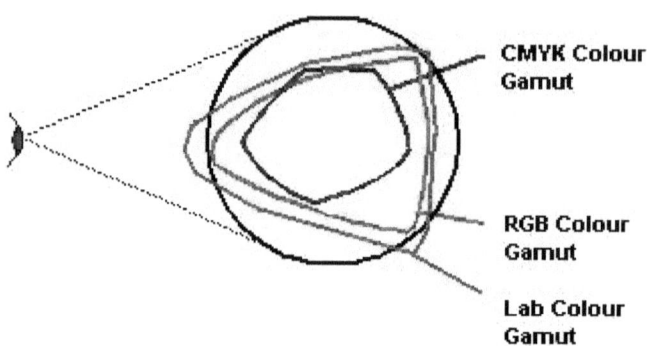

CMYK Colour Gamut

RGB Colour Gamut

Lab Colour Gamut

Fig 3.1 The colour Gamut

Photography gamut mapping is used for electronic assessment of the gamut of devices you use and the reassignment of out-of-gamut colours to other colours that can be reproduced.

As you could see in the figure that L*a*b has the largest gamut, encompassing all colours in the Pantone, RGB and CMYK gamuts. (In Photoshop, Pantone Model is not available). Typically, colours of the RGB gamut are viewed on a computer or television monitor and colours of CMYK gamut can be printed using the process colour ink. Thus you can view many colours on the screen which can't be printed. For example, pure Cyan or pure Yellow can't be displayed on the monitor.

COLOUR CHANNELS

A channel is an 8-bit grayscale version of your image that functions like a plate used in the commercial printing process: each channel represents one level of colour in your image. When all the channels are printed together, they produce the entire range of colours in the image.

Every Adobe Photoshop image has one or more channels, each storing information about colour elements in the image. For example, an RGB image comprises three channels (red, green, and blue). When all three channels are printed or displayed together, they create the entire range of colours in the image. Similarly, a CMYK image has at least four channels, one each for cyan, magenta, yellow and black information.

In addition you can add extra channels, called alpha channels, to these default colour channels for storing and editing selections as masks. You can also add spot colour channels to add spot colour plates for printing.

An image can have up to 24 channels, including all colour and alpha channels. By default, most of the modes, which includes Bitmap-mode, grayscale, duotone, and indexed-colour images, have one channel; RGB and Lab images have three; and CMYK images have four channels. You can add channels to all image types except Bitmap-mode images.

THE INFO PALETTE

Info palette gives information about the colour at different location and coordinates of the location. You can select any tool, position the pointer over any part of an image, and determine the colour value under the pointer. You can also customize the Info palette to express colour values using the HSB, RGB, CMYK, Lab, or Grayscale modes without changing the mode of the image itself.

You can also display colour values of specific target points in your image using colour samplers and use the measure tool to measure distances and angles.

To display the info palette, Choose Window ➤ Info. The Info palette, by default, displays the following specific information:

- The RGB and CMYK numeric values for the colour beneath the pointer, the x- and y-coordinates of the pointer.

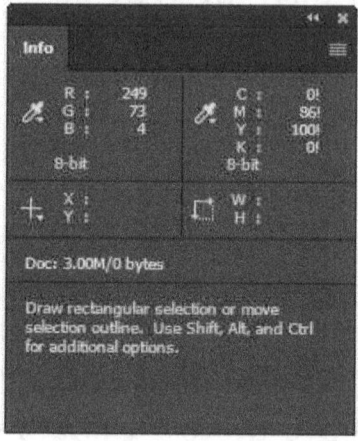

Fig 3.2 Info palette

- Info palette displays an exclamation point if the pointer is on a colour, which is out of the printable CMYK colour gamut.

- If you use the marquee tool, the Info palette displays starting point coordinates (x,y), current pointer position and the width (W) and height (H) of the marquee as you drag.

- If you use the crop tool, the Info palette displays starting point coordinates (x,y), current pointer position and the width (W) and height (H) of the marquee as you drag. Once you have made the selection, the palette also shows the angle of rotation of the crop marquee.

- If you use line tool, pen tool, gradient tool or move a selection, the Info palette displays the starting position coordinates, the change in X (DX), the change in Y (DY), the angle (A), and the distance (D) as you drag. In case of two-dimensional transformation command, the Info palette displays the same information except distance(D). Instead of D it displays the angle of horizontal skew (H) or vertical skew (V).

- If you are using any colour adjustment dialog box (for example, Image ➤ Adjust ➤ Levels), and place the pointer on the image, the Info palette displays the values of both before and after colour values of the pixels.

To change the info palette options :

- Choose Panel Options from the Info palette menu.

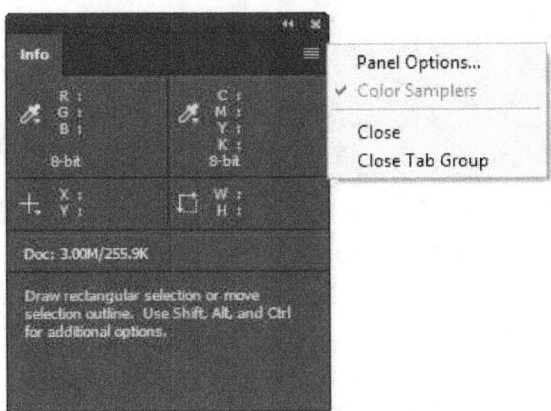

Fig 3.3 Selecting Info Palette options

It brings the Info option dialog box.

- As the info palette, by default, displays two colour modes, you can change both the modes by selecting a different option in First colour Readout and Second colour readout area.

  - Actual colour displays values in the current colour mode of the image.

  - Total Ink displays the total percentage of all CMYK ink.

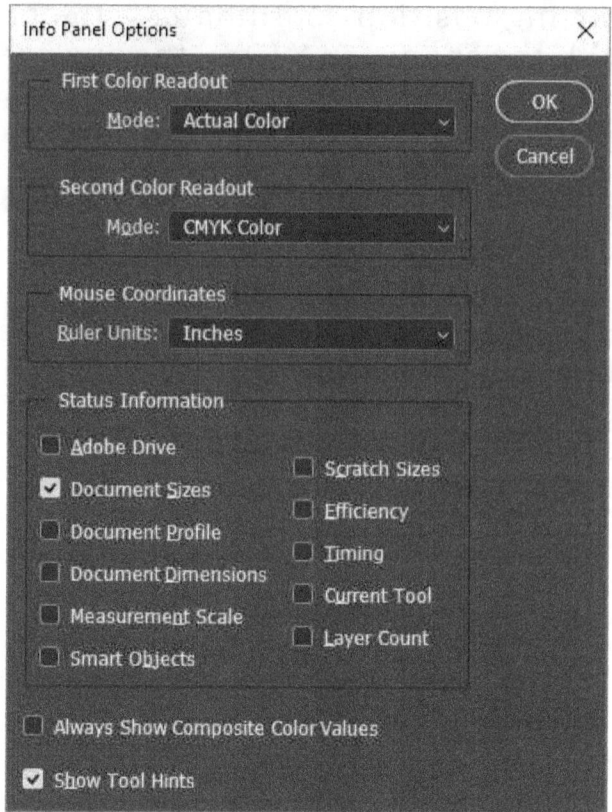

Fig 3.4 Infor Option dialog box

- Opacity displays the opacity of the current layer.
- Any other option to display the colour values in that colour mode.
- You can also select a unit for measurement from Ruler Units option.
- Click OK.

USING THE MEASURING TOOL

The measure tool ( ) lets you calculates the distance between any two points in the work area. When you measure from one point to another, a non-printing line is drawn and the Info palette shows the starting location (X and Y), horizontal (W) and vertical (H) distances travelled from the x and y axes, total distance travelled (D) and the angle measured relative to the axis (A).

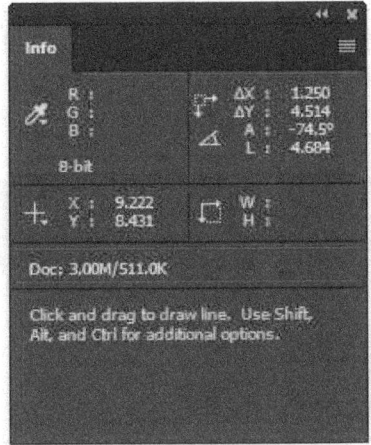

Fig 3.5 Using Measuring Tool

DISPLAYING COLOUR VALUES OF THE PIXELS

By default, Info palette displays two sets of colour values for a pixel under pointer. When any changes are made to colour, each set displays two colour values, separated by "/".

In Photoshop, you can view the colour at five places at a time - At one place, using the eye dropper tool and at rest four places, using the colour sampler tool.

Fig 3.6 Eyedropper flyout

Once you mark these colour samples in the image, these samplers are saved in the image, even if you close and reopen the image.

To mark these samples, select colour sampler tool (), and choose a sampling method from the pop-up menu in colour sampler tool options:

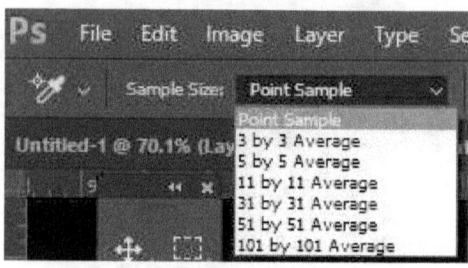

Fig 3.7 Specifying Point Sample

Point Sample   Reads the value of the pixel beneath the pointer.

3 by 3 average   Reads the average value of a 3-by-3 pixel area.

5 by 5 average   Reads the average value of a 5-by-5 pixel area.

11 by 11 average   Reads the average value of a 11-by-11 pixel area.

31 by 31 average   Reads the average value of a 31-by-31 pixel area.

51 by 51 average   Reads the average value of a 51-by-51 pixel area.

101 by 101 average   Reads the average value of a 101-by-101 pixel area.

- Now click on the image where you want to place the sampler. A circle appears at that place with a number (from 1 to 6 in Fig) and Info palette displays the colour value at that point.

- To move a colour sampler, select the colour sampler tool, and drag the sampler to the new location.

- To delete a colour sampler, select the colour sampler tool, and drag the sampler out of image window or Press Alt and click on the colour sampler.

- To change the colour mode, in which colour sampler displays the values, click on the colour sampler icon in the Info palette, and choose another colour mode from the menu that appears as shown in Fig 3.8.

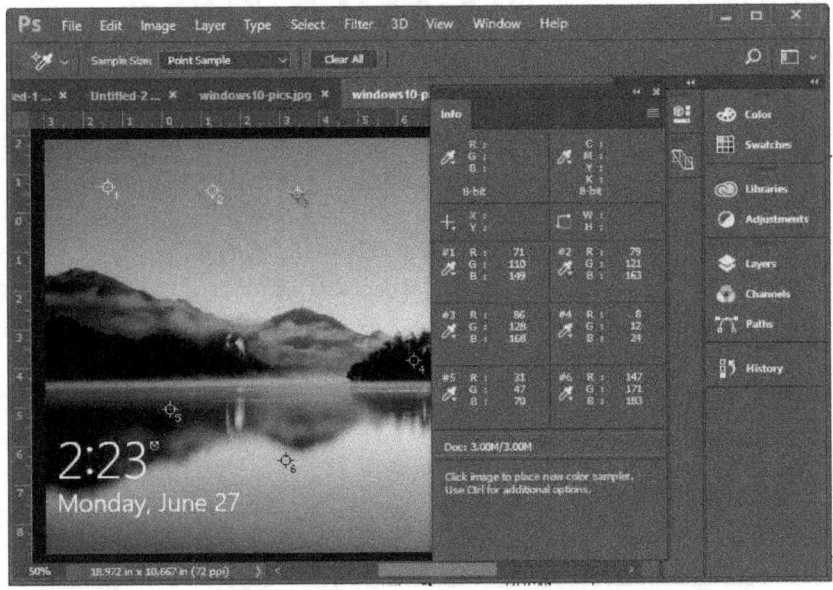

Fig 3.8 Selectingdifferent mode for colour sampler

BIT DEPTH

Bit depth - also called pixel depth or colour depth - measures number of binary bits that define the shade or colour of each pixel in an image. For example, a pixel in a black-and-white image has a depth of 1 bit, because it can only be white or black. A grayscale image is an 8-bit file, with 256 increments, ranging from black to white. The number of colour values that a given bit depth can produce is equal to 2 to the power of the bit depth. A pixel with a bit depth of 24 has 2^{24}, or roughly 16 million, possible values. Common values for bit depth range from 1 to 64 bits per pixel.

Photoshop supports up to 16 bits per pixel for each channel in an image. A 24-bit RGB image, for example, would have 8 bits per pixel for each of the red, green, and blue channels. The higher the colour depth supported by a file, the more space the file takes up on disk.

CONVERTING BETWEEN BIT DEPTHS

Converting is the process of changing something from one form to another. At times you might want to convert an image from one colour mode to another.

As we discussed earlier, colour mode is a system that defines the number and kind of colours that make up a bitmap image. When you convert an image from one colour mode to another, you can change the look of an image. You might also want to convert to a less memory-intensive colour mode to decrease file size, for example converting to the Grayscale colour mode.

You can select from Black and White (1-bit), Grayscale (8-bit), Duotone (8-bit), Indexed colour (8-bit), RGB colour (24-bit), LAB colour (24-bit) or CMYK colour (32-bit) colour modes. The 24 and 32 bit setting has the same amount of colors. They both have around 16.7 million colors (also called true color). The only difference between 24 and 32 bit is that the 32 bit setting has an 8 bit alpha channel that some 3D programs and games can use for different things.

As Photoshop can support upto 32-bit-per channel, it could read and import 96-bit RGB (32 bit x 3 channels), 48-bit RGB (16 bit x 3 channels), 64-bit CMYK (16 bit x 4 channels), and 16-bit grayscale images (16 bit x 1 channel). But few tools such as Gradient, text, blur, burn tool etc. do not support the 16/32 bit channel. If you try to use these tools in 16/32-bit-per-channel image, you will get the dialog box informing you that the selected tool can't be used.

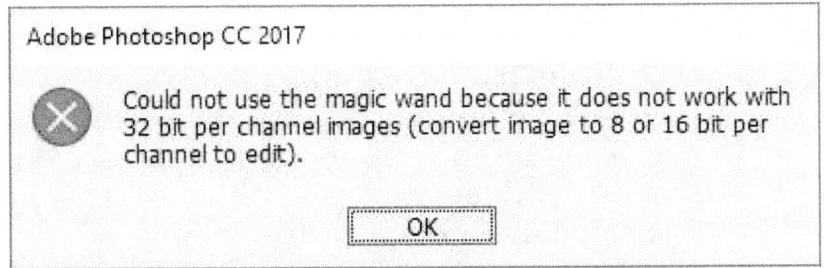

Fig 3.9 Error Message diisplaying that Magic wand tool can't be used on 32 bit channel

Therefore it is advisable that you convert a 32-bit-per-channel image to an 8/16-bit-channel image, to take full advantage of Photoshop's features .

- To convert from 32 bits per channel to 8 bits per channel, choose Image ➤ Mode ➤ 8 Bits/Channel. To convert from 8 bits per channel to 16 bits per channel, select Image ➤ Mode ➤ 16 Bits/Channel.

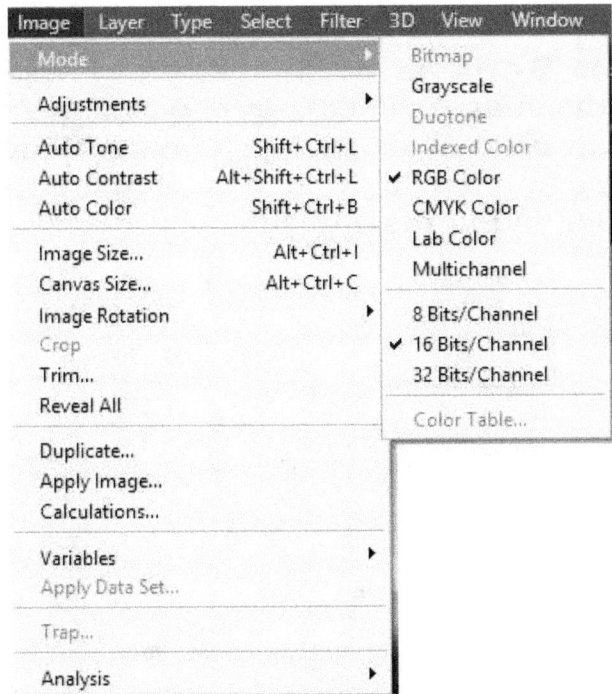

Fig 3.10 Converting Mode of the Image

- The active colour mode of the bitmap can be viewed using Image ➤ Mode submenu. The active colour mode, the mode the image is currently using, has a right check mark along it in the submenu. (Fig 3.10)

- To convert an image to another mode, choose Image ➤ Mode and the mode you want from the submenu. Modes not available for the active image appear dimmed in the menu.

Converting Between Grayscale Mode and Bitmap Mode

The Grayscale colour mode uses 256 shades of gray to represent an image. Every pixel in a grayscale image has a brightness value ranging from 0, which is black, to 255, which is white. In some cases, you must convert an image to grayscale before you can convert it to other modes. For example, you must convert an image to the Grayscale colour mode before you can convert it to the Duotone or Bitmap colour mode.

To convert an image to bitmap mode, do one of the following:

- If the image is in colour, choose Image ➤ Mode ➤ Grayscale. Then choose Image ➤ Mode ➤ Bitmap (Image must br 8 bit per channel). It confirms from you to discard the colour information (Fig 3.11).

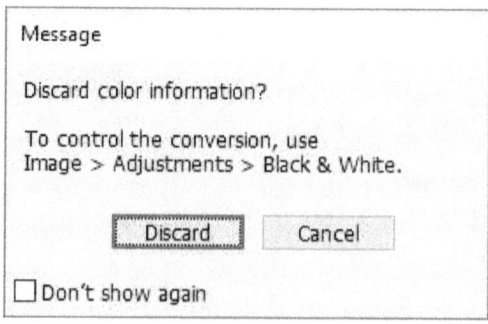

Fig 3.11 Converting to Grayscale

- If the image is grayscale, choose Image ➤ Mode ➤ Bitmap to display Bitmap dialog box (Fig 3.12).

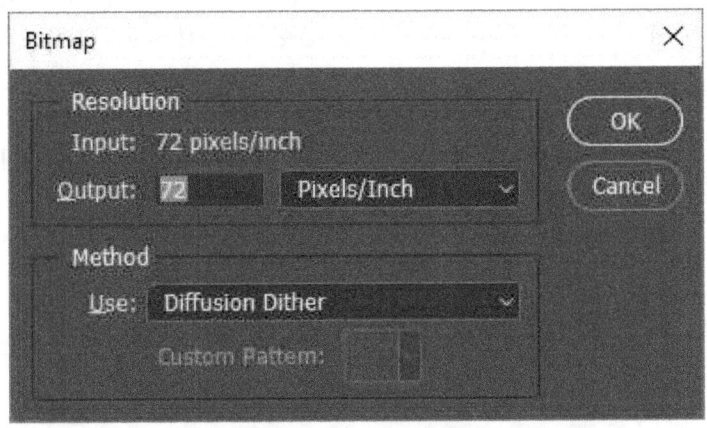

Fig 3.12 Specifying resolution for Bitmap

- For Output, enter a value for the output resolution of the Bitmap-mode image, and choose a unit of measurement.

- Select a bitmap conversion method from the drop down menu, and click OK.

50 % Threshold Converts pixels having gray values more than 128 (the middle gray level) to white and below to black. The output is a very high-contrast.

Pattern Dither Converts an image into geometric configurations of black-and-white dots.

Halftone Screen When you select this option, it brings another dialog box, which lets you define various factors related to halftone. The screen frequency specifies the ruling of the halftone screen in lines per inch (lpi). The frequency depends on the paper grains and type of press used for printing. Newspapers/ screen printers commonly use an 85-line screen. Magazines through offset/ web process use higher resolution screens, such as 133 lpi and 150 lpi. The screen angle, which refers to the orientation of the screen may vary in degrees from -180 to +180. Also select a required shape.

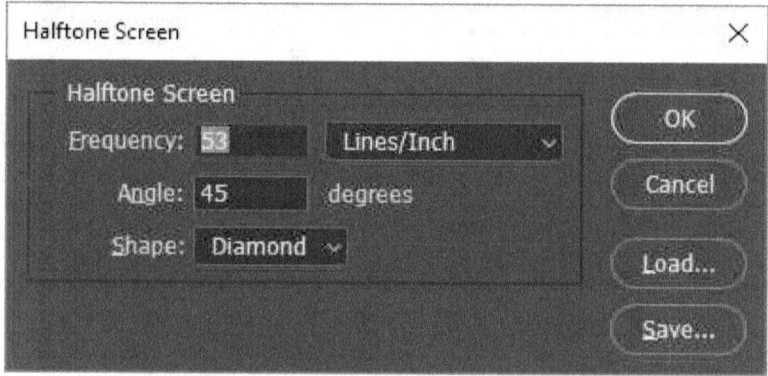

Fig 3.13 Specifying options for Halftone

Diffusion dither   Converts an image to bitmap using an error-diffusion process. In this process, first the upper left corner pixel is converted to black or white pixel according to its gray level (gray value > 128 - white, < 128, black). While converting in such a way, error is introduced, which is transferred to surrounding pixels throughout the image. This results in a grainy, filmlike texture.

Custom Pattern   This method converts the image according to the custom pattern selected from the drop-down me

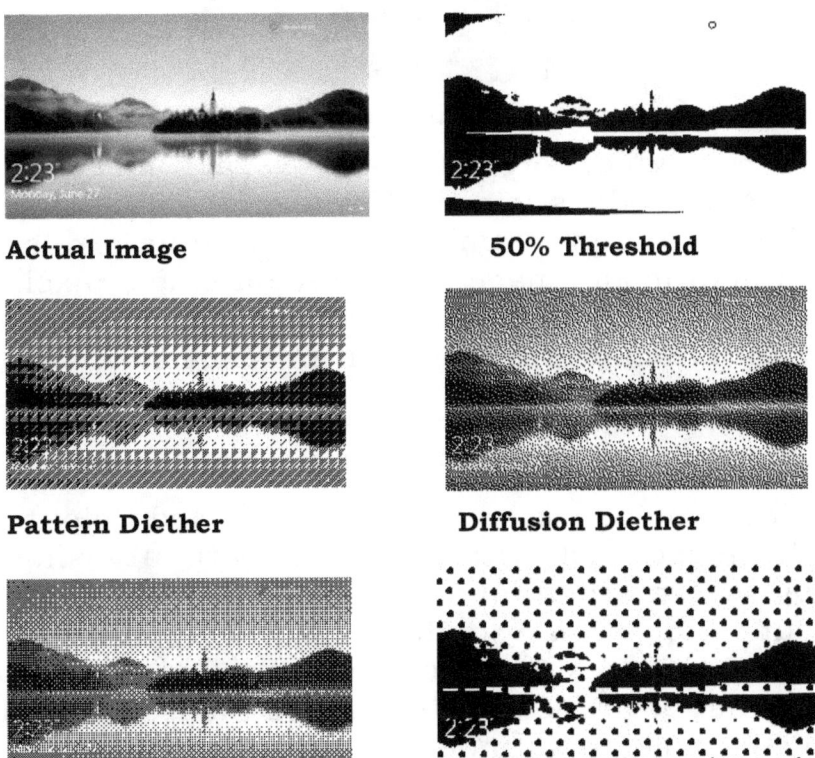

Actual Image   50% Threshold

Pattern Diether   Diffusion Diether

Halftone screen   Custom Pattern

Fig 3.14

You can also convert a Bitmap to Grayscale. To convert a bitmap mode image to grayscale, Choose Image ➤ Mode ➤ Grayscale. This brings Grayscale dialog box asking for a value for size ratio.

The size ratio is the factor for scaling down the image. The more size ratio you enter, the smaller will be the image. At value 1, the image will be of actual size but will not contain any gray pixel. As you reduce the size of the image, the new pixels, of grayscale image, are generated by averaging the multiple pixels as per the ratio.

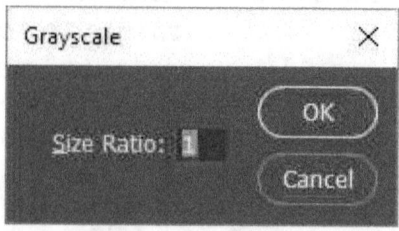

Fig 3.15 Specifying Size Ratio for Grayscale

For example, to reduce a grayscale image by 50%, enter 2 for the size ratio. If you enter a number greater than 1, the program averages multiple pixels in the Bitmap-mode image to produce a single pixel in the grayscale image. This process lets you generate multiple shades of gray from an image scanned on a 1-bit scanner.

Converting to Indexed Colour

When you convert an image to Indexed Colour mode, the image is left with 256 colour without losing much of the information. This mode is standard mode supported by many multimedia animation applications and Web pages. To convert an image to Indexed colour, it must be first converted to RGB mode. To convert an RGB image to an indexed colour image

- Choose Image ➤ Mode ➤ Indexed Colour to bring the Indexed colour dialog box (Fig 3.16).
- Select Preview to display a preview of the changes.
- Select a palette from the drop down menu.

Exact   If the image is using 256 or lower number of colours in RGB mode, then you can select this option to exactly produce the same colour in indexed colour mode.

System   It converts the image on the basis of Windows System's default 8-bit palette.

Web   If you want to convert the image for web usage, use this option. This palette is a subset of the Windows and Macintosh systems palettes.

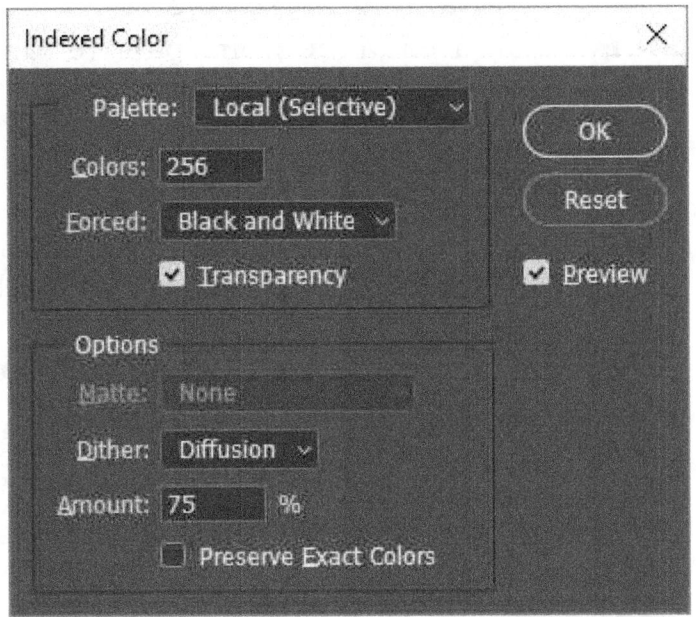

Fig 3.16 Specifying options for Indexed colour

Uniform   In this case, Photoshop produces a uniform palette of 6 evenly spaced colour levels each of red, green, and blue. In case of 8-bit image, it calculates the combinations of these colours to produce a uniform palette of 216 colours (6 x 6 x 6 = 216). A smaller bit depth creates a uniform palette composed of lesser number of colours.

Perceptual Selects the colour in the palette so that the colours having greater sensitivity in human eye are selected.

Selective Creates a colour table similar to the Perceptual colour table, but it favours broad areas of colour and gives preference to those colours.

Adaptive   Here the palette contains the colours that are most commonly appear in the image. To make few colour more prominent, select a part of the image containing those colours.

Custom   Creates a custom palette using the colour Table dialog box. The details of the colour table dialog box are discussed in the following section.

Previous   Uses the custom palette from the previous conversion, which helps in converting several images with the same custom palette.

- Select the bit depth for the image using uniform or adaptive palette.

- Select the dithering option from the drop down menu. Dithering mixes the pixels of the available colours to simulate the missing colours. If you are using Exact colour table option, the dithering option will not be available.

None   Uses the colour closest to the missing colour.

Diffusion   Uses an error-diffusion method which produces a less structured dither than the Pattern option.

Pattern   Available with Mac OS, Web or Uniform palette. It uses a halftone-like pattern to simulate any colours not in the colour table.

Noise   Helps to reduce seam patterns along the edges of image slices.

- If you select diffusion for dithering option, you can preserve exact colours from being dithering.

Customizing Colour Table

Photoshop also gives you the option to change one or more colour in the colour Table. This is helpful in producing special effects, model the colours after a predefined colour table, and save a colour table for reuse with other indexed-colour images.

To edit colours in the colour table:

- Open the indexed-colour image.
- Choose Image ➢ Mode ➢ Colour Table to bring up the colour table dialog box (Fig 3.17).

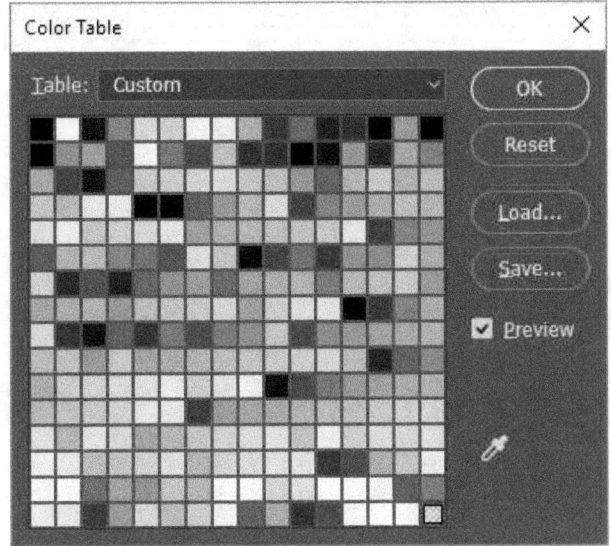

Fig 3.17 Colour Table dialog box

- Click on a colour to choose a colour from the colour Picker dialog box.
- Click and drag to select a range of colours. If you select a range of colours, PhotoShop will create a gradient from the standing colour to the ending colour. Select the first colour in the range and colour picker reappears to let you select the last colour of the range.
- Click on the colour picker and select a colour from the image. The colour is selected in the Table.
- Press Ctrl and the pointer is converted into a scissor. Click once and the entire left column of colour is removed. If you press Alt and click on

a colour in the colour table, the colour is selected in the image.

- Click OK in the colour Table dialog box to apply the new colours to the indexed-colour image.

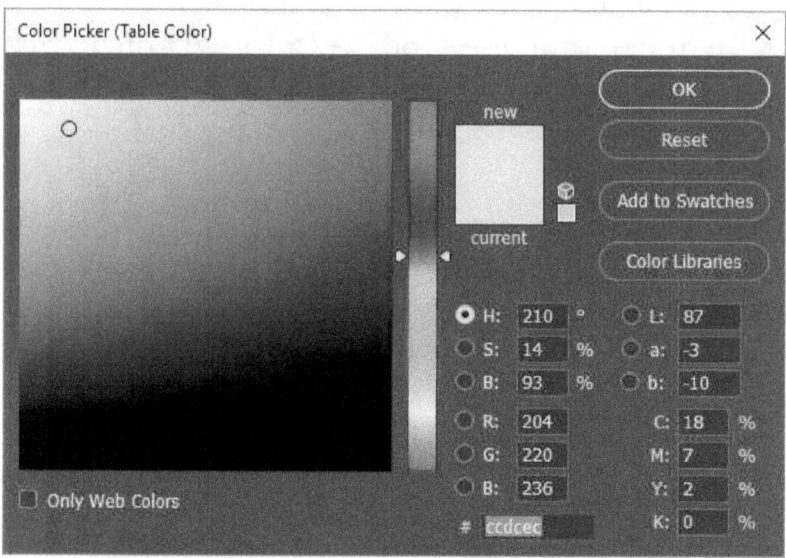

Fig 3.18 Using the colour Picker

- To model your indexed table after the predefined tables, select the option from the Table drop down menu.

Custom	Creates a customized palette.
Black Body	Displays a palette based on the different colours a blackbody radiator emits.
Grayscale	Displays a palette based on 256 levels of gray-from black to white.
Spectrum	Displays a palette based on the colours produced as white light passes through a prism (VIBGYOR)
Windows System	Displays the standard Windows 256-colour system palette.

Macintosh System Displays the standard Mac OS 256-colour system palette.

- You can use the Save and Load buttons in the colour Table dialog box to save your indexed colour tables for use with other Adobe Photoshop images.

IMPROVING IMAGES

Photoshop offers wide range of commands to control the relationship between the shadows, midtones, and highlights in objects in a drawing. You can also use these effects to adjust the brightness, intensity, lightness, and darkness of colours. The adjustment effects let you restore the detail lost in shadows or highlights, correct underexposure or overexposure, and improve the quality of images.

But before you adjust image, you must ensure that your monitor has been calibrated. Then use the following colour-correction workflow for more precise and flexible adjustments.

- Check the scan quality and tonal range.
- Adjust the tonal range.
- Adjust the colour balance.
- Make other special colour adjustments.
- Sharpen the edges of the image.

USING HISTOGRAM

The histogram is a read-only horizontal bar chart that plots the brightness values of the pixels in your image on a scale from 0 (dark) to 255 (light). You can use the histogram to view a visual representation of the tonal values in an image. Shadows are shown in the left part of the histogram, midtones are shown in the middle, and highlights are shown in the right part. A low-key image has detail concentrated in the shadows; a high-key image has detail concentrated in the highlights;

and an average-key image has detail concentrated in the midtones. When you adjust the tonal values, you change the level and distribution of dark and light areas in an image.

To view tonal values in your image

- Click Windows ➤ Histogram.

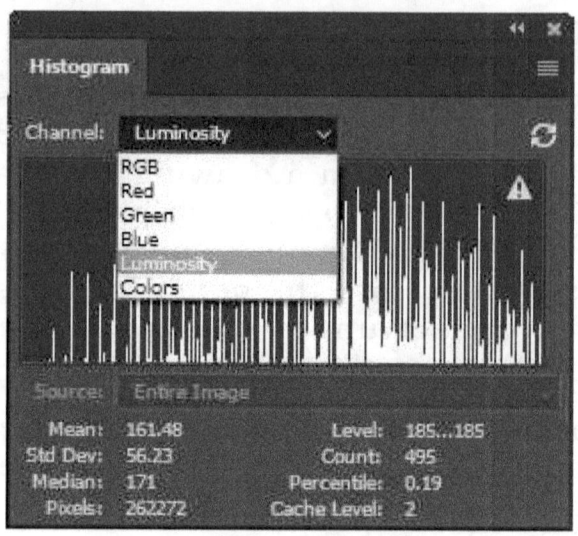

Fig 3.19 Histogram dialog box

- Choose a colour channel from the Channel list box.
- Drag to select a range of pixels which displays the following Range information:

Mean displays the average distribution of the pixel brightness.

Median displays the median distribution of the pixel brightness.

Std Dev displays the standard deviation of the pixel brightness.

Percentile indicates the percentage of image pixels which fall within the selected range.

Level displays the brightness level (between 0 and 255).

Pixels   displays the total number of pixels used to calculate the histogram.

Count   displays the total number of pixels corresponding to the intensity level of the selected range.

Catch Level displays the setting for the image cache.

ADJUSTING COLOURS

You can improve the quality of images by changing their colour and tone. Photoshop effects let you change the hue, saturation, lightness, balance, mixture, and behavior of the colours in images. It also offers tools and effects that you can use to alter the shadows, midtones, and highlights in images.

Levels

This option lets you change shadow, midtone, and highlighted areas by redistributing shades from darkest to lightest. Levels filter lets you preserve shadow and highlight detail that is lost when you adjust the brightness, contrast, and intensity of the tone of an image.

To change the shadows, midtones, and highlights of an image

- Click Image ➢ Adjustments ➢ Levels to bring the Levels dialog box.

- Choose a colour channel from the Channel list box. To select the multiple channels, select the channels in the Channel Palette and then select Image ➢ Adjustments ➢ Levels option.

- Now drag the left (black)and right (white) Input Levels sliders to the edge of the first group of pixels on either end of the   histogram. You can also move the sliders by entering values directly into the first and third Input Levels text boxes.

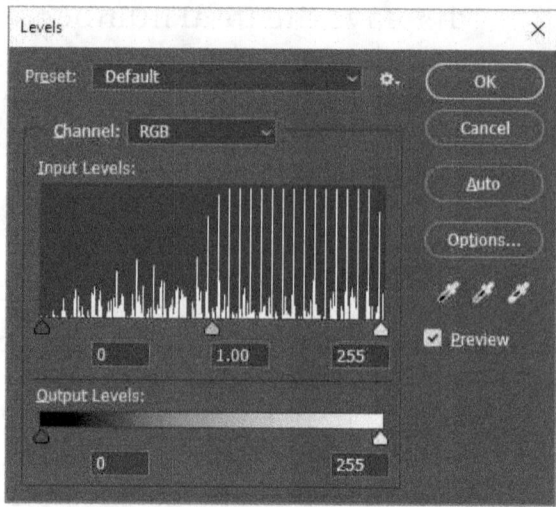

Fig 3.20 Levels dialog box

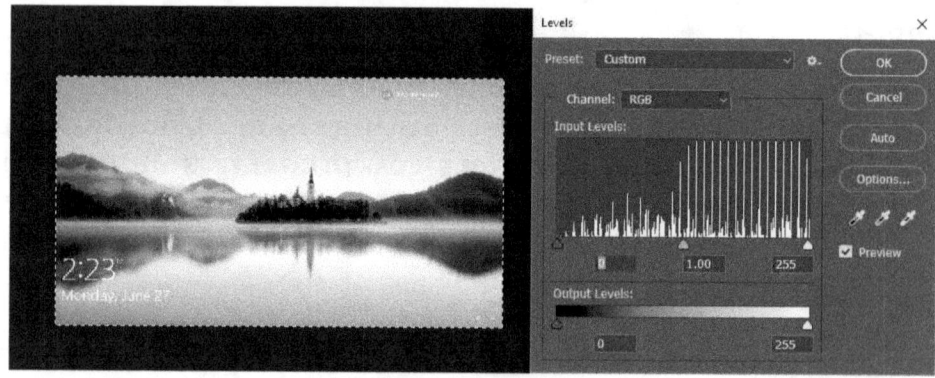

Fig 3.21 Adjusting level

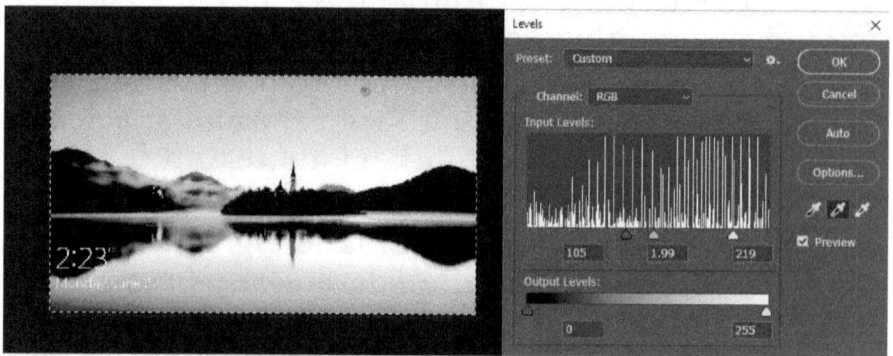

Fig 3.22 Image after adjusting level (Although the difference may not be visible in the black and white, but you can note down the difference in the graph

- To define shadow and highlight values, drag the black and white Output Levels sliders or enter the values directly in the Output Levels text boxes.

- Move the Grey Input Level slider to set the midtones.

- You can also click Auto to move the highlight and shadow sliders automatically to the brightest and darkest points.

- If you want to adjust the percentage of outlying pixels on either end of the tonal range, select Option button. Now click the Options button to bring Auto Range dialog box.

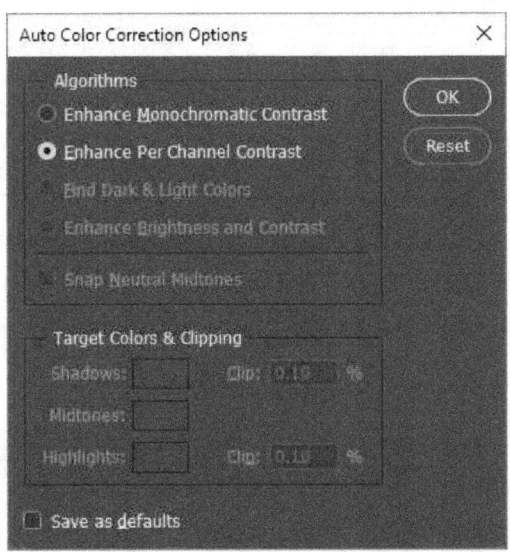

Fig 3.23 Specifying Auto Range option

- Now click OK button to let the effects take place.

Auto Levels

The Image ➤ Adjustments ➤ Auto Levels command performs automatic adjusting of the shadows, midtones, and highlights in an image by automatically redistributing the significant pixel values throughout the tonal range.

Auto Contrast

The Image ➤ Adjustments ➤ Auto Contrast command adjusts the overall contrast and mixture of colours in an image. As it does not adjust channels individually, Auto Contrast does not introduce or remove colour casts.

Curves

The Curves option lets you perform colour corrections precisely by controlling individual pixel values. You can pinpoint a problem area and produce a subtle or pronounced change in that area, which dissipates according to the tone curve, as you move away from the targeted area.

The Curves option also lets you take current pixel brightness values as input and change them to different values. The response curve represents the balance between shadows, midtones, and highlights.

To change the image using curves

● Click Image ➤ Adjustments ➤ Curves to bring the Curves dialog box.

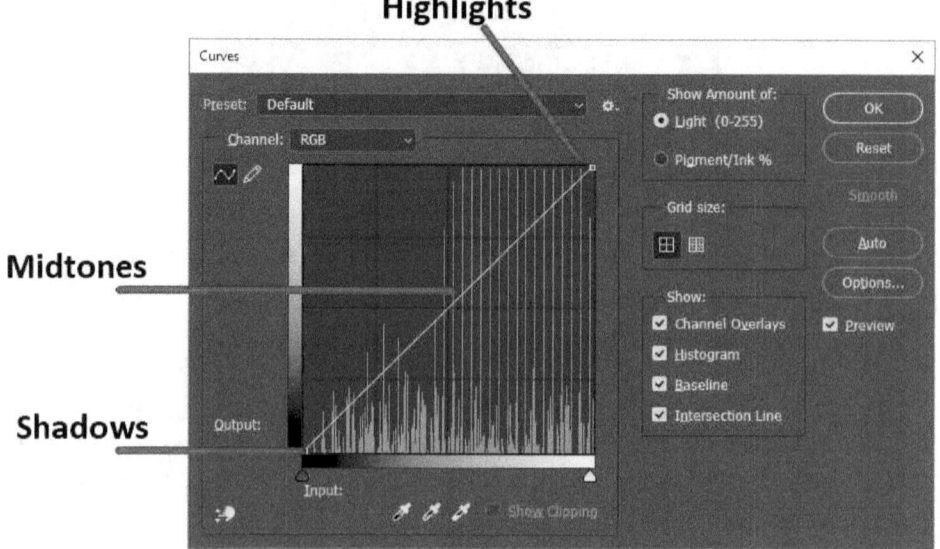

Fig 3.24 Adjusting Highlights, Midtones and shadows using Curves

- Choose a colour channel from the Channel list box. To select the multiple channels, select the channels in the Channel Palette and then select Image ➤ Adjustments ➤ Curves option.

- The Curves dialog box display the Highlights, Midtones and Shadows. By default, shadows are shown on the left at 0 value, and Highlights at right. (value 255 for RGB and 100 for CMYK). Click the double arrow below the curve, to reverse the display of shadows and highlights at any time.

- Press Alt to make grid finer. Now drag the curve to adjust the image. You can also click on a point on the curve and give Input and Output values. Or you can draw entirely a new curve using the Pencil icon.

- Use the smooth option button to smoothen the curve. You can Press Ctrl + Click to mark a point on the curve and then drag the curve around that point. Press Ctrl+D or click on the grid to deselect all selected points.

- Select the point to Delete the point.

Colour Balance

The Colour Balance option lets you change the mixture of colours in an image. This allows you to shift between CMY colour values and RGB colour values. This is done as per colour wheel. The colour wheel is handy tool for correcting colour casts. You can decrease the amount of any colour in an image by increasing the amount of its opposite on the colour wheel - and vice versa.

As displayed in the figure, to increase the green in the image, you can reduce magenta (increase Green) or reduce Blue or red.

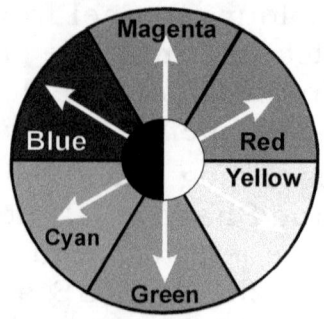

Fig 3.25 The colour Circle

To colour balance the image

- Click Image ➤ Adjustments ➤ Colour Balance to bring the colour Balance dialog box.

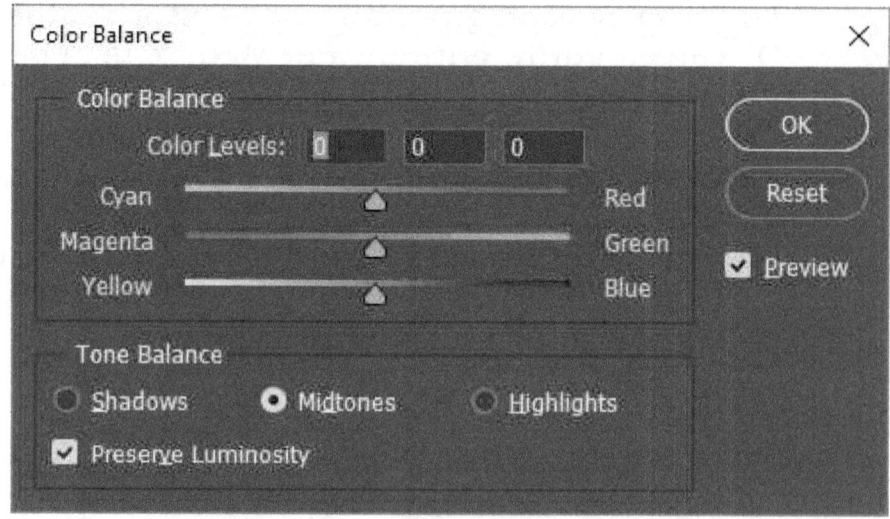

Fig 3.26 The colour Balance dialog box

- Select Shadows, Midtones, or Highlights. It balances the tone of the selected option.

- Select Preserve Luminosity to prevent changing the luminosity values in the image while changing the colour.

- Now drag the slider on any of the three lines - move the slider toward a colour if you want to increase that colour in the image; or away from a colour, if you want to decrease that colour in the image.

Click OK, when you achieve the required result.

Brightness Contrast

The Image ➤ Adjustments ➤ Brightness-Contrast option lets you change the brightness and contrast of image. You can move the slider in the right side to increase brightness and contrast and left side to decrease the brightness and contrast. Adjusting the brightness lightens or darkens all colours equally.

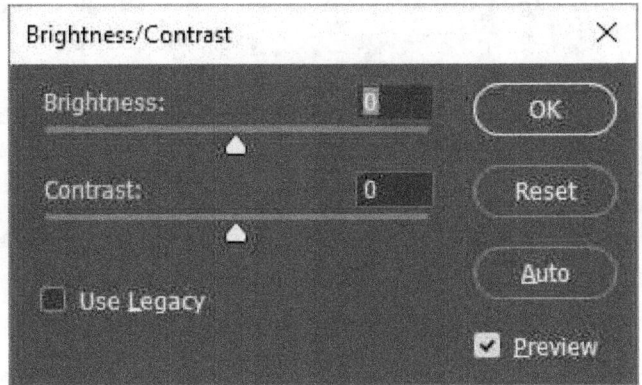

Fig 3.27 Controlling Brightness and Contrast

Hue/ Saturation

The Image ➤ Adjustments ➤ Hue/Saturation option lets you change the hue, saturation, and lightness values of an image all at once or channel by channel. When you change the hue, saturation, and lightness values of the colours in an image, you change the colour intensity by changing the richness and white values or by changing the colour entirely. Hue represents colour; saturation represents colour depth or richness; and lightness represents the overall percentage of white in an image.

The two bars at the bottom displays the colours before and after changing the hue and saturation.

To change the hue, saturation and lightness of the image

- Click Image ➢ Adjustments ➢ Hue/Saturation to bring the Hue/Saturation dialog box (Fig 3.28).

- Drag the slider in left or right as per your requirement or enter the value in the text box. The values can vary from -180 to +180.

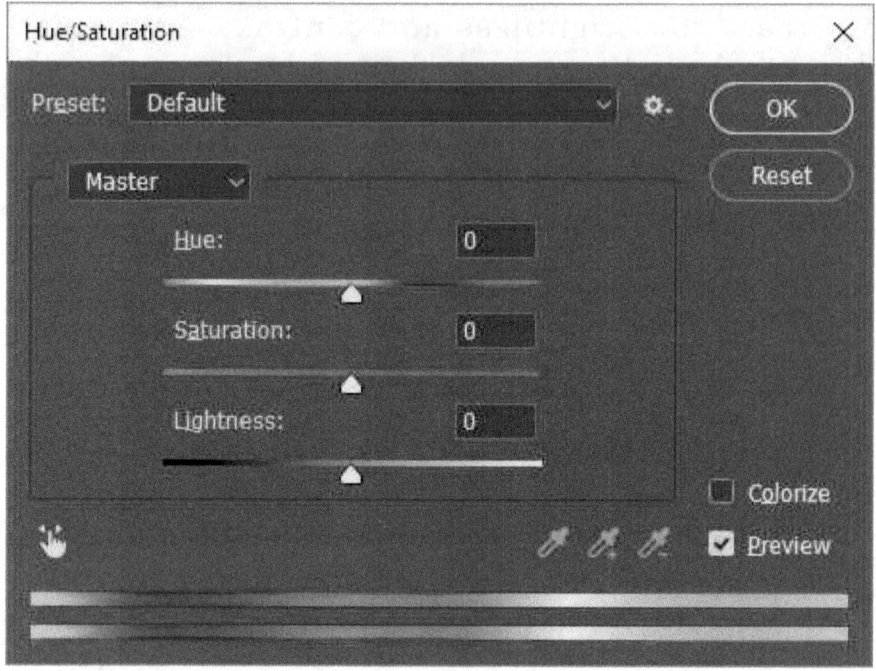

Fig 3.28 Controlling Hue and Saturation

- For Saturation, enter a value or drag the slider to the right to increase the saturation or to the left to decrease it. If you choose to enter the value, it may vary from -100 to + 100.

- For lightness also, you can enter a value between -100 to +100 or drag the slider to the right to increase the lightness or to the left to decrease it.

Desaturate

Image ➢ Adjustments ➢ Desaturate command automatically reduces the saturation of each colour to zero, removes the hue component, and converts each colour to its grayscale equivalent.

Replace Colour

The Replace Colours option lets you replace one image colour with another colour. Depending on the range you set, you can use the Replace Colours filter to replace one colour or to shift an entire image from one colour range to another.

To change the hue, saturation and lightness of the image

- Click Image ➤ Adjustments ➤ Replace Colour to bring the Replace colour dialog box.

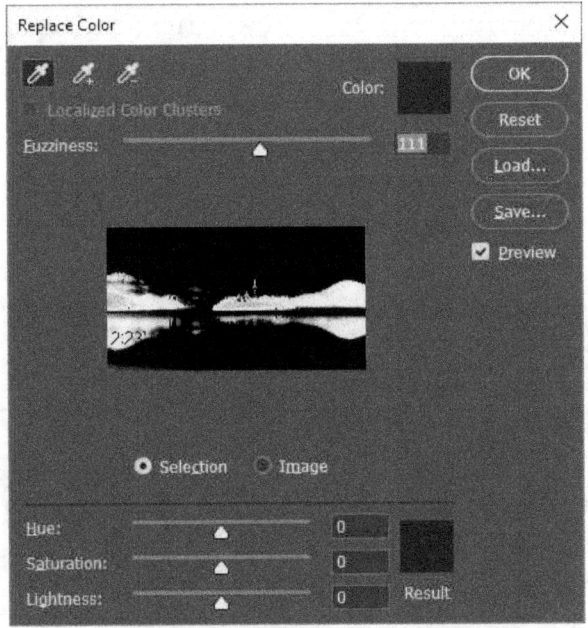

Fig 3.29 Replace Colour dialog box

- Select on the Eye dropper tool in the Replace dialog box, and click the colour that you want to replace. Select the Eye Dropper + to select an additional colour and Eye Dropper - to deselect a selected colour.

- To include colours that are near to the selected colour, increase the Fuzziness. This increases the range of selected colours.

- Now move any of the following Adjust sliders:

Hue   sets the hue level of the new colour.

Saturation sets the saturation level of the new colour.

Lightness   sets the lightness level of the new colour.

Selective Colour

The Selective Colour option lets you change colour by changing the percentage of the component process colours (CMYK values) in a colour spectrum (reds, yellows, greens, cyans, blues, and magentas). You can also use this filter to add process colour to the grayscale tonal component of an image.

- Select Image ➢ Adjustments ➢ Selective Colour to bring Selective colour dialog box.

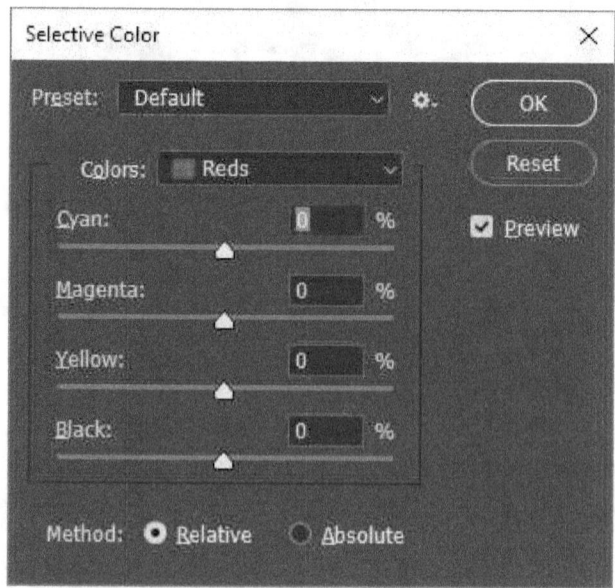

Fig 3.30 Selective Colour dialog box

- To increase or decrease the percentage of cyan, magenta, yellow, and black pixels that make up each primary colour in the colour spectrum, move the slider in right or left direction respectively.

• The extent of colour modification depends largely on the adjustment percentage method you choose. You could select Relative or Absolute method.

Gradient Map

The Gradient Map option fills the equivalent grayscale range of an image to the colours of the selected gradient fill. To use the Gradient Map command :

• Click Image ➤ Adjustments ➤ Gradient Map to bring the Gradient Map dialog box.

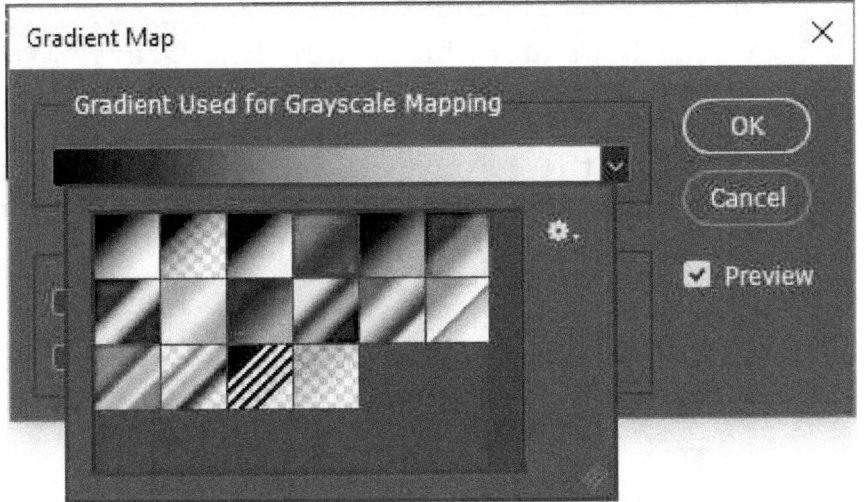

Fig 3.31 Applying Gradient Map

• Choose a Gradient Map from the drop down menu and Click OK.

Invert

The Invert option automatically reverses the colours in an image creating the appearance of a photographic negative.

91

Equalize

The Equalization option enhances the contrast near image edges and reveals details in both light and dark regions.

Threshold

The Threshold option lets you set a brightness value as a threshold. Pixels, with brightness values above or below the threshold, are displayed in white or black respectively. You can change the threshold value.

To use threshold to change the image into black and white

- Click Image ➤ Adjustments ➤ Threshold to bring the Threshold dialog box.

- Move the slider, below the histogram, in the right direction to bring more pixels in black by increasing the threshold level. If you move the slider in the left direction, you decrease the threshold value and thus more white pixel appear in the image.

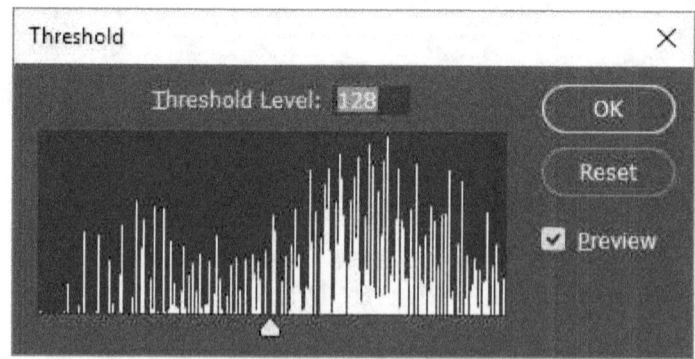

Fig 3.32 Specifying Threshold Level

Posterize

The Posterize option reduces the number of tonal values in the colours used to create an image. All existing colours are mapped to the closest match.

Posterizing removes tonal gradations and creates larger areas of flat colour.

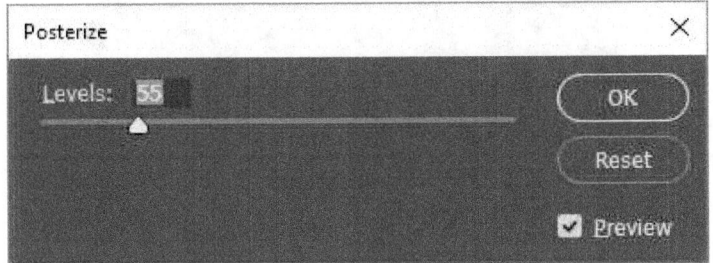

Fig 3.33 Specifying Posterize

Shadows/Highlights

The Shadow/Highlight command is used for correcting photos with silhouetted images due to strong backlighting. It can also be used to correct subjects that have been slightly washed out because they were too close to the camera flash.

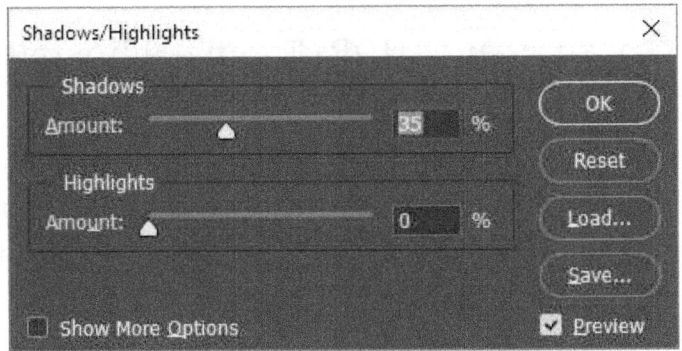

Fig 3.34 Specifying Shadows and Highlights

Click Show more option to display Midtone Contrast slider, Black Clip option, and White Clip option for adjusting the overall contrast of the image, and a Color Correction slider for adjusting saturation.

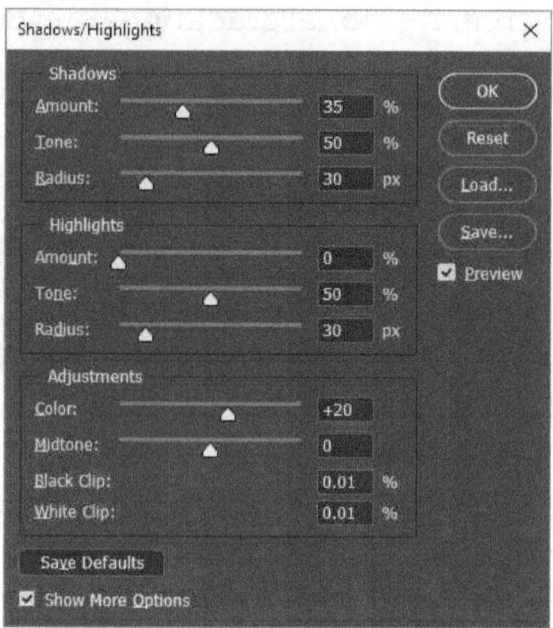

Fig 3.35 Specifying more options in Shadows and Highlights

Exposure and HDR Toning

The Exposure and HDR Toning adjustments are primarily designed for 32-bit HDR images, but you can also apply them to 16- and 8-bit images to create HDR-like effects. High Dynamic Range (HDR) technique are used in photography and imaging to reproduce a greater dynamic range of luminosity than is possible with standard digital imaging or photographic techniques.

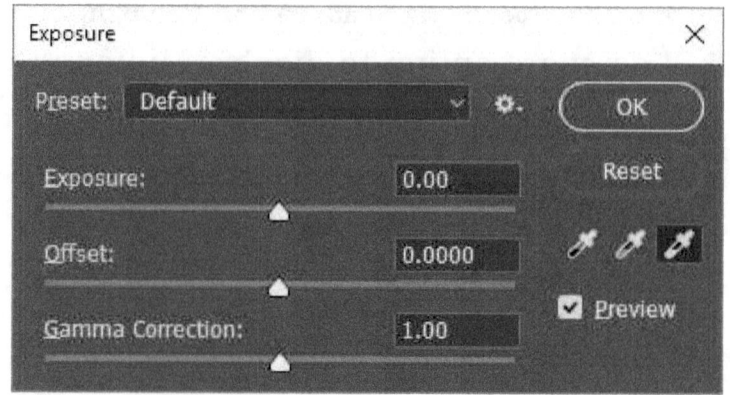

Fig 3.36 Specifying Exposure

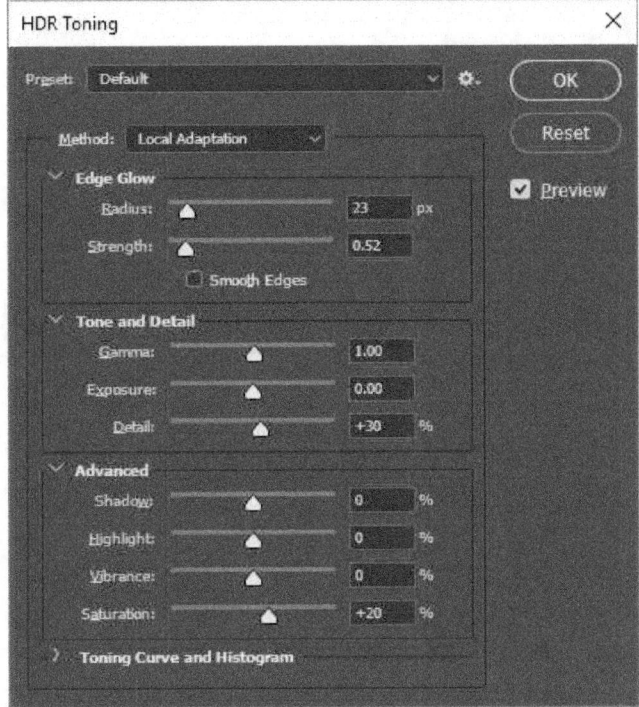

Fig 3.37 Specifying more options in Exposure

WORKING WITH SELECTIONS

You can use selections to do advanced image editing. A selection is an area of an image that you isolate so that you can modify it. After selecting a part of image, you can move selections, expand and reduce them, or apply transformations to them, such as rotating, scaling, and skewing.

Photoshop offers many tools for making selections. You can make select entire image or part of image by clicking and dragging with the marquee, lasso, polygon lasso, or magnetic lasso tool, or by targeting colour areas with the magic wand tool or the Colour Range command. The option palette of selection tool also offers useful options.

THE MARQUEE TOOLS

You can select areas with a specific shape using the marquee tools in rectangular or elliptical shape.

You can use one marquee tool to create a simple selection, or you can use a combination of marquee tools to create complex selections. When you choose a tool from the MarqueeTools flyout, controls that apply specifically to the active tool are displayed on the Option Palette.

Fig 4.1 Marquee Tool flyout menu

- Marquee tool flyout offers four options:
  - Rectangular marquee to make a rectangular selection.
  - Elliptical marquee to make an elliptical selection.

- Single row or single column marquee to define the border as a 1-pixel-wide row or column.

Selecting Rectangular or Elliptical Area

You can select a rectangular or elliptical area by drawing in the Image Window or by specifying its dimensions.

To select a rectangular or Elliptical area

- Open the marquee tools flyout, and click the Rectangle or Elliptical marquee tool.

- Select the required style from the drop down menu from the option palette.

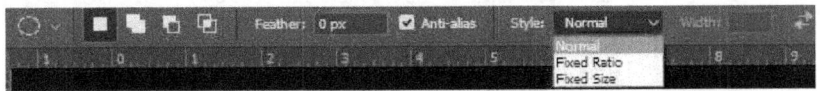

Fig 4.2 Specifying options for Marquee Tool flyout

- Select Normal option to determine marquee dimension by dragging.

- Select Constrained Aspect Ratio to set a height-to-width ratio. With this option selected, the selected portion on the image will have the same aspect ratio. When you select this option, the Width and Height text box becomes active, and you can define the aspect ratio there.

- Select Fixed Size to select marquee of already defined dimension. When you select this option, the Width and Height text box becomes active, and you can define the dimension there.

- To make a selection, do one of the following:

  - With Normal or Constrained Aspect Ratio style selected, drag over the image to select the required area.

  - With Fixed size option selected, click in the image to position the top left corner of the selection.

W : 5.792 in
H : 5.583 in

Fig 4.3 Selecting area using Rectangular Marquee Tool. While selecting the area, you can use the following key combination for
perfect shapes. Start dragging the marquee and

- Hold down CTRL, to select a perfect square.
- Hold down SHIFT, to select a rectangle drawn from the center.
- Hold down CTRL + SHIFT, to select a perfect square drawn from the center.
- You can create feathered edges for the selection by using the Feather Width box on the Option Palette.

Selecting Single Row/Column

Photoshop also offers Marquee tools that let you select single pixel row (Row height 1 pixel) or single pixel column (Column width 1 pixel). To select an area of 1 pixel height/width through entire image,

- Select the Single Row marquee/Single Column marquee tool.
- The option palette offers only the feather option. Select the option if required.
- Click on the image to select the row or column.

Using the Lasso, Polygon Lasso, and Magnetic Lasso Tools

These tools lets you define the area to be selected in the image. These tools let you draw both straight-edged and freehand segments of a selection border whereas magnetic lasso tool snaps to the edges of defined areas in the image. You can use the magnetic lasso tool for quickly selecting objects with complex edges set against high-contrast backgrounds.

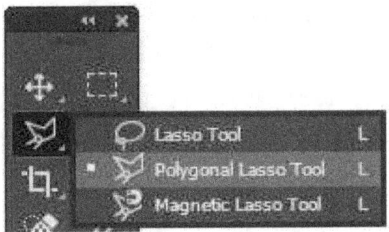

Fig 4.4 The Lasso Tool flyout

To use the lasso tool:

- Select the lasso tool from the flyout. You can create feathered edges for the selection by using the Feather Width box on the Option Palette.

- Now click and drag to draw a freehand selection border.

- Release the mouse to close the selection border.

- If you press Alt key with lasso tool, it becomes the polygon lasso tool.

To use the polygon lasso tool

- Select the polygon lasso tool from the option palette to display its Options palette, and select the required option.

- Click in the image to set the starting point. Now click on more points so as to select the desired area. As you click, new segments of straight line are created. Press Del to delete the recent click.

  - To enclose the area, position the polygon lasso tool pointer over the starting point (a closed circle appears next to the pointer) and click.

  - If you are away from the starting point and want to connect the starting position and present position by a straight line segment, double-click the lasso tool pointer, or Ctrl-click.

To use the magnetic lasso tool

● Select the magnetic lasso tool from the flyout menu. The Option palette lets you define various options for magnetic lasso tool.

● Define feather width in the options palette to select feathered edges. Enter a pixel value between 1 and 40 to specify a detection width. To specify the rate at which the lasso sets fastening points, enter a value between 0 and 100 for Frequency. To specify the lasso's sensitivity to edges in the image, enter a value between 1% and 100% for Edge Contrast.

Fig 4.5 Specifying values for Magnetic Lasso Tool

● Now, click in the image to set the first fastening point. Move the pointer along the edge you want to trace.

Fig 4.6 Using Magnetic Lasso Tool

As you move the pointer, the active segment snaps to the strongest edge in the image. The magnetic lasso tool adds fastening points to the selection border to anchor previous segments.

- Press Del if you want to delete the recent added fastening point. You can add the fastening point manually if the border doesn't snap to the desired edge. Continue to trace the edge and add fastening points as needed.

- You can use other lasso tools also while selecting the image. To activate lasso tool, hold down Alt and drag with the mouse button depressed . To activate polygon lasso tool, hold down Alt and click.

- Close the selection border by double-clicking or Alt-Double clicking.

A greater lasso width and higher edge contrast trace the border roughly whereas the smaller width and lower edge contrast will trace the border more precisely.

MAGIC WAND TOOL

The Magic Wand tool lets you select adjacent colours for editing without having to trace the outline. Using Magic wand tool, you click on the colour to be selected. It also lets you define the tolerance range so that the selected colour and all other colours falling within the specified tolerance range and lying adjacent to the selected colour are selected.

To use the magic wand tool:

- Click on the magic wand tool. Enter value in pixel for tolerance, ranging from 0 to 255. A small value lets you pick colour similar to the pixel you click, whereas a higher value to select a broader range of colours.

- To define a smooth edge, select Anti-aliased. To select colours using data from all the visible layers, select Use All Layers.

- In the image, click the colour you want to select. All adjacent pixels within the tolerance range are selected.

To select all pixels on a layer within the canvas boundaries,

- Select the layer, on which you want to make selection, in the Layers palette.

- Choose Select ➤ All from the menu or right click on the image to bring the context sensitive menu and Select All from the menu.

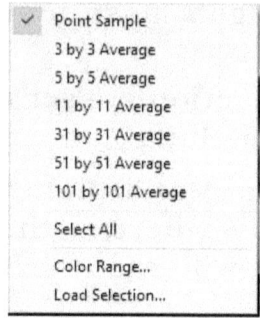

Fig 4.7 Selecting entire area using Magic Wand Tool

- To deselect selections, choose Select ➤ Deselect or click anywhere in the image outside the selected area using the rectangular marquee, elliptical marquee or lasso tool

- To reselect the most recent selection, choose Select ➤ Reselect.

Using the Colour Range Command

The Colour Range command lets you select a specified colour and all other colours falling within the specified tolerance range, within an existing selection or an entire image. To replace the existing selection, you must deselect the entire selection.

To select a colour range using sampled colours

- Choose Select ➤ Colour Range from the menu or colour range option from the context menu. (Fig 4.8)

- The Colour range dialog box lets you select the colour of your choice or any of the preset colours. For selecting colour of your choice, select

Sampled Colours from the Select drop down menu.

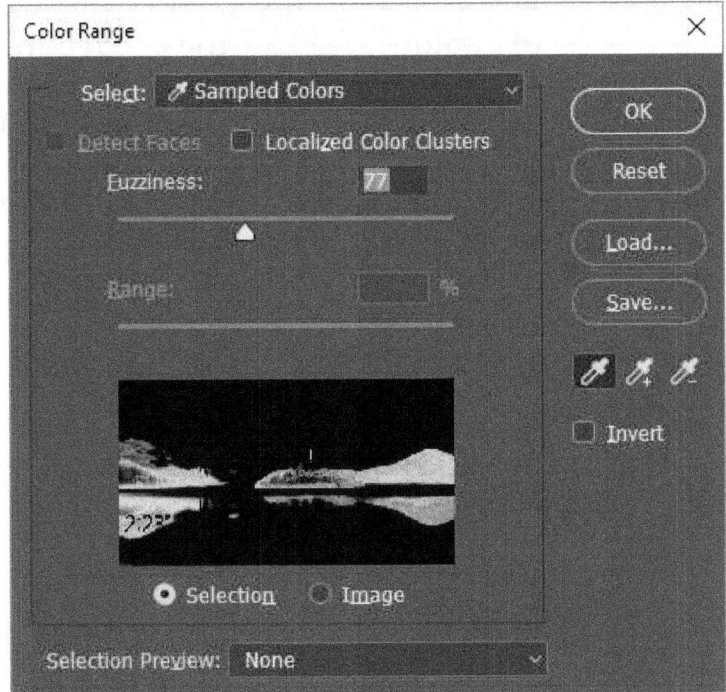

Fig 4.8 Using Colour Range dialog box

To select any preset colours, select the required option from the Select drop down menu.

- To select the range of colour, use Fuzziness slider or enter a value (Max 200). To decrease the range of colours selected, decrease the value.

- Select one of the following options listed below the preview box:

  - Selection to preview only the selection.

  - Image to preview the entire image. You can use Ctrl to toggle between Image and Selection.

- Now, position the eyedropper over the image or preview area, and click on the pixel of the colours you want to include.

- Adjust the selection by moving the Fuzziness slider.

- The Colour Range also lets you add or subtract colours from the selected colours. You could use eyedropper+ or eyedropper- tool respectively.
  - To add colours, select the eyedropper+ tool or hold down Shift with normal eyedropper tool and click on the image or preview area.
  - To subtract colours, select the eyedropper- tool or hold down Alt with normal eyedropper and click in the preview area or image.
- To preview the selection in the image window, choose an option for Selection Preview:

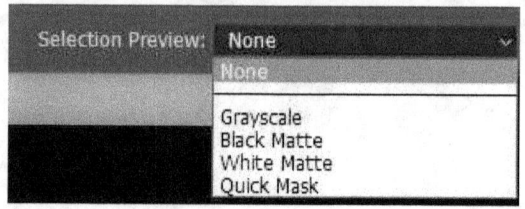

Fig 4.9 Selection Perview drop down menu

- **None**   -   No preview.
- **Grayscale** -   Selected portion as would appear in grayscale channel.
- **Black Matte** -selection in colour against a black background.
- **White Matte**- selection in colour against a white background.
- **Quick Mask** - selection using the current quick mask settings.
- Select the Invert option to select the opposite of original selection.

  Hold down Alt key to make Reset button active, to reset to the original selection.
- Click OK to make the selection.

You can also save the settings to reuse it at later stage by using the Save and Load buttons in the Colour Range dialog box.

ALTERING SELECTION

EXPANDING AND REDUCING SELECTIONS

You can expand or reduce a selection by using various selection tools defined in the option palette. Option palette of all selection tool provides four options - New Selection (Default), Add to selection, Subtract from selection and Intersect with selection.

Adding to Selection

To add to the selection or select an additional area in the image, select the selection tool and then select Add to selection option from Option palette.

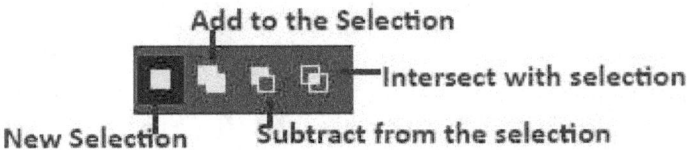

Fig 4.10 Altering Selection using various options

Selecting this option is equivalent to holding down Shift with New Selection option (a plus sign appears next to the pointer). Now select the area or areas you want to add.

Subtract from Selection

To subtract an area from a selection, select the selection tool and then select Subtract from selection option from Option palette. Selecting this option is equivalent to holding down Alt with New Selection option (a minus sign appears next to the pointer). Now select the area or areas you want to subtract.

Intersect with Selection

To intersect selections, select the selection tool and then select Intersect with selection option from Option palette. Selecting this option is equivalent to holding down Alt+Shift with New Selection (a cross appears next to the pointer), Now select an area that intersects the original selection. Photoshop retains only that portion that is common of two areas.

ADJUSTING SELECTIONS NUMERICALLY

Select menu offers tools in the Modify submenu to expand or contract the image numerically. Using these tools you can increase or decrease the pixels in an existing selection.

Expanding or Contracting Numerically

To expand or contract a selection border, choose Select ➤ Modify ➤ Expand or Contract.

- For Expand By or Contract By, enter a pixel value between 1 and 16, and click OK.

This increases or decreases the value of the border by the specified amount. If a portion of selection is running along the image's edge, it remains unaffected.

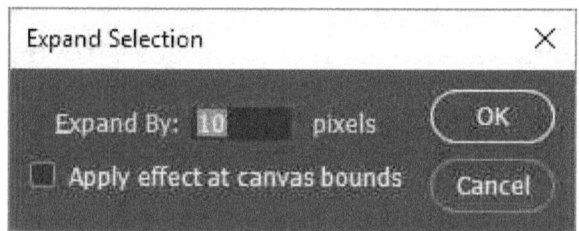

Fig 4.11 Expanding selection

Bordering the Selected Area

Photoshop also lets you select a border around the selected pixels. To frame an existing selection with a selection

- Use a selection tool to make a selection and choose Select ➤ Modify ➤ Border.

Enter a value between 1 and 64 pixels for the width of the border, and click OK. This selects the border of specified width around the selected area.

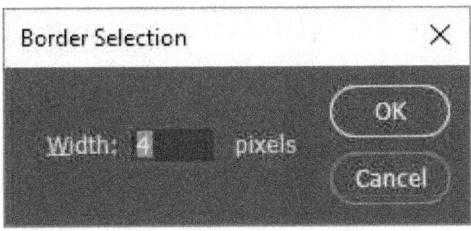

Fig 4.12 Selecting Border around the selected area

Smoothening the selection

Smoothening removes the hard edges in the selected area. To smooth a selection, choose Select ➤ Modify ➤ Smooth.

- For Sample Radius, enter a pixel value between 1 and 16, and click OK.

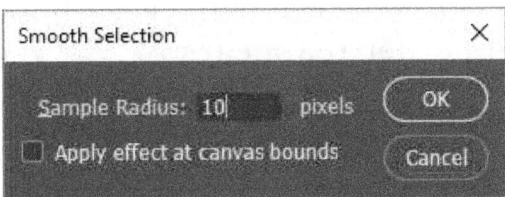

Fig 4.13 Smoothening the selection

Growing Selection

You can also grow the selected area on the basis of colour. To extend a selection based on colour, you can one of two options Grow or Similar, defined in the Select menu.

- Select ➤ Grow command expands a selection by adding pixels that are of similar colour to the pixels in the selection and adjacent to them. The Grow command operates on the basis of the colour tolerance you specify for the Magic Wand tool, but it modifies a selection created with any of the selection tools.

- Select ➤ Similar command expands a selection by adding pixels that are of similar colour to the pixels in the selection and located anywhere in the image, not just adjacent ones.

ADJUSTING SELECTION

PhotoShop also provides many options to adjust and refine your selections. This you can do using the selection tools or a variety of commands in the Select menu.

Moving the Border

To move the selection border within the image, select any selection tool and place the pointer inside the selection border.

Now drag the selection border to enclose a different area of the image. If you drag the selection border beyond the canvas and drop it there, the selection is deleted. But if you drag it back without dropping it, the original border reappears.

If you drag the selection border to another image window, the same border reappears there to select the area of that image.

You can use the following methods to control the motion of selection border:

- To constrain the motion of selection border vertically, horizontally or diagonally, begin dragging, and then hold down Shift as you continue to drag.
- To move the selection in 1-pixel increments in any of the four direction, use the keyboard arrow keys.
- To move the selection in 10-pixel increments in any of the four direction, hold down Shift, and press an arrow key.

Hiding the Border

To hide or show selection border, choose View ➤ Hide Edges or Show Edges to toggle between hiding and showing.

Selecting Inverse

To select the unselected parts of an image, choose Select ➤ Inverse. This tool at times is very effective when you want to select all the colours except one colour. First you select that colour using any tool and then invert the selection.

Fig 4.14 Figures displaying selected portion and Inverse selected portion

SOFTENING EDGES OF A SELECTION

You can adjust the edges of selections by applying anti-aliasing or feathering effects.

Anti Aliasing

Anti-aliasing makes some of the pixels located on the edge of a selection semitransparent, thus creating a smoother outline. It is especially useful for smoothing the uneven edges that often result from creating selections along curved or diagonal regions.

Anti-aliasing is enabled by default for the lasso, polygon lasso, magnetic lasso, elliptical marquee, and magic wand tools. also you can apply Anti-aliasing only if you enable it before you create a selection. Once a selection is made, you cannot add anti-aliasing.

To use anti-aliasing, select Anti-aliased in the Options palette for the selected tool.

Feathering

Feathering blends the edges of a selection with the underlying background by gradually increasing the transparency of the pixels along the edge of a selection.

You can define feathering for the marquee, lasso, polygon lasso, or magnetic lasso tool as you use the tool, or you can add feathering to an existing selection. Feathering effects become apparent when you move, cut, or copy the selection.

To define a feathered edge for a selection tool, enter a Feather value in the Options palette. This value defines the width of the feathered edge and can range from 1 to 250 pixels.

To define a feathered edge for an existing selection

• Choose Select ➢ Modify ➢ Feather.

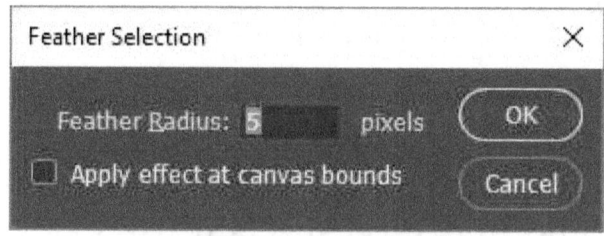

Fig 4.15 Specifying Feather Selection

• Enter a value for the Feather Radius, and click OK.

You may note that if selected selection is small and you define a large feather radius, then an error message appears as the selection may be faint that edges are invisible and thus not selectable.

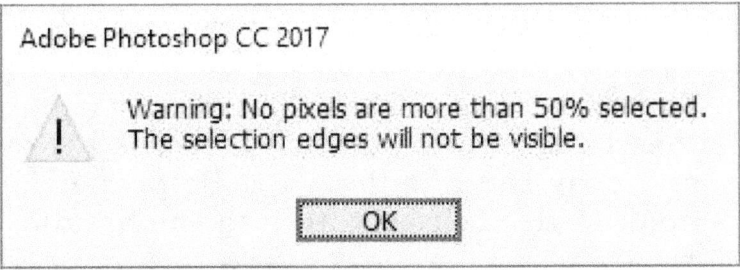

Fig 4.16 Error message on specifying Large Feather Radius

TRANSFORMING SELECTION

You can transform a selection by rotating, resizing, scaling, mirroring, skewing, distorting or applying perspective to its marquee. PhotoShop lets you transform selection border as well as the selected portion of the image.

To transform the selection border, create or load a selection border and choose the option Select ➤ Transform Selection. This brings the bounding box around the selection. If you want to combined selection border with the underlying image choose the option Edit ➤ Free Transform or select the Move tool (⊕) and select the option Show bounding box from the option palette. The difference between transforming a selection border and the selections is displayed in the Fig. 4.17.

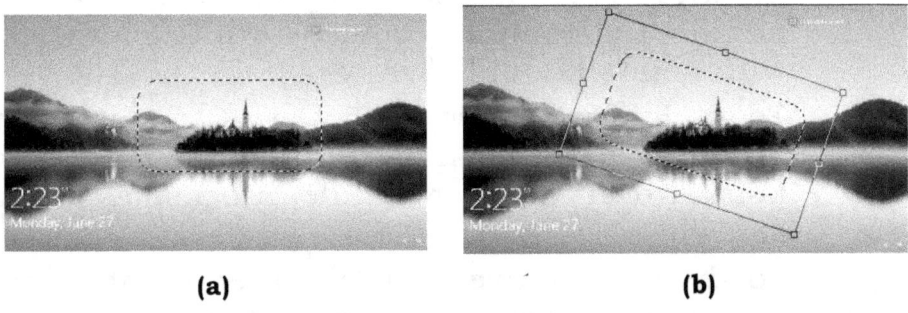

(a)   (b)

Fig 4.17 (a) Original Selection, (b) Transformed selection border

In both the cases, eight handles surrounds the selection and as you move the cursor towards the handles, it changes shape.

Now you can apply following transformation to the selection border or the selections.

- To scale, position the cursor over a handle so that it becomes a double arrow (↖). Now click and drag the handle. To scale proportionately, hold down Shift as you drag the handle.

- To rotate, move the pointer outside of the bounding border so as to make it a curved double-arrow (↷)and then drag. To constrain the rotation to 15° increments, hold down Shift key as you drag. If you want to change the centre point around which rotation takes place, drag the center point to a new position.

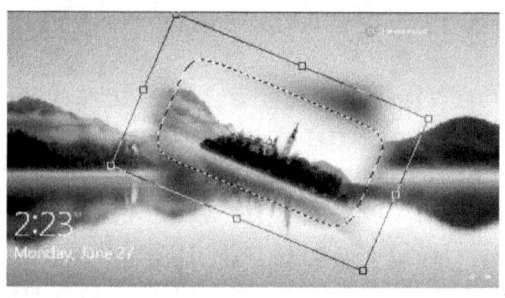

(c)

Fig 4.17 (c) Transformed selection

- To skew, hold down Ctrl+Shift and drag the handle. If you position the pointer over a side handle, the pointer becomes a white arrowhead with a small double arrow (▸).

- To apply perspective, hold down Ctrl+Alt+Shift, and drag a corner handle. If you position the pointer over a corner handle, it becomes a gray arrowhead.

- To distort relative to the center point of the bounding border, hold down Alt key and drag a handle.

- To distort freely, hold down Ctrl and drag a handle.

DRAWING IN PHOTOSHOP

DRAWING SHAPES

You can draw squares, rectangles, circles, ellipses, and polygons on your images using the Shape tools. Besides these standard shapes that Photoshop offers, you can draw your own shapes from scratch with the pen, magnetic pen, or freeform pen tool. Shapes can be outlined or filled with colour, and can be rendered as separate objects or merged directly with the image background or active object. You can also draw straight line segments on your images. When you create line segments using the Line tool, you can control the width of the line, the way that multiple line segments join together, and the transparency of the lines.

Shapes are line and curve segments connected by square endpoints called nodes or anchor points. Anchor points connecting curve segments have two direction line ending into direction point that determine the angle of the curve you are creating or shaping. Direction point look like small nodes and are connected with a line that passes through the node.

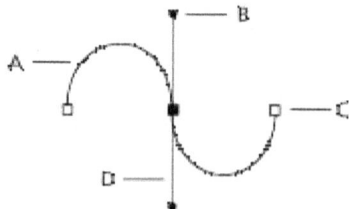

Fig 5.1 A. Curved segment B. Control or Direction point C. Node or Anchor point D. Direction line

As shapes are created from line and curve segments, they are vector objects and contain no pixels. Shapes are easy to work with as you can quickly select, resize, edit, and move a shape. You can also use shapes to make selections and create libraries of custom shapes. Moreover, As shapes are vector objects, they are resolution-independent, thus they maintain their crisp edges and attributes even if you resize them.

You can draw simple shapes and lines using a tool in the Shape Tools flyout or using a pen tool. If you create the shape or line as an object, you can edit it independent of the background image as the shape is created on a separate layer. This layer, on which you create a new shape, is consist of two parts - a fill layer with a layer clipping path.

The fill layer defines the colour of the shape, while the layer clipping path defines the geometric outline of the shape. If you want to change the colour and other attributes of a shape, you can do so by editing its fill layer and applying layer styles to it. If you want to change the outline of the shape, you can edit its layer clipping path. The clipping path also appears in the Paths palette.

CREATING NEW SHAPES

You can create new shapes using shape tools or pen. You can specify the foreground colour similar to the colour, you want to fill in the shape. To create a new shape

- Click on the rectangle tool, rounded rectangle tool, ellipse tool, polygon tool or line tool from the flyout. To create any custom shape from the predefined set, select the Custom Shape tool. Additionally, you can select pen tool or freeform tool from the toolbox to draw shapes.

 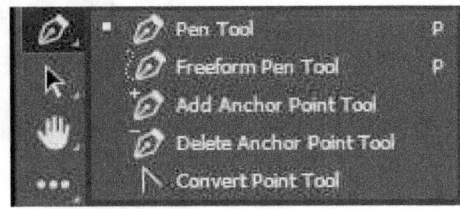

Fig 5.2 Shape and Pen flyout

- Once you select the tool, look at the option palette. Option palette offers you options to create a new shape layer or a new work path. Click on the new shape layer option. There is also another option of creating filled regions for few tools like rectangle, ellipse etc.

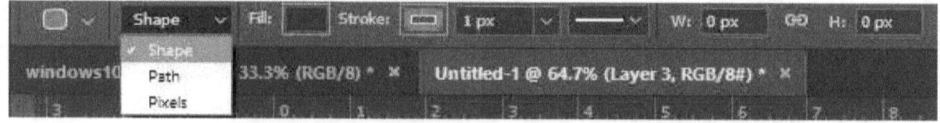

Fig 5.3 Selecting options for drawing Shapes

- When you select the New shape layer option, option palette offers others options.

  - To choose a layer style from predefined layer styles, click on the Layer Style pop-up palette.

  - Specify a layer blending mode from the Mode drop-down menu.

  - Specify a layer opacity using the Opacity slider.

- Now, click on the image and drag the mouse to draw the specific image. If you are using the pen tool or freeform tool, then draw the image as required.

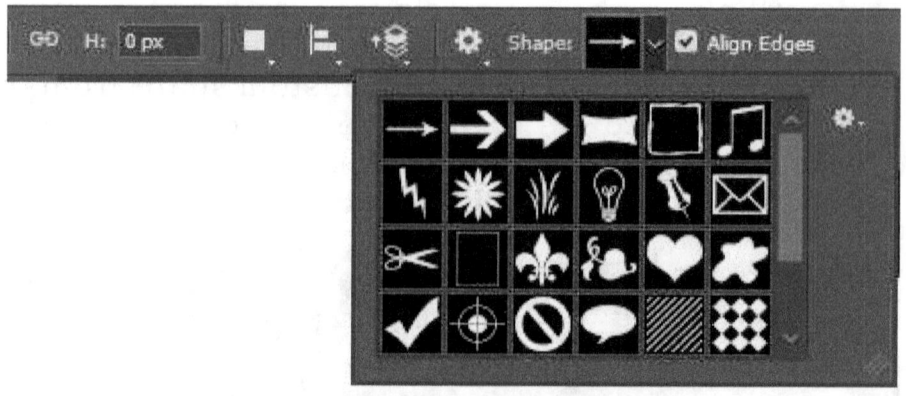

Fig 5.4 Selecting Custom Shapes

- Once you draw a shape, the option palette changes and displays the options for that particular shape. You can draw multiple shapes on the same layer using the same tool or the other tools defined in the fresh option palette. If you want to select a custom shape, click on the Custom shape tool and then click on the Shape drop down menu to display all the custom shapes.

- When you are finished, click on the Ok ☑ button.

Fig 5.5 The image after adding different shape

- You can set the properties for different shapes using option palette. To define the tool specific properties, select the tool and the click the inverted arrow (₊) next to the shape buttons to view additional options as shown in Fig 5.6 for Rounded rectangle tool.

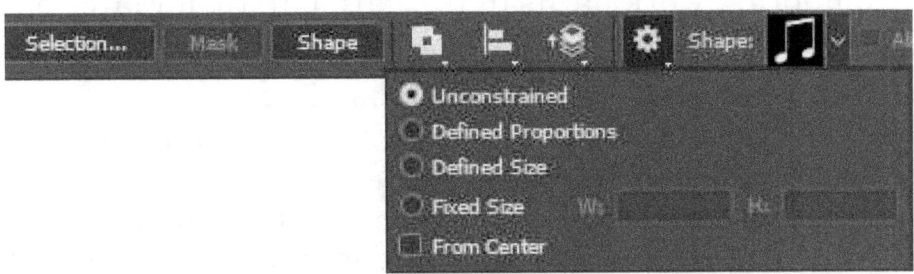

Fig 5.6 Specifying Custom Shaped options

- To save any custom shape, select Edit ➢ Define Custom Shape to bring Shape Name dialog box.

Once saved, the shape appears in the custom shape drop down menu shown in Fig 5.4.

Fig 5.7 Saving custom shape

PATHS

Just now you have learned to create shapes. At times you need to draw the paths only so as to develop a particular shape as vector image, which you can use at a later stage for different purpose.

If you remove the fill layer from the shapes, you are left with clipping paths only. Photoshop also lets you only the path. Paths , similar to shapes, are line and curve segments connected by nodes. The only difference is that they are not filled, are created on the same layer as of image and are not a part of image.

Paths are also vector objects and contain no pixels. The advantage of paths is that you can create temporary paths, which is not part of your image, unlike shapes, until you apply it in some way. You can save these temporary work paths in the Path palette for later use-

- Save the path for a later use as they take up less disk space than pixel-based data.

- Convert the path to a selection, which lets you edit only the area enclosed by the path. Because paths let you modify isolated segments of the outline you create, they provide more flexibility than selection. You can edit each line and curve segment on a path with precision, and you can move, add, remove, or transform the connecting nodes.

You can also convert a selection to a path.

- Apply a brush stroke along the path or fill the path with colour.

- Export the contents of the path as an irregularly shaped bitmap for placement in a drawing or page layout program.

CREATING NEW PATHS

You can create a path by placing nodes on your image using the pen or freeform tool or using any shape tool. If you are using pen tool, straight or curved line segments join the nodes. As you create a path using pen tool, Photoshop determines the type of node to use based on whether you create a straight line or curved line segment. If you using shape tool, then a predefined path similar to shape selected (rectangle, ellipse, polygon or custom shape) is created.

When you create a new path, it appears as temporary workpath in the Paths palette. You can save the workpath to avoid losing its contents. You can also create a new path from the path palette and then start drawing the path. This way the path contents are saved automatically.

To create a new path, do one of the following:

- Click on the rectangle tool, rounded rectangle tool, ellipse tool, polygon tool or line tool from the flyout. To create any custom path from the predefined set, select the Custom Shape tool. Additionally, you can select pen tool or freeform tool from the toolbox to draw paths.

  Once you select the tool of your choice, do one of the following-

  - Select create new work path (▨) option from the Path palette and start drawing the path. The new path is created as temporary workpath.

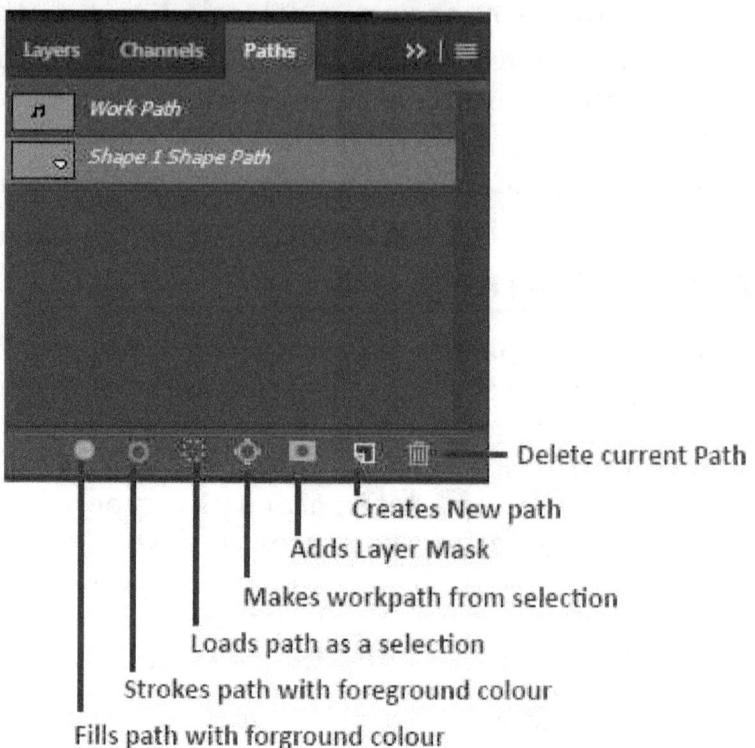

Delete current Path

Creates New path

Adds Layer Mask

Makes workpath from selection

Loads path as a selection

Strokes path with foreground colour

Fills path with forground colour

Fig 5.8 The Path palette

- You can also click the New Path button (Fig 5.9) at the bottom of the palette, to create a path without naming it.

Fig 5.9 Creating New Path

- To create and name a path, make sure no work path is selected. Choose New Path from the Paths palette menu, or Alt-click the New Path button at the bottom of the palette. Enter a name for the path in the New Path dialog box (Fig 5.9), and click OK.

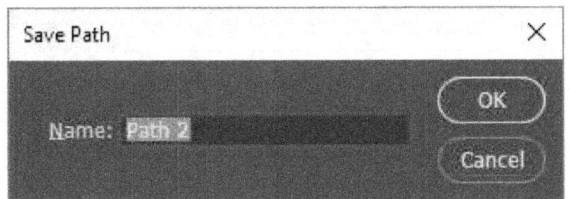

Fig 5.10 Saving a Path

Saving a Workpath

To save a work path, do one of the following:

- To save without renaming, drag the Work Path name to the New Path button at the bottom of the Paths palette.
- To save and rename, Choose Save Path from the Paths palette menu, enter a new path name, and click OK.

To rename a saved path

- Double-click the path's name in the Paths palette.
- Enter a new name in the Rename Path dialog box, and click OK.

Deleting a Path

To delete a path

- Select the path name in the Paths palette.
- Do one of the following:
  - Drag the path to the Trash button at the bottom of the Paths palette.
  - Click the Trash button at the bottom of the Paths palette, and click Yes.

Fig 5.11 Deleting a Path

- Choose Delete Path from the Paths palette menu.
- To delete a path automatically, Alt-click the Trash button at the bottom of the Paths palette.

CREATING MULTIPLE SUB PATHS

Each time you draw a connected series of straight or curved segments, you create a subpath. You can create several subpaths and save them as a single path in the Paths palette. To create additional subpaths, close or end the current subpath, and begin drawing again to create a new, disconnected segment.

USING THE PATHS PALETTE

Path palette displays the list of paths as well as clipping paths of the shape. But clipping path is visible only if the layer containing the shape is selected. In other words, if the layer containing the shape is active layer, the Path palette displays the clipping path. If you select a layer, which doesn't contain the shape, the clipping path will not be displayed.

On the other hand, the work paths are always displayed in the Path palette if they are saved. Path palette can also displays the thumbnails of the paths to have a quick look at the path. To view a path in the image, you must select the path in the Path palette.

- To display the Paths palette, select Windows ➢ Show Paths. This displays the Path palette.
- To select a path, click the path name in the Paths palette. You can select only one path at a time. Click on the blank area in the Option palette to deselect the path or click on the path name in the palette while holding down the Shift key.
- To change the size of a path thumbnail or hide the thumbnail, select Palette Options from the Paths palette menu. From the Path palette

options, select the size of the thumbnail or select none to hide the thumbnails.

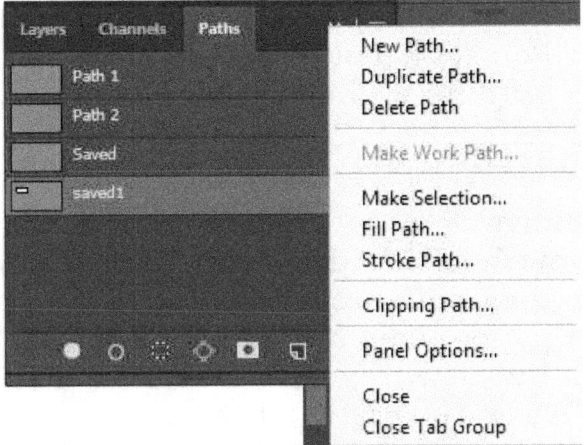

Fig 5.12 The Path palette menu

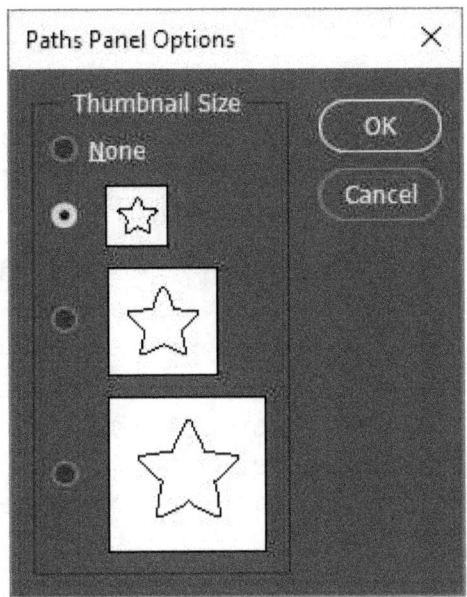

Fig 5.13 Specifying Path palette options

You can also drag the paths, except the clipping paths, up or down in the option palette to change a path's stacking order.

FREEHAND DRAWING

As discussed earlier, Photoshop offers two tools to draw your own shapes and paths - Pen tool and Freeform Pen tool. The Freeform Pen tool also offers magnetic options to make it Magnetic pen tool.

USING FREEFORM PEN TOOL

The Freeform Pen tool provides the most straight forward method for drawing. It lets you draw by dragging the mouse cursor across the page like a pencil on paper. This method is closest to traditional drawing, but the results are often imprecise and rough. As you draw, the anchor points are automatically positioned. You can improve these results by adjusting the position of anchor points after you complete your drawing.

To use the Freeform pen tool

● Select the freeform pen tool to display its Options palette. Select the option of drawing a shape or work path from the option palette.

Fig 5.14 Specifying options for freehand tool

● To control the sensitivity of the path as compared to mouse movement, specify the Curve Fit in Setting. The higher the value of Curve Fit, the simpler will be the path with less number of anchor points.

● Now, click and drag the mouse over the image to draw the path. A path is created along the movement of mouse. Release the mouse to create the workpath.

● If you have not enclosed the existing path, you can continue to draw the path from the endpoint of existing path.

- To enclosed the path, drag the mouse over the starting point (a circle appears next to the pointer when it is aligned) and release the mouse.

USING MAGNETIC PEN TOOL

The magnetic pen tool lets you draw a path that snaps to the edges of defined areas in your image. You can define the range and sensitivity of the snapping behavior, as well as the complexity of the resulting path. The magnetic pen and magnetic lasso tools share many of the same options.

To use the magnetic pen tool

- Select the magnetic option from the Setting option of the Freeform Pen tool. The Freeform Pen tool is converted into Magnetic Pen tool.

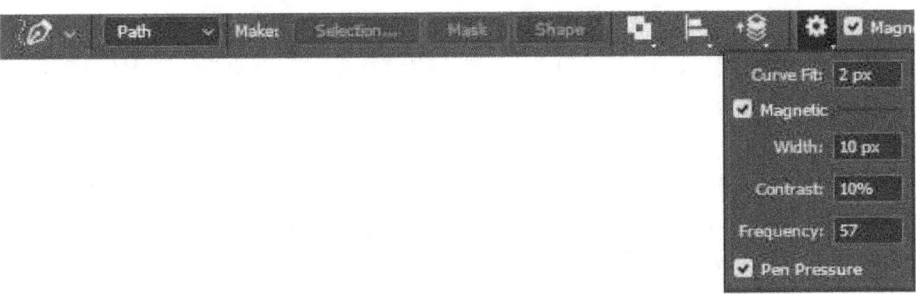

Fig 5.15 Specifying options for Magnetic Tool

- The Magnetic pen options becomes active. Click on the drop down menu to display various options.
  - To control the sensitivity of the path as compared to mouse movement, specify the Curve Fit. The higher the value of Control Fit, the simpler will be the path with less number of anchor points.
  - The width controls the distance of the edges to be detected from magnetic pen. It can have values between 1 to 40.
  - Contrast can have value from 0 to 100 percent and it controls the contrast

required between the pixels to be considered as an edge. A higher value will let you pick the border even if the contrast is less.

- Specify Frequency to define the rate at which anchor points are created. It can have a value between 0 to 100.

- Click on the image to set the first point. Now, move the mouse along the border of the object to be selected. As you move the pointer, the active segment snaps to the strongest edge in the image. The magnetic pen tool adds anchor points to the selection border to anchor previous segments.

- Press Del if you want to delete the recent added anchor point. You can add the anchor point manually if the border doesn't snap to the desired edge. Continue to trace the edge and add anchor points as needed.

- To turn off magnetic properties temporarily, hold down Alt key and drag the mouse button depressed to draw a freehand path or click and move the mouse to draw straight lines.

- To enclosed the path, drag the mouse over the starting point (a circle appears next to the pointer when it is aligned) and release the mouse. You can also double-click the magnetic pen to complete the path. Press Alt-Double click to have a last segment as straight line.

USING PEN TOOL

You can draw path and shape segments using the Pen tool. This tool gives you option to draw straight line or curves by defining the nodes or anchor points, thus giving you a better and precise control to define your path. You can draw line segments or curves by placing start and end nodes on an image. As you create curve segments, direction lines move to indicate the direction of the curve segment and its angle relative to the node. You can draw any number of subpaths within a path by drawing nonconnected segments.

Drawing Straight Lines

Using Pen, you can draw straight lines as well as curves. To draw a straight line :

● Click on a starting point and immediately release the mouse button. This will display a solid black square at starting point which is a node or anchor point.

● Move the mouse to the end point of line. Unlike freeform pen tool, no line appears while you move the mouse. Click at a point where you want to place the end point of the segment. You can hold down Shift key to draw the straight line segment at an angle, which is multiple of 45°.

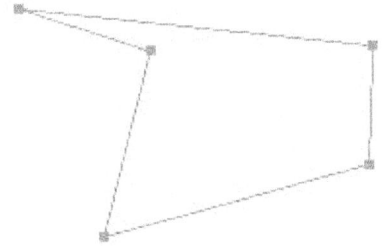

Fig. 5.16 Drawing straight lines

● You can continue to draw straight lines, by clicking on more end point. This way, end point of one segment becomes starting point of next segment.

● To enclosed the path, move the mouse over the starting point (a circle appears next to the pointer when it is aligned) and click at the starting point. You can press Ctrl key and click any where to end an open path.

Drawing Curves

The curves drawn using the freeform tool, normally, are not smooth & precise. To draw a curve using Pen tool-

- Select a point where curve is to be started click at that point, A small anchor point [filled box] is displayed.

- Click and hold down the mouse where the curve is to end, drag the mouse until the direction points, two small boxes, connected to the anchor point by a thin line (Direction line) are displayed.

- Drag the direction point in the direction the curve is to take. Dragging away from the anchor point increases the height and depth. Dragging towards the anchor point would decrease the height & depth.

- Hold down Shift key to move the direction points at an angle which is multiple of 45°.

- To draw a smooth curve, drag away from the curve. To change the direction of the curve sharply, press Alt, and then drag the direction point in the direction of the curve.

- Release the mouse when the curve is the required shape.

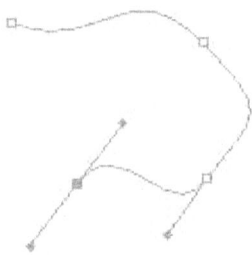

Fig. 5.17 Drawing curves

- Repeat above steps for each curve to be added.

- To enclosed the path, move the mouse over the starting point (a circle appears next to the pointer when it is aligned) and click at the starting point. You can press Ctrl key and click any where to end an open path.

EDITING PATHS AND SHAPES

Photoshop offers various tools to modify the shapes and paths. Once you have created a path, you can move, resize, reshape or delete the complete path or the segment in a path. Before applying the editing tool on the path or shape, you must first select the path name in the Paths palette to display the path. (In case of shapes, you can select the layer containing the shape).

If you select a path, all of the anchor points on the selected portion are displayed. If you select a path segment, all direction lines and direction points are displayed, if the selected segment is curved. If you select the segment, direction points appear as filled circles, selected anchor points as filled squares, unselected anchor points as hollow squares.

SELECTING PATHS & SHAPES

Photoshop offers two tools to select the shapes. These are Path Component Selection Tool and Direct Selection Tool.

Fig 5.18 Tools for selecting Paths and Anchor Points

- The Path Component Selection tool selects the entire path when clicked on the path. All the anchor points in the path are also displayed. If there are more than one component in path, only one component is selected on which you click. To select more than one component, drag the

131

marquee over all the components using the Path Component Selection Tool as Shown in Fig 5.19.

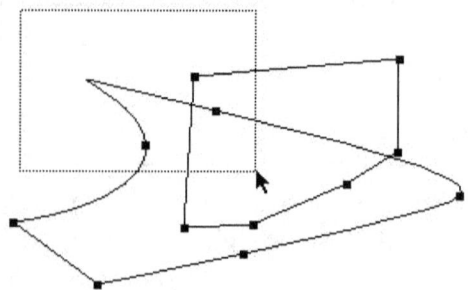

Fig 5.19 Selecting Paths using the Path Component selection Tool

● To select a path segment, select the direct selection tool. You can also activate this tool, even if some other tool is selected, by holding down Ctrl key. Now click on the segment to select it, or click on any anchor point to select it or drag a marquee to select more than one anchor point as shown in Fig 5.20.

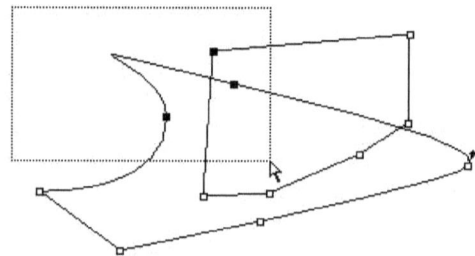

Fig 5.20 Drag a marquee to select anchor points

● If you click on a curve segment to select it, the direction points and direction line of that segment are displayed.

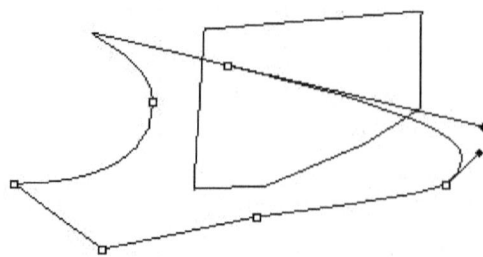

Fig 5.21 The direction points on the selected segment are shown

- If you want to select more than one anchor point, you cam hold down the Shift key and click on the various anchor points.

Moving Paths and Segments

As you have seen in previous section that you can select the entire path, a segment or a number of segments. Once you have selected the the required segments, you can apply any operation including moving, resizing, deleting or reshaping.

- To move an anchor, select the anchor point using the direct selection tool and drag the anchor point to the new position.

- To move a curve segment, select both the anchor points anchoring the segment that you want to move. To move more than one segment, select the starting and end anchor points of all the segments.

  Once selected, you can click and drag the anchor points to reshape the curve.

- To move the entire path, select the path using the Path Component Selection tool and then drag the mouse to move the path.

Reshaping Paths and Segments

To reshape a curve segment, you must select the curve segment by clicking over it using the Direct Pen tool. If the segment, you selected, has previous and next segment as curved segment, two direction line are displayed, one at both anchor.

To adjust the curve, drag the segment to make the changes to that segment only. You can also move the anchor point or direction line to reshape the curve but the effect of moving the anchor point or direction line will be on the adjacent segment also. Hold down Shift as you drag to constrain the movement to multiples of 45°.

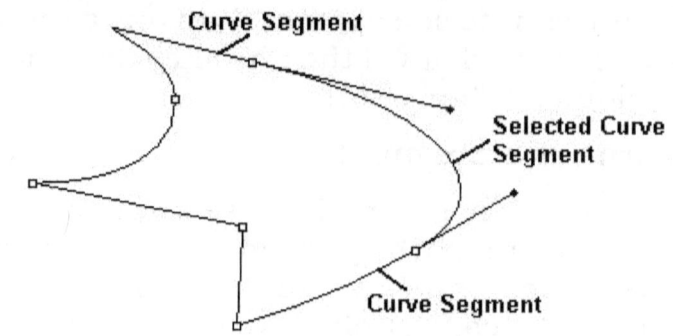

Fig 5.22 Reshaping segments

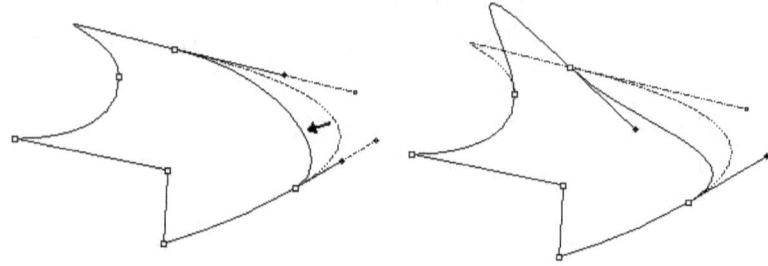

Fig 5.23 (a) Moving Segment (b) Moving Direction line to reshape

Erasing a Paths

To erase a path segment, select the segment you want to delete and click Del. If you select an anchor point and press Del, it will erase two segments. To erase the entire path, select the path using the Path Component Selection Tool and press Del.

If after removing a segment or anchor point, you again press Del, entire path is removed.

Copying Paths and Segments

You can copy paths or segments within an image or between two Photoshop images. If you paste the copied path or component in the same image, it becomes another component of that path. You can also use the Copy and Paste commands to duplicate paths, between a Photoshop image and an image in another application, such as Adobe Illustrator, Adobe Streamline, or Adobe Dimensions®.

To copy a path, do any of the following:

- To copy a path as you move it, select the path name in the Paths palette, and use the direct-selection tool to select the path in the image. Hold down Alt as you drag the path.

- To copy a path without renaming, drag the path in the Paths palette to the New Path button at the bottom of the palette.

- To copy and rename a path, Alt-drag the path in the Paths palette to the New Path button at the bottom of the palette. Or select the path to copy, and choose Duplicate Path from the Paths palette menu. Enter a new name for the path, and click OK.

- You can also use Ctrl+C to copy a path to clipboard and then press Ctrl+V to paste the path on the same path, new path or new image or another application.

To copy a segment :

- Click on the segment using Direct selection tool to select the segment. Now, press Ctrl+C (Edit ➤ Copy) to copy and press Ctrl +V (Edit + Paste) to paste the copied path on same path, new path, new image or another application.

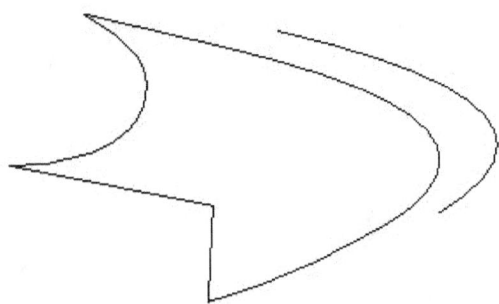

Fig 5.24 Copying Segment

Merging Paths

Photoshop also lets you combine the two path so as they behave as one single path. The final output of combining two paths depends upon the option selected for combining the two paths. The available options are - Add to shape area(⬕), subtract from shape area (⬔), Intersect shape area (⬔) or exclude overlapping shape area (⬔).

To merge the two paths, select both the paths using the Path Component selection tool. Now click on the type of the option to combine the two paths and click on the Combine button.

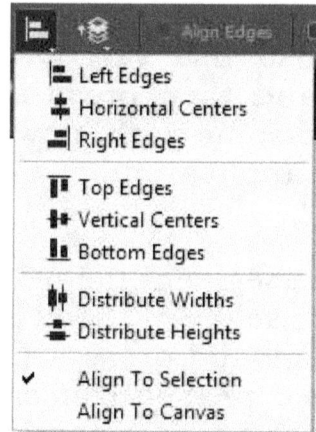

Fig 5.25 Aligning and distributing options in option bar

Fig 5.26 displays the merged path of the two paths shown in Fig 5.25 using the Add to Shape area option.

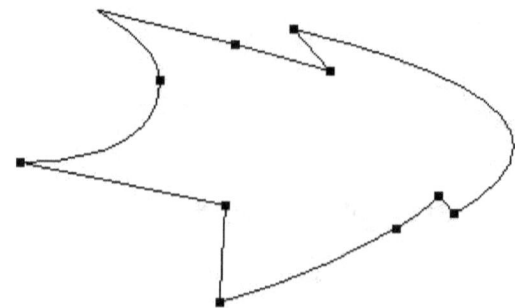

Fig 5.26 Merging the two paths shown in Fig 5.24

Aligning Paths

Photoshop lets you distribute and align the paths on the same layer. To align various paths, select the paths using Path Component Tool and then select the required alignment option from the Option bar (Fig 5.25).

To distribute components, select the components you want to distribute, then select one of the distribute options from the options   bar.

Transforming Paths & Shapes

You can transform a path or shape by rotating, resizing, scaling, mirroring, skewing, distorting or applying perspective. To transform the path or shape, select the path or shape using the Path Component selection tool and choose the option Show Bounding Box to bring the bounding box around the selection. Eight handles surrounds the path or shape and as you move the cursor towards the handles, it changes shape.

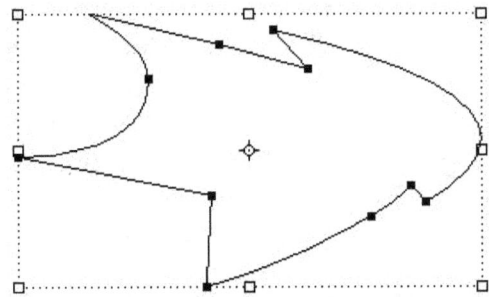

Fig 5.27 Transforming Shapes

Now you can apply following transformation to the selected path or shape.

- To scale, position the cursor over a handle so that it becomes a double arrow ($\nwarrow$). Now click and drag the handle. To scale proportionately, hold down Shift as you drag the handle.

- To rotate, move the pointer outside of the bounding border so as to make it a curved double-arrow (↰)and then drag. To constrain the rotation to 15° increments, hold down Shift key as you drag. If you want to change the centre point around which rotation takes place, drag the center point to a new position.

- To skew, hold down Ctrl+Shift and drag the handle. If you position the pointer over a side handle, the pointer becomes a white arrowhead with a small double arrow (▸₊).

- To apply perspective, hold down Ctrl+Alt+Shift, and drag a corner handle. If you position the pointer over a corner handle, it becomes a gray arrowhead.

- To distort relative to the center point of the bounding border, hold down Alt key and drag a handle.

- To distort freely, hold down Ctrl and drag a handle.

EDITING ANCHOR POINTS

The anchor points on a curve can be edited i.e. added, removed, cornered or smoothened. It can be done by using the add-anchor-point and delete-anchor-point tools, which let you add and delete anchor points on a path or shape. The convert-direction-point tool lets you convert a smooth curve to a sharp curve or to a straight segment, and vice versa.

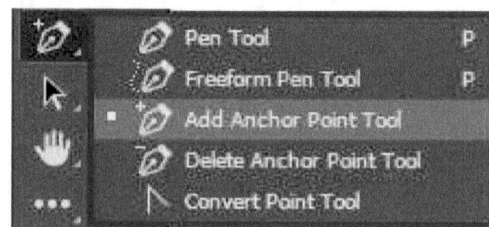

Fig 5.28 Various tools for editing Anchor Points

Before moving forward, you must understand the difference between smooth anchor point and cornered anchor point.

Smooth Anchor Point

Have two direction points which always lie on a straight line. Whenever one direction point is moved, the other one moves to maintain the smoothness of the line.

Cornered Anchor Point

Their direction points are not necessarily in a straight line. Therefore each direction point can be moved independently, which, in effect control either of the segments meeting at the anchor point. Cornered anchor point is used when a shape change of direction is required between two segments.

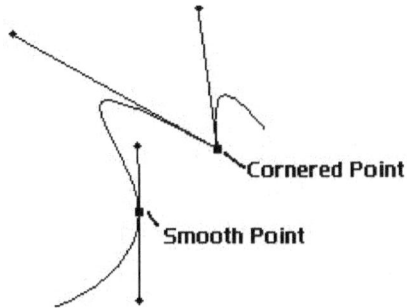

Fig 5.29 Smooth and Cornered Anchor points

Adding Anchor Points

To gain more control over curve shaping, anchor points can be added onto the curve.

- To add the anchor point, select the add-anchor-point tool, and position the pointer on the path where you want the anchor point added (a plus sign appears next to the pointer).

- Click to add an anchor point without changing the shape of the segment.

Fig 5.30 Adding New Anchor Points

Deleting Anchor Points

The anchor points can also be deleted from the curve to create a smoother shape. It is common to delete unwanted extra anchor points. To delete an anchor point, select the delete-anchor-point tool and click on the anchor point you want to delete.

Converting Anchor Point

Photoshop allows you to convert curve segment to line segment and vice-versa. The basic difference between a curved segment and a line segment is that a curve segment has two direction points whereas a straight line segment has none.

You can use the Convert Point tool to convert between a smooth point and a corner point.

- Select the convert-anchor-point tool :
  - Click on the smooth anchor point to convert into an corner point.
  - You can also break the pair of direction line to convert a smooth line to corner point. To do so, ensure that both the direction lines of the smooth anchor point are visible and then drag a direction point to break the pair of direction lines.
  - Click on a corner point and drag it away from the anchor point to make it a smooth curve. (Fig 5.31)

FILLING AND STROKING PATHS

Photoshop also lets you add colour to the path. You can fill the path with a specified colour or paint the path border by striking it. You can apply the stroke or fill command to entire path or a subpath.

Filling a Path

You can fill the path using current Fill path settings or select various options to fill the path.

To fill the path with the current fill settings, click the Fill Path button at the bottom of the Paths palette. (Refer to Fig 5.8).

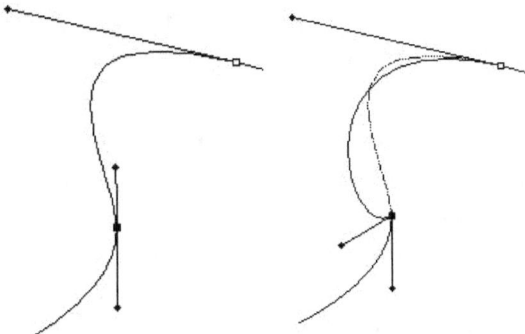

Fig 5.31 Converting Anchor Point

To define options to fill a path, select the path in the Paths palette. Now Alt-click the Fill Path button at the bottom of the Paths palette or choose Fill Path from the Paths palette menu to bring the Fill Path/Subpath dialog box.

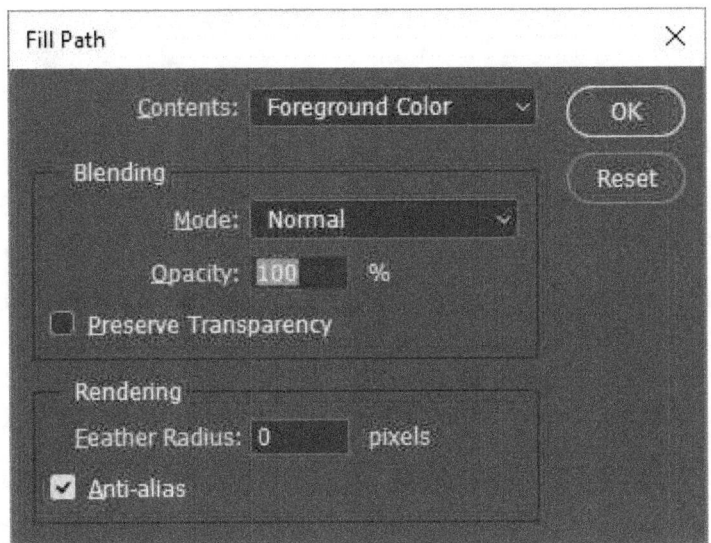

Fig 5.32 Fill Path dialog box

- For Use, choose the contents for the fill from the drop down menu.

- Specify an opacity for the fill. The higher the value of opacity, the lesser will be the transparency.

- Choose a blending mode for the fill (The modes has been discussed in detail in next chapter). Select Preserve Transparency to limit the fill to layer areas that contain pixels.

- Select a Rendering option. Define the Feather Radius extend the feather edge inside and outside the selection border. Select the Anti-aliased option to create a finer transition between the pixels in the selection and the surrounding pixels. Click OK to fill the path.

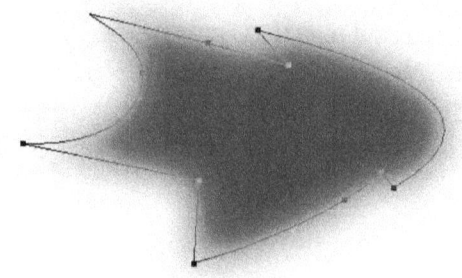

Fig 5.33 Filled path with Feather Radius

Stroking the Path

You can stroke the path using current stroke settings or select various options to strike the path.

To stroke the path with the current stroke settings, click the Stroke Path button at the bottom of the Paths palette. (Refer to Fig 5.8). If you continue clicking at the button, the thickness of the stroke increases.

To specify options stroke a path, select the path in the Paths palette. Now Alt-click the Stroke Path button at the bottom of the Paths palette or choose Stroke Path option from the Paths palette menu to bring the Stroke Path/Subpath dialog box. (Fig 5.34)

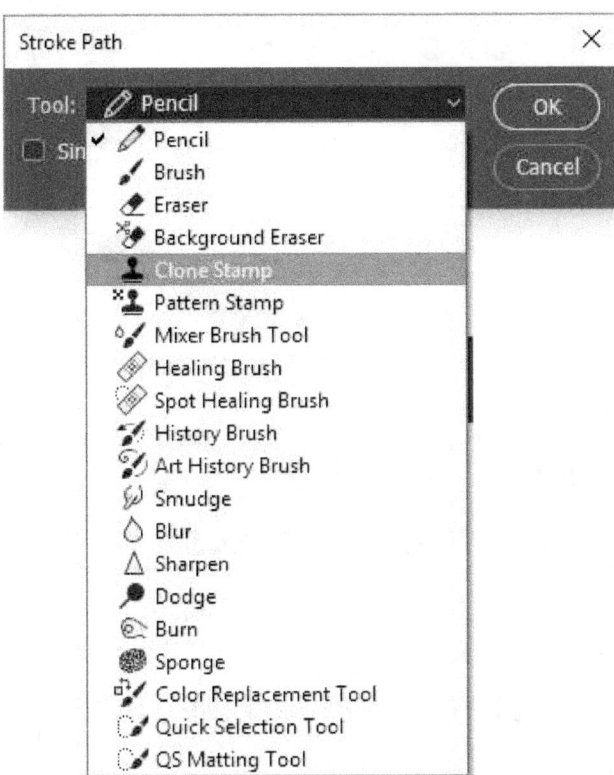

Fig 5.34 Stroking the Path

- Here, you can select the tool for stroking the path. Set the tool options in the Options palette, and specify a brush in the Brushes palette.

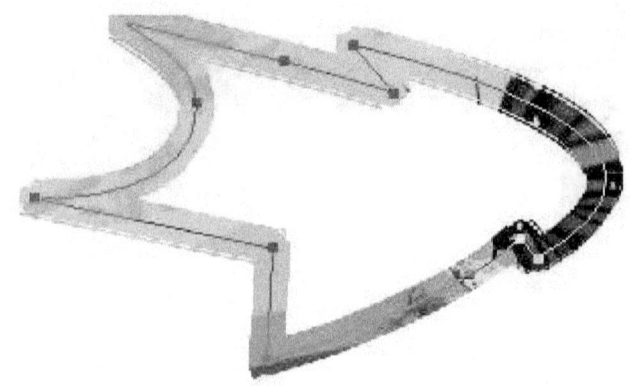

Fig 5.35 Stroked path and Option bar for Stroking path

● Click OK to stroke the path.

PATHS AND SELECTION BORDERS

Photoshop lets you change the selection border to path and path to selection border.

DEFINING PATHS AS SELECTION BORDERS

When you convert a path to a selection, the selection is created in addition to the path so that both appear on the image. You can then create an object from the selection and move the object without affecting the position of the path.

To convert a path to a selection border using the current Make Selection settings, click on the Make selection button at the bottom of the Path Palette.

To specify options while converting path to selection border, select the path to be converted to selection border in the Paths palette. Now Alt-click the Make selection button at the bottom of the Paths palette or choose Make Selection option from the Paths palette menu to bring the Make Selection dialog box (Fig 5.36).

● Define Feather Radius in pixel to control the smoothness of the selection border. Select Anti-aliased option to create a finer transition between the pixels in the selection and the surrounding pixels.

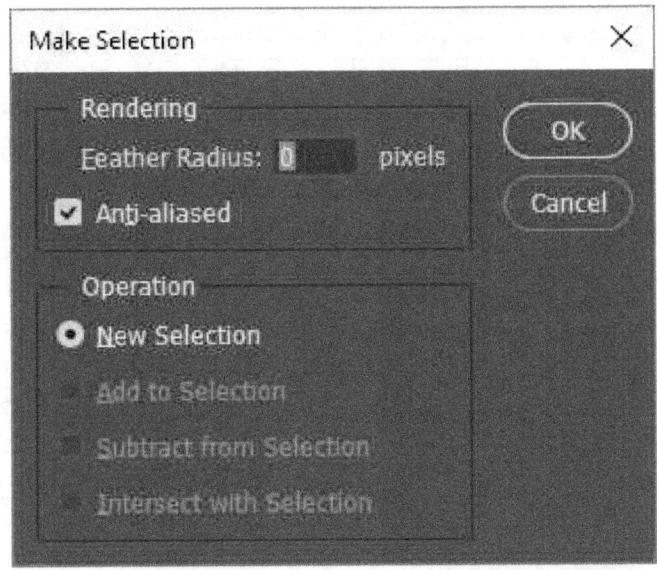

Fig 5.36 Converting Paths to Selection Border

- Select a Operational option:
  - New Selection defines new area as per the Path. (Hold down Ctrl + Click on the path name in the palette).
  - Add to Selection add the path selection to any other previous selection. (Hold down Ctrl + Shift + Click on the path name in the palette).
  - Subtract from Selection removes the path selection from the existing selection. (Hold down Ctrl + Alt + Click on the path name in the palette).
  - Intersect with Selection selects the area common to both the path selection and existing selection. (Hold down Ctrl + Alt + Shift + Click on the path name in the palette).

CONVERTING SELECTION BORDERS INTO PATHS

You can also convert a selection to a path. If you have already defined a selection on your image using any selection tool, you can use the Work Paths from selection button at the bottom of the Path Palette to define the same image area as a path. Converting selection to paths lets you modify the shape using the additional editing power provided by the Path tool.

To convert a selection to a path without tolerance, click the Make Work Path button at the bottom of the Paths palette. To specify the tolerance value (to smoothen the path) while converting it into path, Alt-click the Make Work Path button at the bottom of the Paths palette to bring Make work path dialog box.

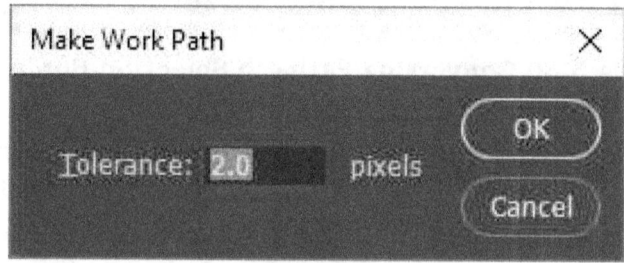

Fig 5.37 Creating Paths from Selection Border

- Enter a Tolerance value. Enter a higher value (Max - 10, Min - 0.5)) to have smoother path with less number of anchor points.

- Click OK to convert the selection as a workpath in the Paths palette.

PAINTING IN PHOTOSHOP
THE COLOUR PICKER
THE PAINTING TOOLS
ERASING
FILLING AN IMAGE
USING HISTORY AIRBRUSH

PAINTING IN PHOTOSHOP

You can create images using the paintbrush, airbrush and pencil tools. You can use the brush tools to draw with the selected colour.

Before you can create using painting tools, you must choose a painting tool and merge mode. You can choose preset brushes or you can create custom brushes. Most brushes are used in the same way: you choose a tool, specify a paint colour, and drag to paint.

After you choose a tool to paint, you can choose a paint colour and merge mode. Merge modes specify how the current paint colour blends with the colours of the image you are creating or editing. When you merge colours, you blend a source colour with a base colour to produce a result colour.

But before moving ahead with painting tools, let us discuss about selecting the colour with which painting is to be done. Photoshop offers various models of colour as we have already discussed in the 3rd chapter. Here we will discuss about selecting various colours for foreground and background application.

THE COLOUR PICKER

The toolbox of Photoshop offers two colour selection box - the upper colour box lets you select the foreground colour, whereas the lower colour box lets you select the background colour.

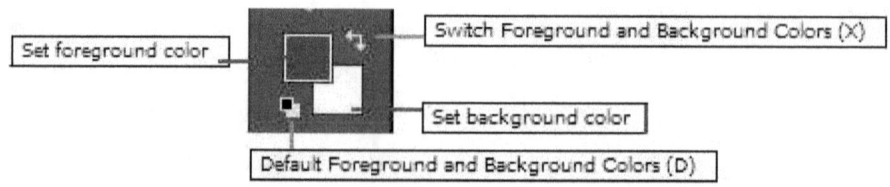

Fig 6.1 Setting foreground and background colour

The double sided arrow at right top corner of colour selection box lets you switch the foreground and background colours. To switch between the foreground and background colours, press X on the keyboard.

To select the foreground or background colour, click on the concerned colour box to bring the Colour Picker dialog box. You can also click on the active colour in the Colour palette to bring the Colour palette.

To choose a colour:

- Click a component next to the HSB, RGB, or Lab values to select a colour model.

Fig 6.2 Using Colour Picker

- To select a colour, drag the white triangles along the slider to choose the nearest of the colour. Now view the Select colour box which displays all the possible combination of the model near about that colour.

You can adjust the colour to be selected using the colour field and colour slider. The rectangle on the right of the slider displays the original colour and the new colour which will be selected.

SPECIFYING A COLOUR USING NUMERIC VALUES

The Colour Picker dialog box also displays the numeric value of the new colour for four different models - HSB, RGC, Lab and CMYK. You can also specify your values to define the colour numerically.

To specify colours using numeric values, use any of the one model:

- CMYK model - define the values as percentage of all the four colours.

- RGB mode - Specify the component values from 0 to 255.

- HSB colour mode - specify saturation and brightness as percentages and specify hue as an angle corresponding to the location of the colour on the Colour wheel.

- Lab mode - Enter a lightness value (L) from 0 to 100, and a axis (green to magenta) and b axis (blue to yellow) values from -128 to +127.

Using Eyedropper Tool

To pick a colour from the image -

- Move the mouse pointer outside the Colour Picker dialog box. The cursor changes to an eyedropper tool. Now click on any colour in any image to select the particular colour as foreground or background colour. You can sample from the active image or from another image. You can also click on the colour in the colour selection box.

Besides displaying the colour in four models, you can also select colours from various Colour Libraries. To select colour from the Colour Libraries, click on the

Colour Libraries button. This brings the Colour Libraries dialog box.

- The Colour Libraries dialog box displays the colour closest to the colour currently selected in the Adobe Photoshop Colour Picker. Move the slider to select entirely different colour. Select a book from the drop down menu to display other colour books.

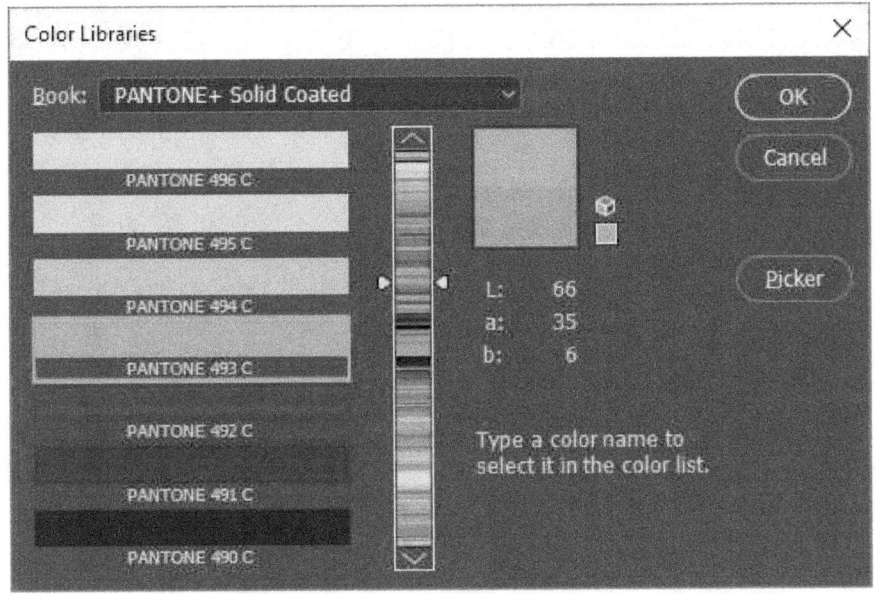

Fig 6.3 Selecting a Custom Colour

- After selecting the required colour, click OK.

WINDOWS COLOUR PICKER

The colour picker discussed in the previous section in the colour picker of Adobe. PhotoShop also offers the familiar Windows Colour Picker. Besides, you can also use a plug-in colour picker to select colours. Any plug-in colour pickers you install appear under Colour Picker in the General Preferences dialog box.

To use the Window Colour Picker

- Choose Edit ➢ Preferences ➢ General.

- From the Colour Picker drop down menu, choose Windows and click OK.

- Now if you click the foreground or background colour selection box in the toolbox, the colour picker that appears is the familiar Windows Colour Picker shown in Fig 6.4. The Windows Colour Picker lets you select colours from 48 basic colours or define up to 16 custom colours based on the HSB or the RGB colour model, but it does not alert you to nonprintable colours.

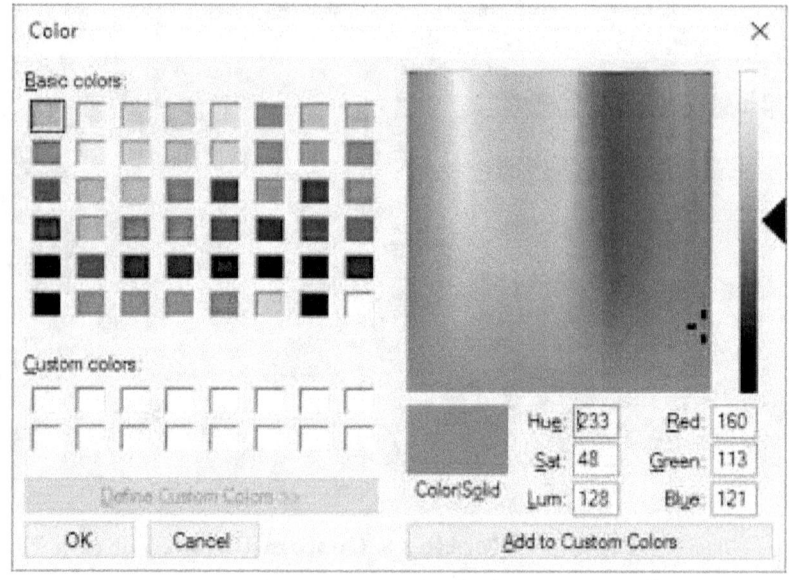

Fig 6.4 Using Windows Colour Picker

- Click Define Custom Colours ≫ to open the Custom Colour Selector. Here again you can specify a colour by using the colour field and colour slider or by entering numerical values for each colour component.

- The additional advantage of this dialog box is that you can save upto 16 custom colours, which you can select at a later stage also. To save the custom colour, click Add to Custom Colours. Select the colour from the Custom Colour and Click OK.

USING SWATCHES PALETTE

Swatch palette lets you choose a foreground or background colour. You can also add or delete colours to create a custom swatch set. The concept of swatch palette is used to save the swatch set which can be reloaded for other image. To display the Swatches palette, choose Window ➤ Show Swatches. To choose a colour, do one of the following:

- Simply click in the swatch palette to choose a foreground colour.

- Hold down Alt key while clicking in the swatch palette to choose a background colour.

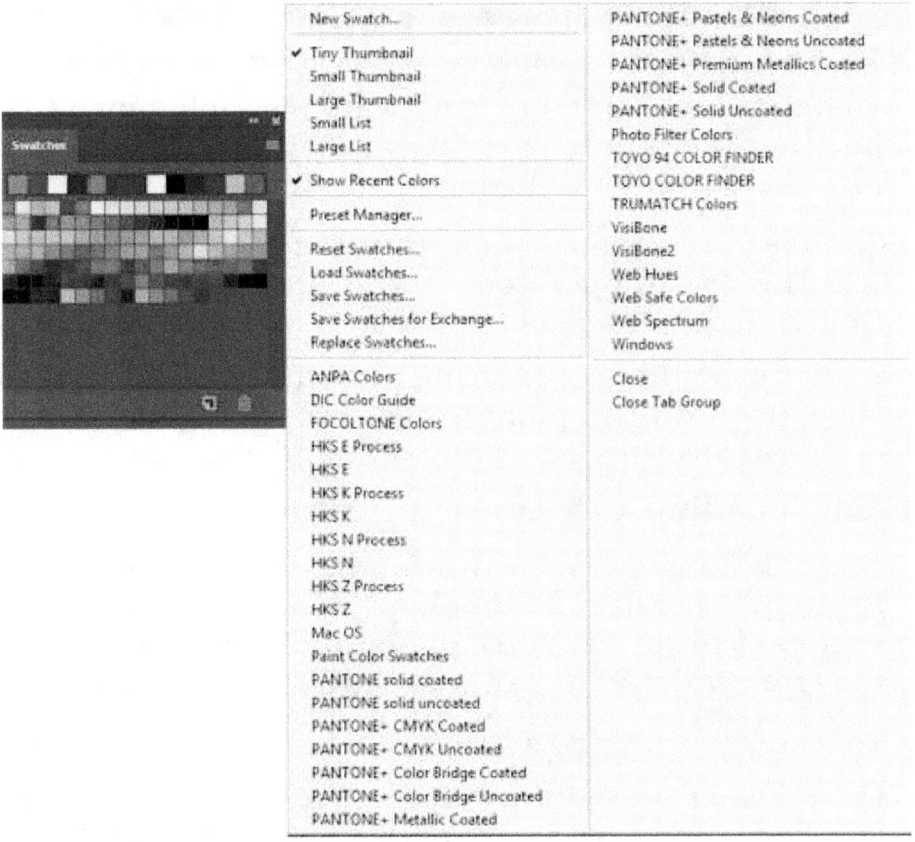

Fig 6.5 The Swatch palette

To add a colour to the Swatches palette, select the colour you want to add to the swatch palette by using the eyedropper tool or Colour Picker.

- Now click in the swatch palette at the bottom row of the swatch palette. The pointer turns into a paint bucket. This brings the colour swatch name dialog box. Specify the name and Click OK.

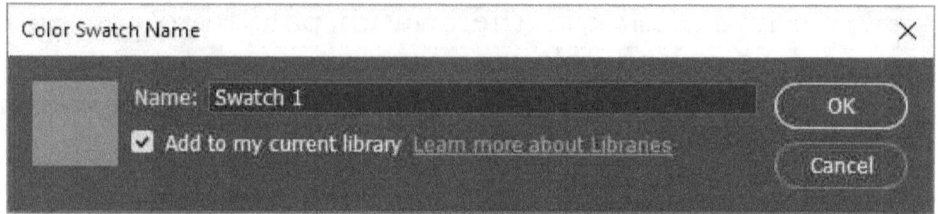

Fig 6.6 Specifying the name of the Colour for Swatch palette

To delete a colour from the Swatches, hold down Ctrl, position the pointer over a swatch (the pointer turns into scissors), and click.

To insert or replace a colour in the Swatches palette, use the eyedropper tool, the Colour palette, or the Colour Picker to select the colour you want to add.

- To replace an existing swatch, hold down Shift, position the pointer over a swatch (the pointer turns into a paint bucket), and click the swatch.

Saving, Loading and Replacing Swatches

You can append as many swatches as you want in the Swatches palette. Photoshop also provides various swatches libraries. You can also define your own set of libraries which you can load into Swatches palette.

To load a predefined swatches set into Swatch palette,

- Select the library from the list in Swatches palette menu or select the option Load Swatches from the menu to select *.ACO files.

- As you select the file, Photoshop gives you option to replace or append the selected library into Swatches palette. Select the required option.

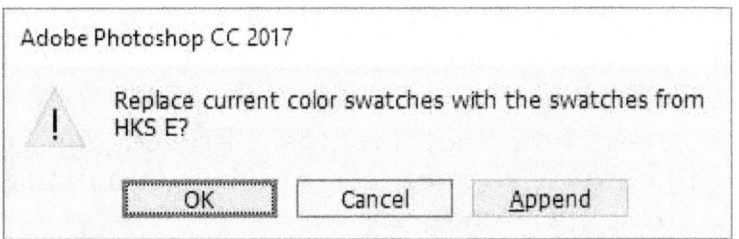

Fig 6.7 Replacing or appending colours in Swatch palette

If you append the selected library, you can mix the various libraries, add custom swatches and remove the unwanted swatches from the palette to create a new library of your choice.

Now select the Save Swatches option to save the new set of swatches as a library.

Select the other options from the Swatches palette menu, shown in Fig 6.5), as described below:

- Select Reset Swatches option to load the default swatches.
- Select Replace Swatches option to replace the current swatch set with swatches stored in a file.

THE PAINTING TOOLS

Photoshop offers three basic tools - paintbrush, pen, Mixer brush and Colour replacement - to paint the current foreground colour on an image.

Fig 6.8 Selecting Painting Tool

When using them as a painting tools, the three tools gives different effects.

- The paintbrush tool creates soft strokes of colour.

- The airbrush tool simulates traditional airbrush techniques and applies gradual tones to an image.

- The pencil tool creates hard-edged freehand lines and segments, which is most useful for bitmapped images.

To draw a straight line with any painting tool, click a starting point in the image. Then hold down Shift, and click an endpoint.

To use the paintbrush, airbrush, or pencil tool:

- Specify the foreground and background colour using the colour selection box.

- Now select the tool you want to use for painting. To draw with the current setting, simply click and drag on the image with the selected tool.

When you select a painting tool, the option palette displays the options for the selected tool. The common option to all the three tools is that of selecting the brush shape and defining the mode.

SELECTING BRUSH

Photoshop offers number of shapes and sizes of brush by default. Besides that it also offers various libraries containing different brush shapes. You can also create a custom brush shape if no brush from the libraries serves your purpose. You also can use part of an image to create a custom brush shape.

The Brush palette gives you option to append new brush, delete existing brush or edit the properties of selected brush temporarily.

To display the Brush palette, select any of the painting tool, and click on the Brush drop down arrow, as shown in Fig 6.9, to display the Brush palette. Select the brush you want to use in painting. The palette displays the shape of the brush along with the size, if the size is too large to fit on the palette.

Creating New Brush

To create a brush, select the New Brush option from the Brush palette to bring the Brush popup box.

- The dialog box displays the tip of the current brush at the left bottom preview box and angle. The box in the lower left corner shows the current brush angle and roundness. As you enter new options, the brushes in these boxes update.

  - Enter the diameter of the brush to control the size of the brush. It can take a maximum value of 999.

Fig 6.9 The Brush palette and specifying parameters for new Brush

  - Increase the hardness to have a hard centre. A lower value gives soft center and blur the edges.

- Specify spacing to control the brush marks in a stroke. Higher value places the brush mark at a distance.

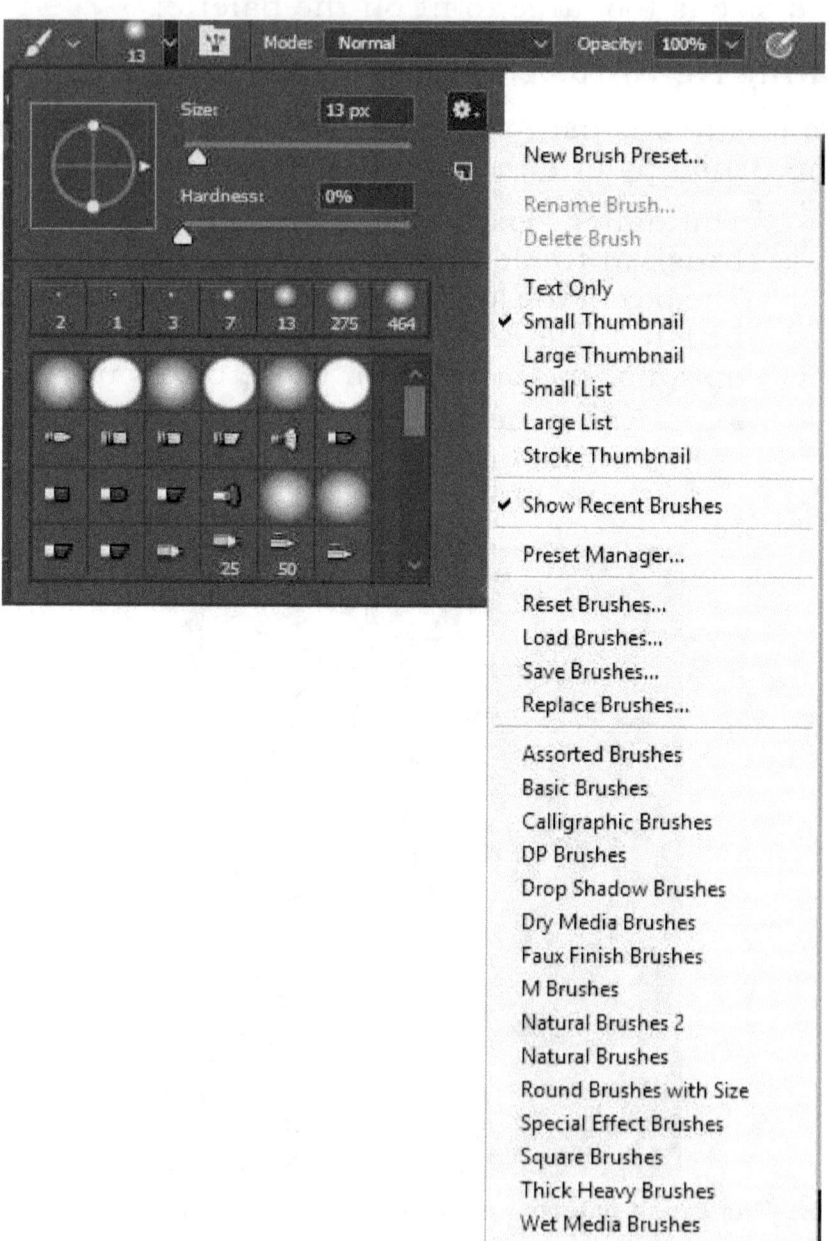

Fig 6.10 Adding Preset Brush or the new Brush

- Click OK. New brushes are added at the bottom of the palette.

Deleting a Brush

To delete a brush, do one of the following:

- Press Alt, and click the brush you want to delete.
- Click the brush in the Brushes palette, and choose Delete Brush from the palette menu or right click on the brush and select Delete Brush from the the menu that appears.

Creating Custom Brush Shape

Photoshop also lets you define a custom brush made of a rectangular part of Image. To create a custom brush shape from the image, you must select the image using rectangle selection tool. The maximum size of such brush could be 1000 pixels by 1000 pixels.

- After selecting the required part, choose Edit ➢ Define Brush. This brings the Brush Name dialog box.

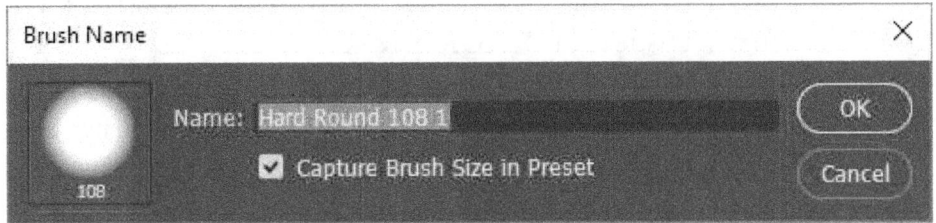

Fig 6.11 Creating Custom Brush

- Specify the name of the brush and click OK. New brushes are added at the bottom of the palette.

Modifying Brush Properties

To modify the properties of the existing brush, select the brush from the Brush palette and click on the brush shape in the option palette.

- Specify spacing to control the brush marks in a stroke. Higher value places the brush mark at a distance. To make the brush placement more accurate, make sure that Anti-aliased is selected.

- Define a new name and click on ⬜ button to create a new preset brush.

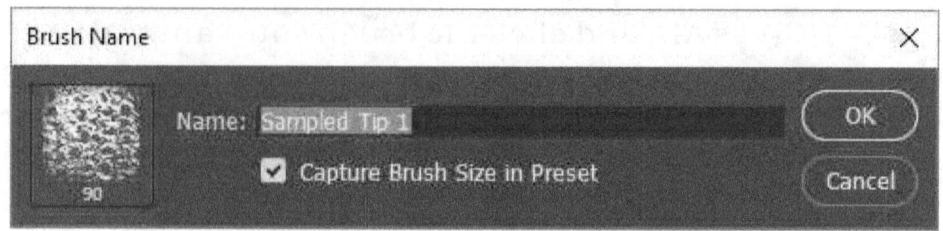

Fig 6.12 Modifying Brush Properties

Saving, Loading and Replacing Brushes

You can append as many brush as you want in the brush palette. Photoshop also provides various brush libraries as shown in Fig 6.6. you can also define your own set of libraries which you can load into brush palette.

To load a predefined brush set into Brush palette,

- Select the library from the list in Brush palette menu or select the option Load Brush from the menu to select *.ABR files.

- As you select the file, Photoshop gives you option to replace or append the selected library into Brush palette. Select the required option.

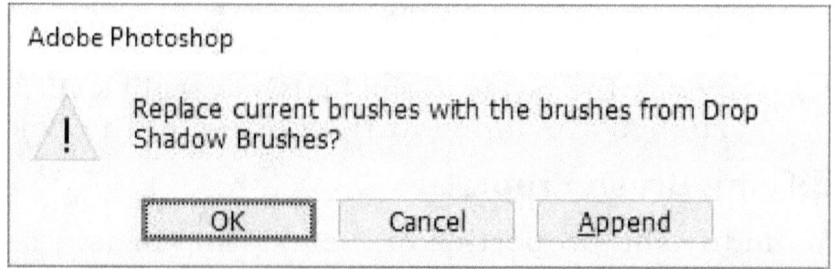

Fig 6.13 Replacing or appending brush library in Brush palette

If you append the selected library, you can mix the various libraries, add custom brush shapes and remove the unwanted brush shapes from the palette to create a new library of your choice.

Now select the Save Brush option to save the new set of brush as a library.

Select the other options from the Brush palette menu, shown in Fig 6.9), as described below:

- Select Reset Brushes option to load the default brushes.
- Select Replace Brushes option to replace the current brush set with brushes stored in a file.
- Select Rename Brush option to change the name of the selected brush.
- Select the option from Text only, Thumbnails or list to change the view of the brush palette.

SELECTING MODE

You can control the effect that a Brush tool has on an image by blending the colours in different ways. Blending colours means that you are merging or combining a source and base colour to produce a result colour. The source colour is the current foreground colour - the colour you are applying to your image using a Brush tool. The base colour is the colour displayed on the original image the colour you are altering. The result colour is the colour that is produced after the colour merge.

To select a blending mode, select a painting tool and click on the Mode drop down menu in the option palette to display the list of modes.

- The **Normal** mode replaces the base colour with the current paint colour. This is the default merge mode.
- The **Dissolve** mode edits or paints each pixel to make it the result colour.
- The **Behind** mode edits or paints only on the transparent part of a layer. The effect that is like looking through the clear, silver-free areas on a 35-mm negative.

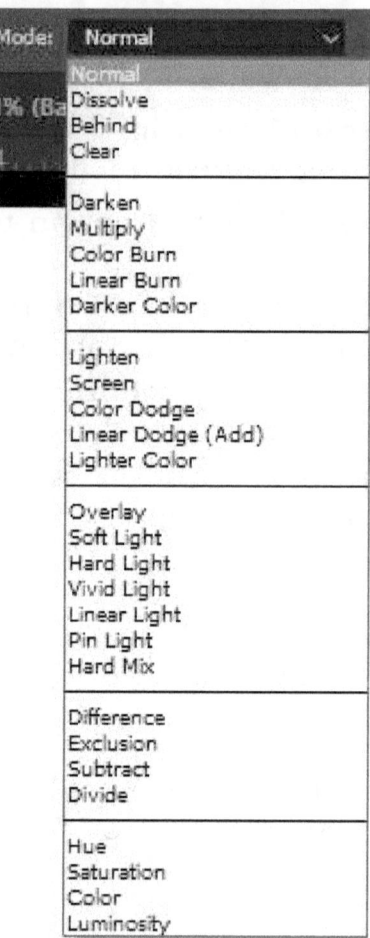

Fig 6.14 Selecting a Mode for painting

- The **Multiple** blend mode multiplies the values of the current colour and base colours and divides the result by 255. Unless you colour on white, the final result is always darker than the original base colour. Multiplying black with any paint colour produces black. Multiplying white with any paint colour leaves the colour unchanged.

- The **Screen** mode inverts and multiplies the values of the current paint and paper colours. The result colour is always lighter than the original base colour.

- The **Overlay** blend mode multiplies or screens the current paint colour, according to the value of the base colour.

- The **Soft** Light mode applies a soft, diffused light to the base colour.

- The **Hard** Light mode applies a hard, direct spotlight to the base colour.

- The **Colour Dodge** mode simulates the photographic technique called dodging (will be discussed later in the book), which lightens image areas by decreasing the exposure.

- The **Colour Burn** mode simulates the photographic technique called burning (Will be discussed later), which darkens image areas by increasing the exposure.

- The **Darken** mode applies the current paint colour to the base colour when the current paint colour is darker than the base colour. If the paint colour is lighter than the base colour, the base colour is not changed.

- The **Lighten** blend mode replaces the base colour with the current paint colour when the current paint colour is lighter than the base colour. If the paint colour is darker than the base colour, the base colour is not changed.

- The **Difference** mode subtracts the current paint colour value from the base colour value and applies the absolute value of the result. If the value of the current paint colour is 0, the base colour does not change.

- The **Exclusion** mode creates an effect similar to but lower in contrast than the Difference mode.

- The **Hue** merge mode uses the hue value of the current paint colour and both the saturation and lightness values of the base colour to create a result colour.

- The **Saturation** merge mode uses the saturation value of the current paint colour and both the lightness and hue values of the base colour to create a result colour.

- The **Colour** merge mode uses both the hue and saturation values of the current paint colour and the lightness value of the base colour to create a result. This merge mode is the opposite of the Lightness merge mode.

- The **Luminosity** mode creates a result colour with the hue and saturation of the base colour and the luminance of the blend colour.

SELECTING TOOLS FOR PAINTING

The properties discussed above i.e. selection of brush and mode, are to be selected for all the three tools - Airbrush, Paintbrush and Pencil tool. Besides these two common properties, the option palette also offers some tool specific options which are discussed below-

Airbrush Tool

Pressure - Specify the pressure of airbrush while painting. The higher percentage gives stronger effect of the colour.

Paintbrush

Opacity - specify opacity to control the transparency of the brush stroke. Specify a high value for more opaque stroke and low value to view the background image.

Wet Edges - Select this option to paint with a water colour effect when Mixer Brush tool  is selected. When you paint with wet edges on, the paint builds up along the edges of the brush stroke.

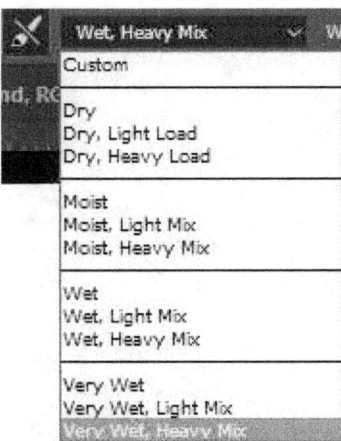

Fig 6.15 Painting with Wet Edges off, and on

Pencil

Opacity - specify opacity to control the transparency of the brush stroke. Specify a high value for more opaque stroke and low value to view the background image.

Auto Erase - Select this option to paint the background colour over areas containing the foreground colour i.e. if you are painting over an image, the image is removed where you paint with this option on.

SETTING BRUSH DYNAMICS

The dynamic options for the three basic painting tool includes size, pressure and colour. Using these options you can fade these three parameters of the brush over a distance defined in steps. Photoshop also gives the option of using Stylus if you have pressure sensitive dizitizing tablets installed on your system.

To control the three parameter of size, pressure and colour, select ant of the basic painting tool - Airbrush, Paintbrush or Pencil. Now select the Brush Dynamics by pressing F5 or Window ➢ Brush to bring up the brush dynamics pallette as shown in Fig 6.16.

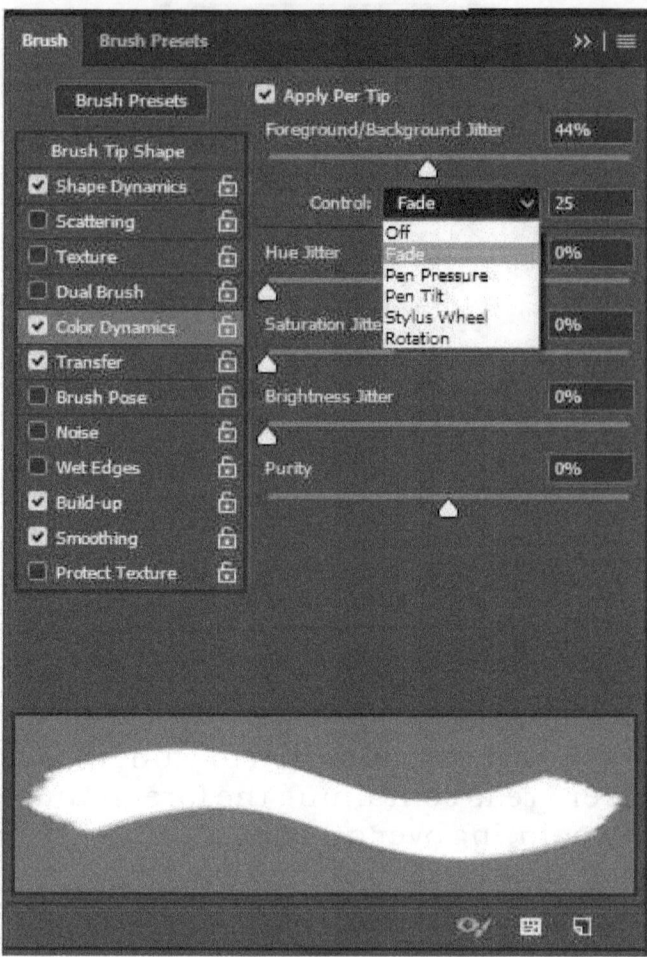

Fig 6.16 Specifying parameters for Brush Dynamics

The pallette offers various parameters to let you select the required option from off, Fade, Pressure, Tilt and Stylus Wheel.

Size parameter fades away the size of the brush in specified number of steps. For example, if you start drawing with 50 pixels wide brush and want to fade away in 50 steps then after 50 steps, brush size will become 0.

Similarly you can fade away the pressure and colour in the brush. The result of fading away the size, pressure and colour is shown in Fig 6.17(a), (b) and (c) respectively.

Fig 6.17 Effect of Fading of various parameters

ERASING

Photoshop offers various erasing tools to let you erase areas of an image to transparency or to the background colour. These include eraser, magic eraser and background eraser tool. To cycle through the eraser tool types, Alt-click the eraser tool, or hold down Shift and press E on the keyboard. The Auto-erase option with the pencil tool also erases the contents.

Fig 6.18 Erasing Tool Flyout

Using Eraser Tool

The eraser tool changes pixels in the image as you drag through them. To use the eraser tool:

- Select the eraser tool. In the option palette, select the mode from the drop down menu, with which you would like to erase. The choices offered are - paintbrush, airbrush, pencil, or block.

- Select a brush size as described in previous section. You can also specify the opacity, fade-out rate, and stylus options with the eraser tool as explained in previous section.

- Select the option Erase to History to erase to a saved state or snapshot of the image.

- Now, drag through the area you want to erase.

Using Magic Eraser

The magic eraser tool lets you erase all the pixels of the similar colour. When all the pixels are removed, you get the transparent background. If the layer below is locked, pixel changes to the background. To use the magic eraser tool -

- Select the magic eraser tool. The option palette displays various options related to magic eraser tool.

- Define a tolerance value. The higher the value the wider will be the colour range that can be deleted.

- If you want to smoothen the edges of the erased portion, select the Anti-aliased option.

- Don't select Contiguous option, if you want to erase all the similar pixels from the image. To remove the data from all the visible layers, select Use All Layers option. Also define the opacity of the erased portion.

- Select Use All Layers to sample the erased colour using combined data from all visible layers. A lower opacity erases pixels to partial transparency.

- Now click any where on the image to remove the pixels.

Using Background Eraser

The background eraser tool lets you erase pixels on a layer to transparency as you drag the mouse. This way you can erase the background while maintaining the foreground.

- Select the background eraser tool.

- Select a brush size as described in previous section.

- Select the Limits from the drop down menu.

- Discontiguous option erases the sampled colour.

- Contiguous erases areas that contain the sampled colour and are connected to one another.

- Find Edges erases connected areas containing the sampled colour, while preserving the sharpness of shape edges.

- Select a value for Tolerance. Check the Protect foreground colour to prevent the erasing of foreground colour.

- Select a sampling option from the drop-down menu.

- Now, drag through the area you want to erase.

FILLING AN IMAGE

You can fill images and backgrounds with a variety of colours, including solid colours, bitmaps and textures. You can also adjust the transparency of the fill colours by applying a gradient fill. You can use fills to create backgrounds, apply textures, and create other effects. You can apply fills to an entire image, or you can use the Fill tool or a selection tool to fill part of an image.

Photoshop offers two tools for filling the images - Gradient tool and Paint bucket tool.

Fig 6.19 Paint Tool Flyout

Using these tools, you can fill following types of fills in the image.

Uniform fills

Uniform fills let you fill images with solid colours. You can create custom colours for a uniform fill by choosing a colour model, fixed palette, mixer, or custom palette.

Pattern fills

Patterns fills let you fill images with textured patterns. You can fill images using a sample pattern or you can create a custom pattern for the fill.

Gradient fills

Gradient fills let you fill images with gradual colour blends. A gradient fill creates smooth transitions between colours by gradually changing their transparency as it progresses from the start colour to the end colour. You can apply a preset gradient fill or create a custom fill.

USING THE PAINT BUCKET TOOL

Paint Bucket lets you fill an entire image or part of an image with a solid colour. You simply have to select the colour, with which you want to fill the image, in foreground colour selection box. You can also use the Paint Bucket tool to fill a selection.

To apply a uniform fill to an entire image or selection:

- Select the foreground colour using the Foreground colour selection box.
- Specify the selection using any selection tool.
- Select the Paint bucket tool from the tool box or select the option Edit ➤ Fill. This brings the Fill dialog box.
- The option palette or the Fill dialog box displays various options related to Paint Bucket tool.

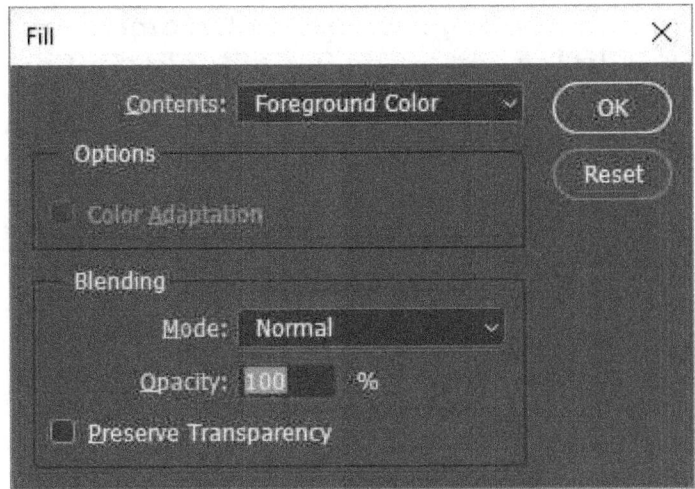

Fig 6.20 Fill dialog box

- In the Fill drop down menu, select the Foreground option as you want to fill the foreground colour. Select a blending mode and opacity as discussed earlier in this chapter.

- Select Preserve Transparency to limit the fill to layer areas that contain pixels.

- Select the tolerance value as required. To smooth the edges of the filled selection, select Anti-aliased. To fill pixels based on the merged colour data from all visible layers, select Use All Layers.

- Click on the image to fill the image or click inside the selection to fill the selection.

FILLING PATTERNS

Using the Paint bucket tool, you can fill various predefined or custom patterns into the image. Photoshop also lets you define any part of the image as pattern.

To fill an image or a selection with a pattern

- Select the part of the image you want to fill.

- Choose Edit ➤ Fill. Select Pattern in the dropdown menu for Use. Or select the Paint bucket tool and choose pattern from the Fill drop down menu. The Pattern option becomes active in the Fill dialog box or the Paint bucket option palette.

- Click on the Pattern drop down menu to display various predefined patterns.

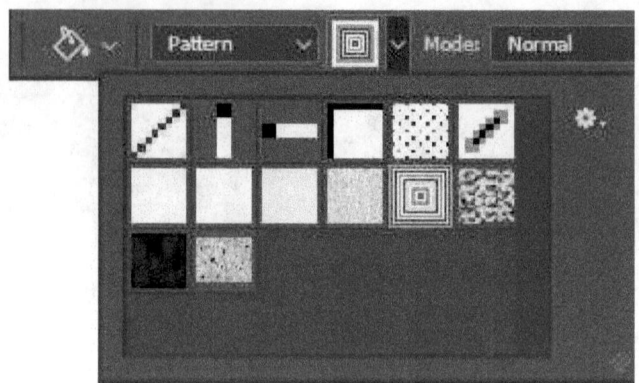

Fig 6.21 The Pattern palette

The pattern you select is repeated as tiles within the selection. Each new pattern replaces the current pattern.

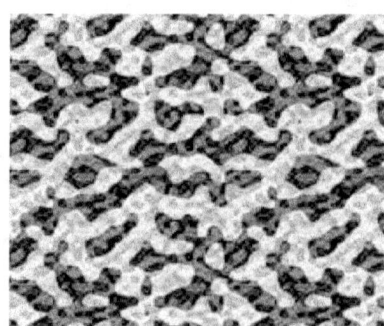

Fig 6.22 Filling a selection with pattern

Deleting a Pattern

To delete a pattern, do one of the following:

- Press Alt, and click the pattern you want to delete.

- Click the pattern in the palette, and choose Delete Pattern from the palette menu or right click on the pattern and select Delete Pattern from the menu that appears.

Creating Custom Pattern

Photoshop also lets you define a custom pattern made of a rectangular part of Image. To create a custom pattern from the image, you must select the image using rectangle selection tool. The maximum size of such pattern could be 1000 pixels by 1000 pixels.

- After selecting the required part, choose Edit ➤ Define pattern. This brings the Pattern Name dialog box.

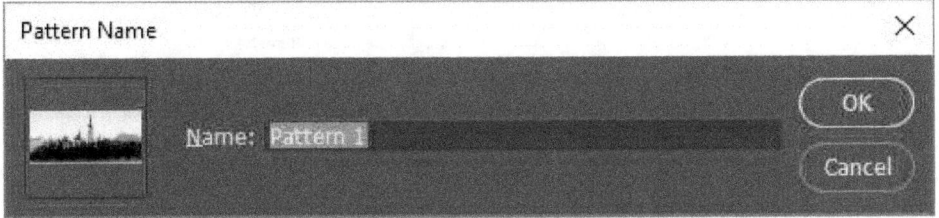

Fig 6.23 Specifying Pattern Name

- Specify the name of the pattern and click OK. New patterns are added at the bottom of the palette.

Saving, Loading and Replacing patterns

You can append as many patterns as you want in the Pattern palette. Photoshop also provides various patterns libraries. You can also define your own set of libraries which you can load into Pattern palette.

To load a predefined patterns into Patterns palette,

- Select the library from the list in Patterns palette menu or select the option Load Patterns from the menu to select *.PAT files.

- As you select the file, Photoshop gives you option to replace or append the selected library into Swatches palette. Select the required option.

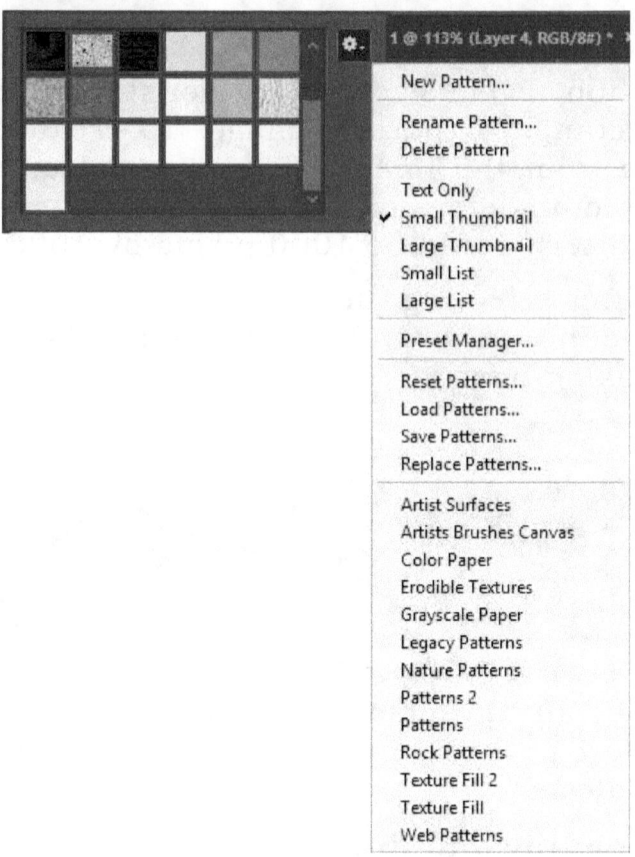

Fig 6.24(a) Replacing or Appending patterns in the palettes

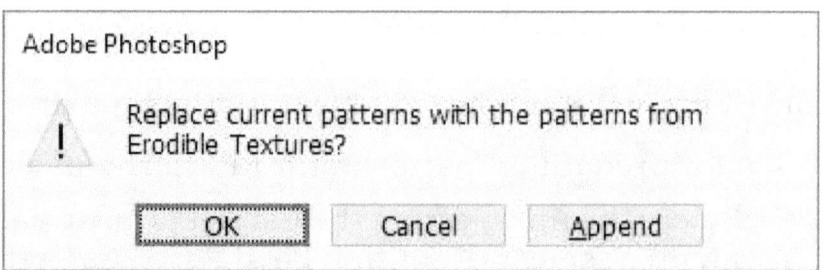

Fig 6.24(b) Replacing or Appending patterns in the palettes

If you append the selected library, you can mix the various libraries, add custom patterns and remove the unwanted patterns from the palette to create a new library of your choice.

Now, select the Save Patterns option to save the new set of patterns as a library. Select the other options from the Patterns palette menu, shown in Fig 6.21), as described below:

- Select Reset patterns option to load the default patterns.

- Select Replace patterns option to replace the current patterns set with patterns stored in a file.

USING THE GRADIENT TOOLS

Gradient tool let you create a gradual blend among multiple colours in the area that you want to fill. You can apply gradient tool to create a fill colour that fades according to the type or shape of the image that you want to fill. Gradient fills are based on flat, linear, elliptical, radial, rectangular, square or conical shapes. You can apply gradient fills to an entire image or to part of an image.

You draw a gradient by dragging in the image from a starting point (where the mouse is pressed) to an ending point (where the mouse is released).

- When you select the gradient tool, the option palette displays various options related to gradient tool. The Option palette lets you pick predefined gradients from the Gradient pop-up palette. Few of the predefined gradients have fixed colours, whereas first and second gradient in the default set of gradients gives you option of "Foreground to background" colour and "Foreground to Transparent" colour respectively.

- The Gradient pop-up palette also lets you load, save and replace gradient in a similar way as you can do with brush, pattern etc.

- After selecting the gradient from the predefined set of gradients, select one type of gradient from the following types :

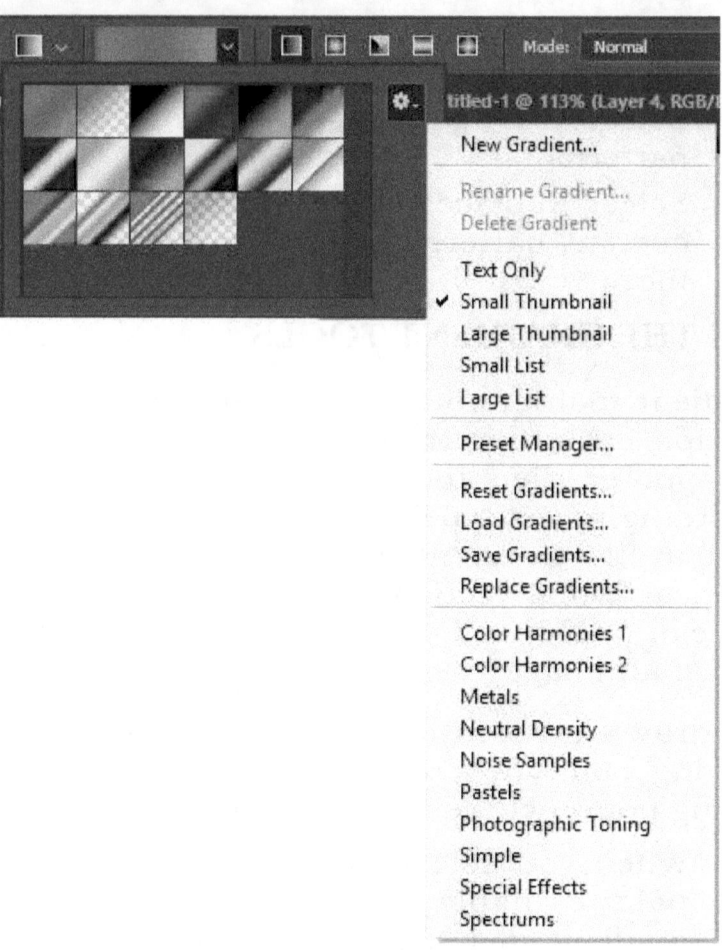

Fig 6.25 The Gradient palette

Linear gradient   Shades from the starting point to the ending point in a straight line.

Radial gradient   Shades from the starting point to the ending point in a circular pattern.

Angular gradient   Shades in a counterclockwise sweep around the starting point.

Reflected gradient Shades using symmetric linear gradients on either side of the starting point.

Diamond gradient Shades from the starting point outward in a diamond pattern. The ending point defines one corner of the diamond.

- Specify the opacity and blending mode as you have defined for other tools - Paintbrush or pencil.

- To use a transparency mask for the gradient fill, select Transparency. Select Dither to create a smoother blend with less banding. You can select Reverse option to reverse the order of colours in the gradient fill.

- To fill only part of the image, select the desired area. Otherwise, the gradient fill is applied to the entire active layer.

- Now, click and drag the mouse in the image from the starting point to the endpoint. A line appears connecting the two points. To constrain the line angle to a multiple of 45°, hold down Shift as you drag. As you leave the mouse at endpoint, the selected gradient is filled perpendicular to the line connecting the starting and end point.

Creating and Editing Gradient Fills

You can edit the existing set of gradients of create a new gradient using the Gradient Editor dialog box. In the Gradient Editor dialog box, you can create new gradient using the foreground, background or custom colour and adding as many layers as you want.

To create or edit a gradient

- Select the gradient tool from the tool box. Now click on the sample gradient (Fig 6.25) displayed in the option palette to display the Gradient Editor box shown in Fig 6.26.

- To base your gradient on an existing one, select it in the list.

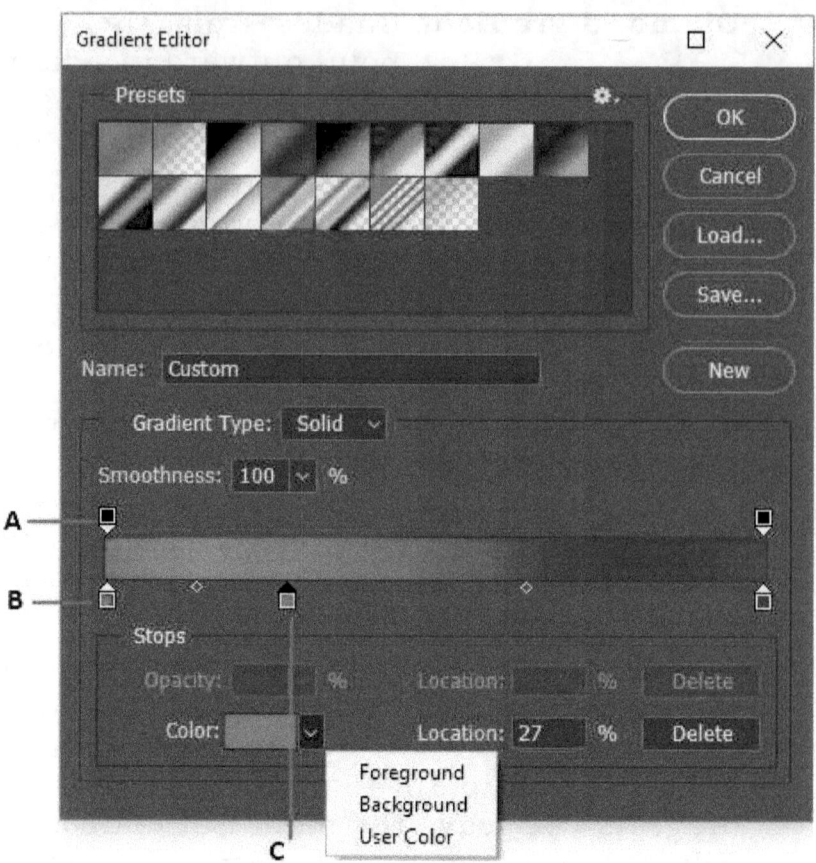

Fig 6.26 A. Starting Colour Stop B. Opacity Stop C. Mid Point

- To define the starting colour of the gradient, click the left colour stop. The triangle above the stop turns black, indicating that the starting colour is being edited.

- To choose a colour, do one of the following:

  - Double-click the colour stop. Choose a colour as described in Using the Adobe Photoshop Colour Picker, and click OK. You can also select foreground, background or user defined option from the Colour option. If you select foreground or background option, the colour of the gradient changes as you change the foreground or background colour.

- To define the ending colour, click the right colour stop. Then choose a colour as described in the previous step.

- Move the starting point or ending point to adjust their location.You can also set the location of the colour stop by specifying it in percentage in Location option.

  To add another colour stop in between the two colour stops, click below the gradient bar, where you want to add the colour stop. Now select this Colour stop and define a colour for this Colour stop.

- The diamond between the two Colour stop displays the Midpoint. At Midpoint, the two colours mixes evenly. To adjust the location of the midpoint, drag the diamond below the gradient bar to the required position.

- You can also control the transparency of the colour by moving the Opacity stop at the required location. Now enter the Opacity value or move the pop-up slider to control the Opacity for the selected stop. Lesser the value of the Opacity, the more transparent will be colour in the gradient bar at Opacity Stop.

- You can also move the midpoint of Opacity to required location by moving the diamond between the Opacity stops.

- To add noise to gradient, you can select the Gradient Type from the drop down menu. A noise gradient contains randomly distributed colours within the specified range of colours.

- To save the newly created gradient, click New. Enter a name for the gradient, and click OK.

USING HISTORY AIRBRUSH

Photoshop offers two history tools to paint complete image of part of image using the source data from a specified history state or snapshot. These tools are - History Brush Tool and Art History Tool.

Fig 6.27 Selecting History Tool from the Flyout

The History Brush Tool reveals the actual image using the source data from a specified history state or snapshot whereas the Art History brush let you paint with different styles.

To use the History Brush Tool :

- Select the History Brush tool.
- Specify the Brush size, blending mode and Opacity for the History Brush tool.
- Specify the fading effect, if required, of the size and opacity from the Brush Dynamics pop-up.
- Now select the snapshot in the History palette. The Snapshot will be discussed in more detail in next chapter - here, you open an image, select a gradient tool and apply the gradient to the image and then apply the History Brush tool to see the effects of the tool.

Fig 6.28 displays the image (A), image with gradient fill (A) and History brush applied on the portion of the image (C) using Fade off property of Brush tool.

To apply the Art History Brush :

- Select the Art History tool.
- Specify the Brush size, blending mode and Opacity for the History Brush tool.
- Specify the fading effect, if required, of the size and opacity from the Brush Dynamics pop-up.
- Besides these options, which are common to History Brush Tool, Art History Brush tool also lets you define various styles with which you can

paint the image. Experiment with various styles from the drop down menu.

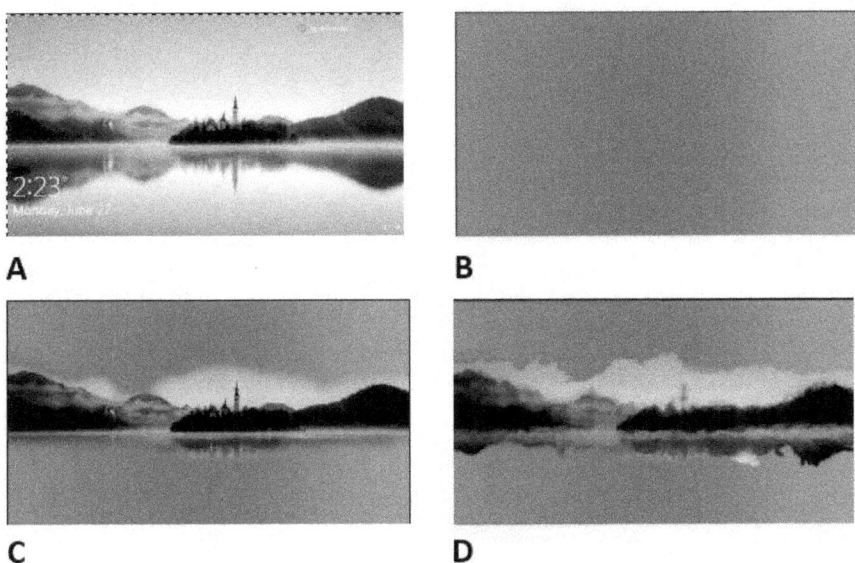

Fig 6.28 Effect of History Brush and Art History Brush

- Specify the Fidelity to control the deviation of the paint colour from the colour in the source state or snapshot.

- Specify the Area to control the area covered in stroke.

- Spacing places the stroke at a distance.

- Now select the snapshot in the History palette. The Snapshot will be discussed in more detail in next chapter - here, you open an image, select a gradient tool and apply the gradient to the image and then apply the History Brush tool to see the effects of the tool.

Fig 6.28(D) display the use of Art History brush on the gradient filled image. You can compare the outcome of History Brush tool and Art History by comparing the Fig 6.28 (C) and 6.28 (D). Fig. (C) is similar to the image whereas (D) is distorted image.

EDITING AND RETOUCHING

MOVING, COPYING AND PASTING SELECTIONS

You can copy selections and layers in an image by duplicating it. To copy selections or layers to other images, use the Copy and Paste commands in the Edit menu. To remove a selection from one image and paste it into another, use the Cut command in the Edit menu. The selection that is cut is placed on the Clipboard.

You can also move or copy selections and layers between images in Photoshop and other applications.

MOVING WITHIN AN IMAGE

Using Move tool, you can drag a selection or layer to a new location in the image. With the Info palette open, you can track the exact distance of the move.

- To move a layer, if any thing is selected on the layer, deselect it. Click on the move tool and drag the layer to the required place.
- To move a selection, select the move tool. To activate the move tool when another tool is selected, hold down Ctrl. Now, move the pointer inside the selection border, and drag the selection to a new position. If you have selected multiple areas, all move as you drag.

COPYING AND PASTING

You can use the move tool to copy selections as you drag them within or between Photoshop images. Or you can copy and move selections using the Copy, Copy Merged, Cut, and Paste commands. These four commands are explained in Edit menu. The difference between the two is that in dragging, Clipboard is not used as in the case of various options from Edit menu. The Edit menu lets you Copy and paste in two different ways.

Copy   Copies the selected area on the active layer.

Copy Merged Makes a merged copy of all the visible layers in the selected area.

Paste   Pastes a cut or copied selection into another part of the image or into another image as a new layer.

Paste Into   Pastes a cut or copied selection inside another selection in the same image or different image.

- To copy a selection, select the area to be copied using the selection tools and Choose Edit ➢ Copy or Edit Copy Merged. Then choose Edit ➢ Paste. The selected area is copied into the image.

- To copy a selection while dragging, select the area and select the move tool or hold Ctrl to convert any tool to move tool. Now, hold down the Alt key as you drag the selection using the move tool. If nothing is selected, the entire active layer is dragged and copied.

- To copy a selection/layer to another image, drag the selection using move tool to the other image. A border highlights the window. Now drop the selection into the windows.

- To create multiple copies of a selection within an image, select the area to be copied, click on the move tool or press Ctrl

  - Hold down Alt and press the arrow key to copy the selection and offset the duplicate by 1 pixel.

  - Hold down Alt + Shift and press the arrow key to copy the selection and offset the duplicate by 10 pixels.

  - Hold down Alt and drag the selection to copy anywhere in the image. Each press of mouse creates a copy of the selection.

COPYING INTO AN IMAGE

To paste one selection into another

- Cut or copy the part of the image you want to paste. Select the area of the image into which you want to paste the selection.

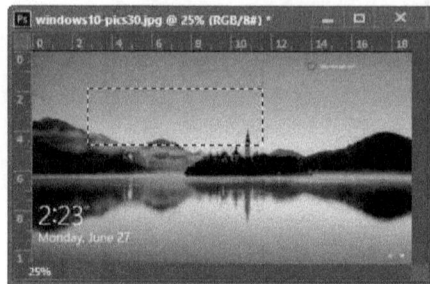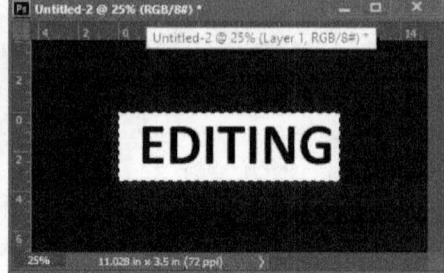

Fig 7.1 Selection dragged to new image

- The source selection and the destination selection can be in the same image or in two different Photoshop images.

- Choose Edit ➢ PAste Special ➢ Paste Into. The contents of the source selection appear masked by the destination selection.

Fig 7.2 And the result

- In the Layers palette, the layer thumbnail for the source selection and layer mask thumbnail appear next to each other. The layer mask thumbnail is the mask created by the selection you made in the destination image. If you move the pasted contents beyond the defined area, you will realize that you are unable to view the pasted contents.

COPYING BETWEEN APPLICATIONS

When you use the Edit ➢ Cut or Copy commands to copy selections or cut selections, the selected part is stored in the Clipboard and it remains there until you cut or copy another selection. (You may note that there is only one Clipboard and if you select another thing from other application, the contents of the Clipborad are replaced.)

In Photoshop, when you store some selection to Clipboard, it is stored in bitmap format (also called raster format). It is because bitmap format is recognised almost all the application and this makes it easy to paste the Clipboard's contents to any other application.

DELETING A SELECTION

To delete a selection, choose Edit ➢ Clear or press Delete. To delete a selection from the image but to store it in the Clipboard, choose Edit ➢ Cut.

REMOVING FRINGE PIXELS FROM A SELECTION

Fringe pixels are the pixels that are included in the anti-aliased selection at border. This can result in a fringe or halo around the edges of the pasted selection. This can be removed by various Layer ➢ Mating commands.

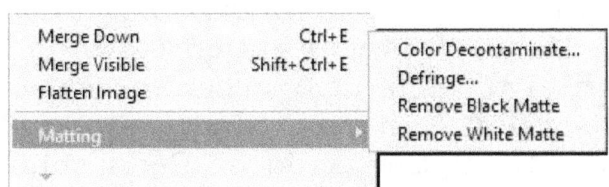

Fig 7.3 Various Mating options

These three Matting commands let you edit these unwanted edge pixels:

- Defringe replaces the colour of any fringe pixels with the colours of nearby pixels containing pure colours. To defringe select the Layer ➤ Matting ➤ Defringe.

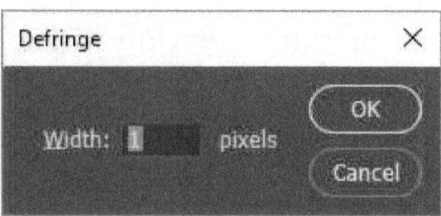

Fig 7.4 Defringing Pixels

- Enter a value in the Width text box for the distance to search for replacement pixels, and then click OK.

- You can use Remove Black Matte and Remove White Matte when you want to paste a selection, which is anti-aliased against a white or black background onto a different background. To remove a matte from a selection, choose Layer ➤ Matting ➤ Remove Black Matte or Remove White Matte.

UNDOING & REDOING CHANGES

You can set up a workspace that makes it easier to correct mistakes. You can undo one action at a time using the standard Edit ➤ Undo option.

You can use the Preference dialog box to activate the undo capabilities, so that you can reverse the changes. The History palette displays the list of actions performed and gives you option to Undo 20 actions consecutively by default. You can increase this to 100 actions so that you can cancel up to 99 actions consecutively. If the Undo or Redo commands are occupying excessive computer resources, you can reduce the number of undo levels. You can also free the memory used by the Undo command, the History palette, the Clipboard, or the Pattern buffer by selecting the option Edit ➤ Purge.

You can also reverse all changes made to the image, since it was last saved, by selecting choose File ➤ Revert, and click Revert.

USING THE HISTORY PALETTE

The History palette records every action that modifies the image. You can jump to any recent state of the image created during the current working session. Each time you apply a change to an image, the new action is added to the palette.

You can display the History palette by choosing Window ➤ Show History. To revert to the previous state of the image, do any of the following:

- Click the name of the state or drag the slider at the left of the state up or down to a different state. You can also revert step by step either by selecting the Step Forward /Step Backward option or by pressing Shift+Ctrl+Z/Alt+Ctrl+Z.

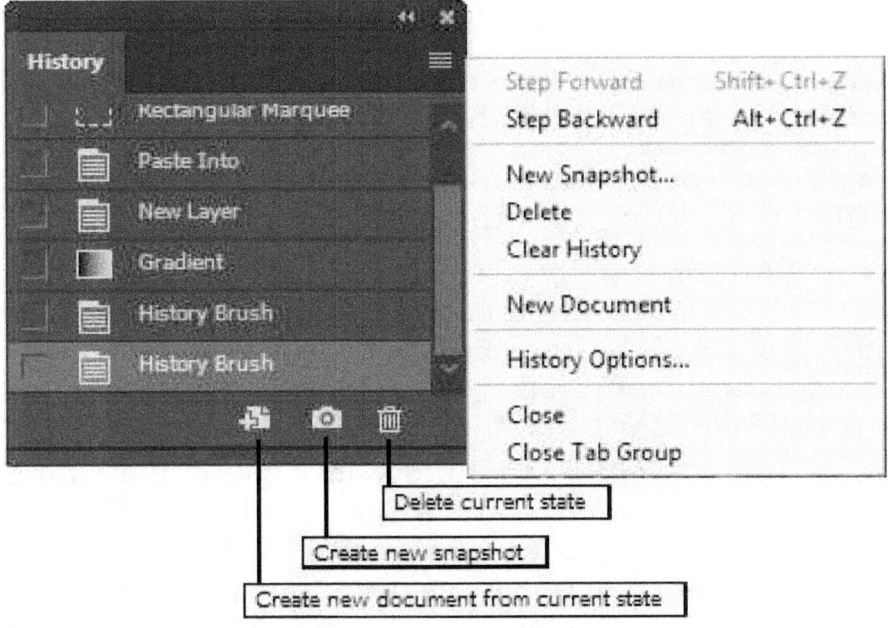

Fig 7.5 The History palette

If you revert back to any previous state and perform a new action, then all steps you revert back, are deleted and the new action is added to the History palette.

To delete one or more states of the image, without performing any new action, you can revert to the required state and choose Delete from the pop-up menu or click on the Trash button.

- To clear history without altering the image, select Clear History from the pop-up menu. All the actions are removed from the History palette except the last action.

Purging

Every action you store in History, it occupies free memory. At times the action consume so much of memory that it is difficult to carry on work. To free all the memory from the History actions, you can use Edit ➤ Purge ➤ History option to purge the list of states from the History palette for all open documents.

You can also hold down Alt and choose Clear History from the pop-up menu to purge the list of states from the History palette without changing the image.

You can specify various History options through the History Option from the palette menu.

- Automatically Create First Snapshot option automatically creates a snapshot of the initial state of the image when the document is opened. The next option creates snapshot automatically, if you save the document.

- Allow Nonlinear History lets you make changes to a selected state without deleting the states that come after. If this option is not selected, History palette stores the action in linear fashion and if you select a state and change the image, all states that come after the selected one are deleted. Enabling this option lets you delete any state in between while maintaining the actions after that state.

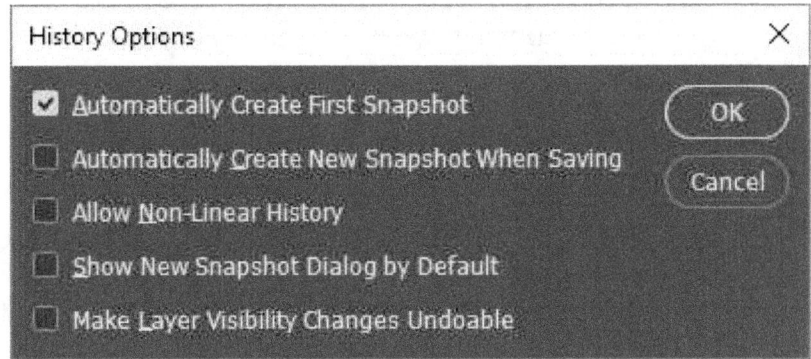

Fig 7.6 The History Option dialog box

CREATING A SNAPSHOT

Snapshots are the states that you can save after reaching a milestone during image editing. This enables you to promptly go back to that state even if you have deleted the History actions. Selecting the snapshot lets you work from that version of the image.

To create a snapshot, select a state and click the New Snapshot button on the History palette, or choose New Snapshot from the History palette pop-up menu to bring the New-Snapshot dialog box.

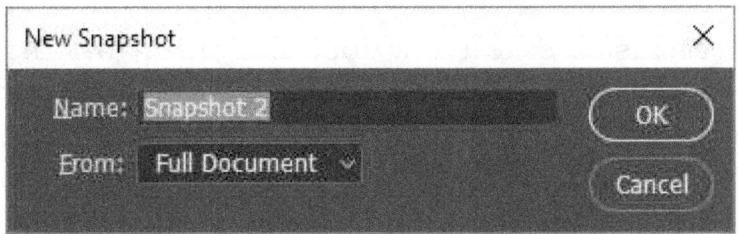

Fig 7.7 Creating a New Snapshot

- Enter the name of the Snapshot in the Name text box. and select the snapshot contents from the drop-down menu.
    - Full Document to make a snapshot of all layers.

- Merged Layers to make a snapshot that merges all layers in the image at that state.
- Current Layer to make a snapshot of only the currently selected layer

- Click OK.

To select a snapshot either click the name of the snapshot or drag the slider at the left of the snapshot up or down to a different snapshot.

To delete a snapshot either select the snapshot and choose Delete from the pop-up menu on the palette or drag the snapshot into Trash button.

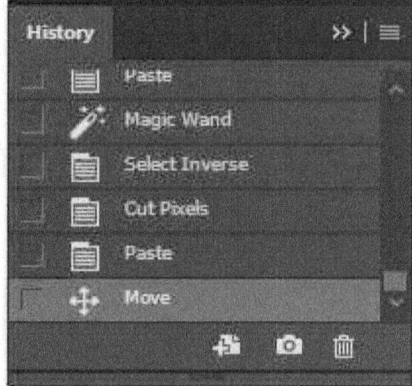

Fig 7.8 History palette before and After creating Snapshot

Creating New Document from Snapshot

You can also create a new document from any snapshot. The document thus created will have empty History list.

To create a new document based on the selected state or snapshot of the image, select a state or snapshot and either click the New Document button or select New Document from the pop-up menu.

Painting a State or Snapshot of the Image

The history brush tool lets you paint a copy of one state or snapshot of an image into the current image window. This tool makes a copy, or sample, of the image and then paints with it.

To paint to a state using history tool is similar to using History tool in a normal way. The only difference is that, while using the history tool or Art History tool, you have to select the snapshot by clicking the left column of the state or snapshot to use as the source for the history brush tool.

Fig 7.9 Selecting Snapshot

DUPLICATING IMAGES

You can duplicate images using the Image ➤ Duplicate option. You can copy an entire image into available memory without saving to disk by using this command or by dragging and dropping.

To copy an image using the Duplicate command, open the image you want to copy and choose Image ➤ Duplicate. This brings the Duplicate Image dialog box. (Fig 7.10)

•   Enter a name for the copied image and select Merged Layers Only option to merge the layers. Click OK.

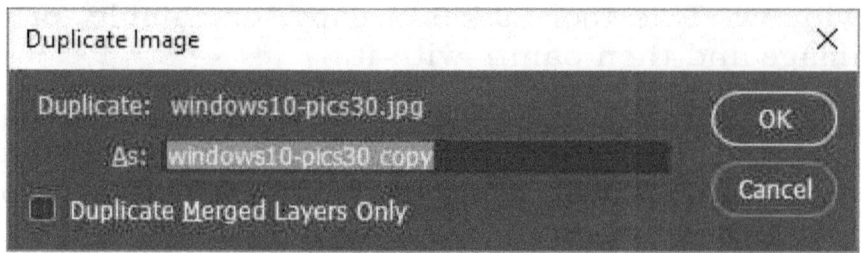

Fig 7.10 Duplicating Image

TRANSFORMING IMAGES

You can transform the entire image by rotating, resizing, scaling, mirroring, skewing, distorting, or applying perspective. You can also transform part or all of a layer, an entire image, path, or selection border. In case of selection, if it is floating above the image, it is automatically combined with the underlying image before the transformation is applied. You can also use the Option Bar to transform a selection precisely.

You can alter a selection directly in the Image Window by dragging the selection handles that surround it when the Move tool is selected and Show Bounding box option is made active.

TRANSFORMING OBJECTS

Rotating and Flipping an Entire Image

You can change the orientation of an image by rotating or flipping it. You can specify a precise angle of rotation in clockwise or anti-clockwise direction. The canvas rotates around its center point. Photoshop lets you flip the image horizontally or vertically.

You can use Image ➢ Rotate Canvas command to rotate or flip an entire image. This command brings a submenu which offers various options.

180°   Rotate the image by a half-turn.

90° CW   Rotate the image clockwise by a quarter-turn.

90° CCW   Rotate the image counterclockwise by a quarter-turn.

Arbitrary   Rotate the image by the specified angle in clockwise or anti-clockwise direction.

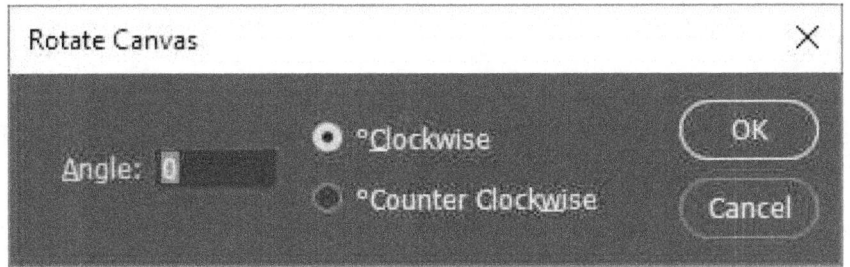

Fig 7.11 Rotating Canvas by specifying the angle

Flip Horizontal   Flips the image horizontally, around the vertical axis.

Flip Vertical   Flip the image vertically, around the horizontal axis.

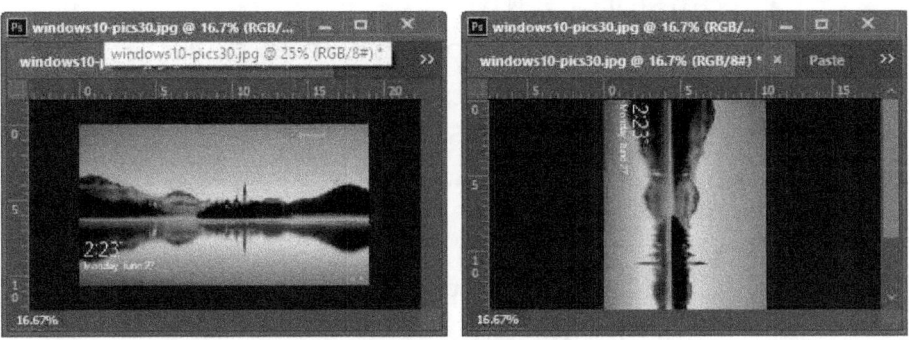

Fig 7.12 The Canvas Rotated

Applying a Specific Transformation

The commands under the Edit ➤ Transform submenu let you apply specific transformations to a selection, layer or path. Photoshop previews the effect and surrounds the selected area with a bounding border that lets you manipulate the selection, layer, or path.

You have already learned about the selection and path transformation. But the commands offered in Edit ➤ Transformation are common commands applicable to all - selection, path, layer or even the anchor point.

These commands lets you apply the selective transformation in succession before applying the cumulative transformation. For example, you can choose Scale, drag a handle to scale, and then choose Distort, drag a handle to distort, and press Enter to apply both transformations.

To scale, rotate, skew, distort, or apply perspective to selection border, path, anchor point or layer, select the selection border, path, anchor point or layer.

- Select Edit ➤ Transform ➤ Scale, Rotate, Skew, Distort, or Perspective. (If you select an anchor point for transformation, the menu is modified and you have to select the option Edit ➤ Transform point ➤ Scale, Rotate, Skew . Distort or Perspective option is not available for Anchor points. Similarly for path, you have to select Edit ➤ Transform Path)

- Drag the handles to achieve the desired effect.

- To apply additional transformations, repeat steps first two steps. To apply the similar transformation again, select Edit ➤ Transformation ➤ again or press Ctrl+Shift+T.

- Press Enter to apply the cumulative transformation. Press Esc to cancel the transformation.

To flip or rotate the selection border, path, anchor point or layer, select the selection border, path, anchor point or layer.

- Choose Edit ➤ Transform (points/path) and from the submenu, choose one of the following commands:

  Rotate 180°   Rotate by a half-turn.

  Rotate 90° CW Rotate clockwise by a quarter-turn.

  Rotate 90° CCW Rotate counterclockwise by a quarter-turn.

Flip Horizontal Flips horizontally, along the vertical axis.

Flip Vertical Flips vertically, along the horizontal axis.

Freely Transforming

The Edit ➤ Free Transform command lets you use the Scale, Rotate, Skew, Distort, and Perspective commands without having to select them from the menu. To access the various transformation modes, you use different shortcut keys as you drag the handles of the transform bounding box.

To freely transform, select selection border, path, anchor point or layer to be transformed and press Ctrl + T (or select Edit ➤ Free Transfer {path/point} depending upon the selected object) to bring the bounding box around the selected object. Now, transform as follows:

- To move, position the pointer inside the bounding border (it turns into a black arrowhead), and drag.

- To scale, position the cursor over a handle so that it becomes a double arrow. Now click and drag the handle. To scale proportionately, hold down Shift as you drag the handle.

Fig 7.13 Drag handle to scale, and result

- To rotate, move the pointer outside of the bounding border so as to make it a curved double-arrow and then drag. To constrain the

197

rotation to 15° increments, hold down Shift key as you drag. If you want to change the centre point around which rotation takes place, drag the center point to a new position.

Fig 7.14 (a) Rotate   **(b) Skew**

- To skew, hold down Ctrl+Shift and drag the handle. If you position the pointer over a side handle, the pointer becomes a white arrowhead with a small double arrow.

- To apply perspective, hold down Ctrl+Alt+Shift, and drag a corner handle. If you position the pointer over a corner handle, it becomes a gray arrowhead.

- To distort relative to the center point of the bounding border, hold down Alt key and drag a handle.

Fig 7.15 (a) Apply perspective   **(b) Distort symmetrically**

- To distort freely, hold down Ctrl and drag a handle.

- To undo the last handle adjustment, choose Edit ➤ Undo.

- Press Enter to apply the transformation. To cancel the transformation, press Esc.

Fig 7.16 Distort freely

Transforming Numerically

To transform the Object precisely, you can define the numeric values in the option bar of Free Transformation (Ctrl + T).

Fig 7.17 Specifying Transformation options in Option Bar

- To move, enter a horizontal distance in the X text box and a vertical distance in the Y text box. To move relative to the existing image, layer, or path, select Relative triangle.
- To resize, enter values for the Width and Height. Select Constrain Proportions to scale proportionally.
- To skew, enter values for the Horizontal and Vertical angles of slant.
- To rotate, enter a value for Angle.
- Click OK.

RETOUCHING IMAGES

Whether you want to repair a damaged image area or improve the quality of an image, Adobe Photoshop provides many correction and enhancement features to assist you with your image-editing tasks. We have already discussed about changing an image's dimensions, resolution, and orientation; adjust colour, tone, and focus; and transform images to create a panoramic effect.

Here, you will come to know about other tools which lets you fine-tune colours and enhance subtle effects. You can use these Effect tools to stamp, sharpen, smudge, blur, sponge, dodge and burn parts of an image. You can apply the editing effects to an entire image or to part of an image using the selection tools. You can use these effects to create high-quality, professional artwork from existing images.

USING THE STAMP TOOL

You can use the Clone stamp tool to create a sample of the image in another image or in the same image at different location. Now, the first thing that will come to your mind is that you can do the same by selecting a part of the image and pasting it into another image. But the difference here is that you can apply the sample of the image using the brush stroke. Each stroke of the tool paints on more of the sampled image.

There is also Pattern stamp tool, which lets you select part of an image and paint with the selection as a pattern.

Fig 7.18 The Stamp Flyout

Using Clone Stamp tool

To use the Clone stamp tool, select the Window ➤ Clone Source.

● In the Option bar define the blending mode and opacity. Also select a brush size. Select Use All Layers to sample data from all visible layers. If left deselected, the tool samples only from the active layer.

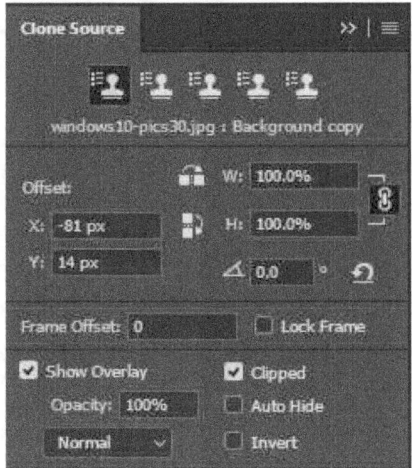

Fig 7.19 Specifying Options for Clone Stamping

- In Brush Dynamics, select Size or Opacity to Fade away or change with changes in stylus pressure.

Fig 7.20 (a) Original Image   **(b) Image Edited with Clone Stamp. Date Removed**

- Select Aligned to apply the entire sampled area once, regardless of how many times you stop and resume painting. Deselect Aligned to apply the sampled area from the initial sampling point each time you stop and resume painting.

- To set the sampling point, position the pointer on the part of any open image you want to sample, press Alt to change the the pointer into a stamp. Now click to take the sample. This sample point is the location from which the image is duplicated as you paint.

- Now drag the mouse at required places to paint as per sampled area.

Using Pattern tool

To use the Pattern stamp tool, select the tool from the flyout.

- In the Option bar define the blending mode and opacity. Also select a brush size.
- With the pattern stamp tool, select Aligned to repeat the pattern as contiguous, uniform tiles, even when you stop and resume painting in different parts of the image.

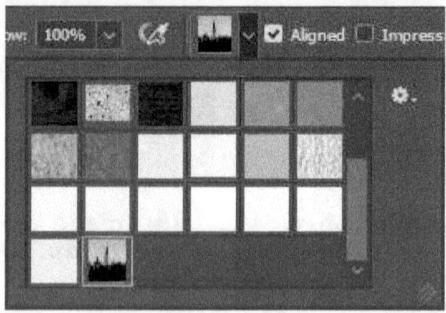

Fig 7.21 Area defined for pattern, and painted

- Now select a pattern from predefined patterns or use the rectangle marquee tool on any open image to select an area to use as a pattern. Then choose Edit ➤ Define Pattern. Reselect the pattern stamp tool.

- Drag to paint with the tool.

USING OTHER TOOLS

You can also retouch images using the smudge, focus, and toning tools.

Fig 7.22 Retouching Tools

The tools work in the following ways:

- The Smudge tool produces the same effect as rubbing your finger across a pastel drawing. The tool picks up colour where the stroke begins and pushes it in the direction you drag.

- The blur tool softens hard edges or areas in an image to reduce detail.

- The sharpen tool focuses soft edges to increase clarity or focus.

- Dodge and burn are photographic terms that describe processes used to lighten and darken areas of an image. You can use the Dodge and Burn tools to respectively decrease or increase the amount of exposure given to an area of an image.

- You can saturate or desaturate the paint in areas of an image by using the Sponge tool. Saturation affects the strength of the paint colour. Fully saturated colours contain no white and are vibrant. Fully desaturated colours are displayed as their grayscale equivalents.

Using Blur, Sharpen or Smudge Tool

To use any of the Blur, Sharpen or Smudge tool :

- Select the tool from the flyout.

- In the option bar, specify the blending mode and pressure. Also select a brush size.

- Select Use All Layers to blur, sharpen or smudge using colour data from all visible layers.

- In Brush Dynamics, select Size or Opacity to Fade away or change with changes in stylus pressure, if you are using a pressure-sensitive drawing tablet.

- Drag in the image to blur, sharpen or smudge the colour. Consider the following Fig. Fig (A) shows the Original image whereas (B), (C) and (D) image show blurred, sharpened and smudged image respectively.

Fig 7.23 Retouched Images - A - Original, B - blurred, C - sharpened and D - smudged

- While using smudge tool, you can also start smudging using the foreground colour. To do so, select Finger Painting option in the option bar. If you have not selected the option, you can press Alt as you drag with the smudge tool, to use the Finger Painting option.

Using Dodge, Burn or Sponge Tool

To use any of the dodge, burn, or sponge tool:

- Select the tool from the flyout menu. Select a brush size from the Option bar.

- For the dodge tool or burn tool, select Range to change in the image:

  Midtones   Changes only the middle range of grays in the image.

  Shadows   Changes the dark portions of the image.

  Highlights   Changes only the light pixels.

- For the sponge tool, select how to change the colour:

  Saturate   Intensify the colour's saturation.

  Desaturate   Dilute the colour's saturation.

- Specify the exposure for the dodge tool and burn tool, or the pressure for the sponge tool.

- Drag over the part of the image you want to modify.

PRINTING IN PHOTOSHOP

In most instances, the default print settings in Adobe Photoshop produce good results. To ensure that your colour images on-screen match your printed colour images, it's important to make sure that your system is correctly calibrated. Calibrating for variations in monitors, printing inks, and output devices is described in Reproducing Colour Accurately

The most common way to print images is to produce a positive or negative image on paper or film and then to transfer the image to a printing plate to be run on a press.

To print any type of image in Photoshop, you first select general printing options, including the halftone screen, and then specify settings for a particular image type. For colour separations, you can also adjust how the various plates are generated and create traps. You then print the image as one or several plates. When you print an image containing spot channels on a composite printer, the spot channels are printed as separate pages.

Choose File ➤ Print to display general printing options. The main area of the dialog box contains the standard printing options for paper type, printer effects, reduction and enlargement, and orientation.

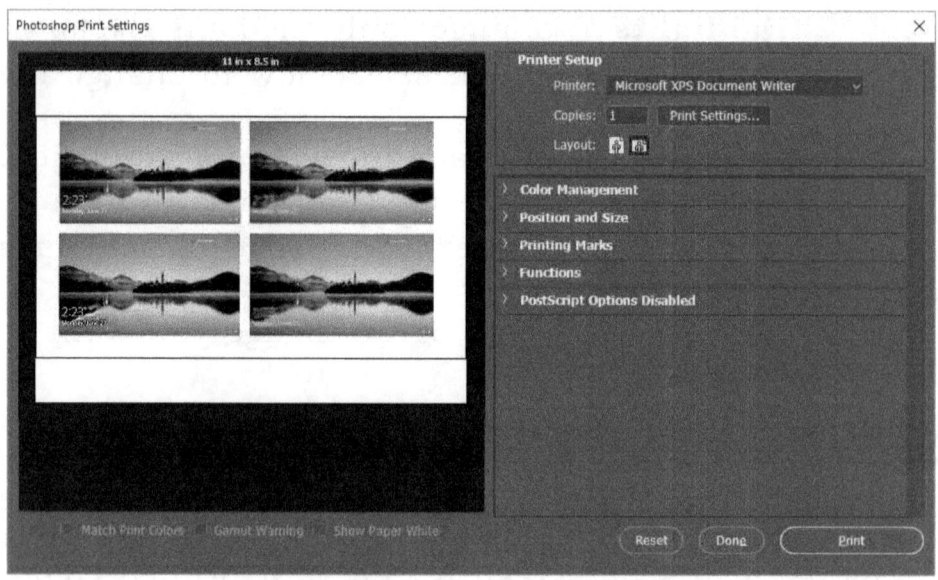

Fig 7.24 Specifying Options in Print

The Print dialog box may include these options:

Orientation

Prints the page using either the Landscape or Portrait setting. Because printing with the Portrait setting is much faster, you may want to rotate your landscape image 90 degrees by using the Rotate Canvas command, and then print using Portrait orientation.

Print Settings

Sets specific options for the printer you have selected.

Printing Marks ➤ Crop Marks

Prints crop marks where the page is to be trimmed. You can print crop marks at the corners, at the center of each edge, or both.

Printing Marks ➤ Labels

Prints filename and the channel name on the image.

Printing Marks ➤ Description

Prints the description with the image.

Printing Marks ➤ Registration Marks

Prints registration marks on the image (including bull's-eyes and star targets), used primarily for aligning colour separations and duotones.

Function ➤ Negative

Prints an inverted version of the image. Unlike the Invert command in the Image menu, the Negative option converts the output, not the on-screen image, to a negative. If you print separations directly to film, you probably want a negative, although in many countries film positives are common. Check with your print shop to determine which is required. If printing to paper, print a positive.

Function ➤ Emulsion Down

Makes type readable when the emulsion is down—that is, when the photosensitive layer on a piece of film or photographic paper is facing away from you. Normally, images printed on paper are printed with emulsion up, with type readable when the photosensitive layer faces you. Images printed on film are often printed down.

Function ➤ Border

Lets you print a black border around an image, specifying its width in the unit of measurement you choose.

Function ➤ Background

Lets you select a background colour to be printed on the page outside the image area. For example, a black or coloured background may be desirable for slides printed to a film recorder. To use this option, click Background, and then select a colour from the Colour Picker dialog box. This is a printing option only and does not affect the image itself.

Function ➤ Bleed

Lets you print crop marks inside rather than outside the image. Use this when you want to trim the image within the graphic. You can specify the width of the bleed.

WORKING WITH TEXT
ENTERING TEXT
FORMATTING ATTRIBUTES
EDITING TYPE LAYERS

WORKING WITH TEXT

Graphics applications create two different kinds of type - Outline and Bitmap type. The page-layout programs such as Adobe Illustrator or Adobe PageMaker create outline type. Outline type consists of mathematically defined shapes and can be scaled to any size without losing its crisp, smooth edges.

Photoshop converts these mathematically defined shapes to bitmap. The sharpness of bitmap type depends on the type size and the resolution of the image. If you zoom up the images, it will show jagged edges. However, Photoshop preserve the mathematically defined shapes of the character, as long as you don't merge the text into the image, so that it you increase or decrease the size of text, it produce type with crisp, resolution-independent edges.

ENTERING TEXT

You can add text to an image by using the Text tool. The text is created on a new type layer that you can select to change with any image-editing tool. You can assign attributes to text, such as style, colour, size, alignment, character spacing, and line spacing.

Photoshop divides the text in two types - point type and paragraph type. Point type is useful for entering a single word or a line of   characters. You can also write paragraph style text using the same tool. Paragraph style is more useful for entering and formatting the type as one or more paragraphs.

Entering Point Type Text

To enter point type text, select the type tool and click in the image to set an insertion point. To enter the text with current setting, start typing. The character appears in the foreground colour. If you have a look at the layer palette, you will see a new type layer added.

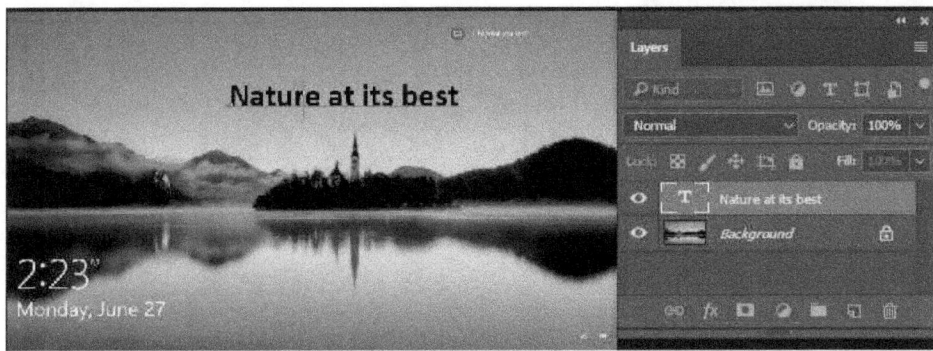

Fig 8.1 Writing Text on a New Layer

Entering Paragraph Type Text

To enter paragraph type text, select the type tool and click-drag the mouse diagonally to create a marquee. As you release the marquee, a bounding box appears with an insertion point on a new layer. To enter the text with current setting, start typing in the box.

In paragraph type, as you type, the lines of type wrap to fit the dimensions of the bounding box. You can enter multiple paragraphs and select a paragraph justification option. The character appears in the foreground colour.

Fig 8.2 Writing Paragraph Text

USING VARIOUS OPTIONS

The option bar displays various parameters that can be changed for the type tool.

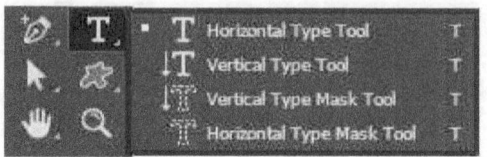

Fig 8.3 Selecting Options for Text in Option Bar

● You can type the text on a new layer or create a mask for selection in the form of text. To type the text on a new type layer, select the "Create a text layer" option. To create a mask for the selection, select "Create a mask or selection" option.

Fig 8.4(a) Creating a text layer Fig 8.4 (b) Creating a Mask

● Fig 8.4 displays the difference in the two types of usage of text tool. Fig (a) displays the text using the first option whereas Fig (b) selects the area in form of text.

Fig 8.5 Horizontal and Vertical Text

- You can also select the text horizontally or vertically. To do so, select the horizontal type or vertical type tool from the option bar.

  The pointer changes to an I-beam pointer. The small line through the I-beam marks the position of the type baseline. The baseline, in case of horizontal type, is the line on which the type rests. For vertical type, the baseline marks the center axis of the type characters.

Setting Simple Characters Attributes

Photoshop also lets you control individual characters in type layers by controlling the properties including font, size, colour, etc. You can also control other properties including leading, kerning, tracking, baseline shift, and alignment.

- Font is a complete set of characters - letters, numbers, and symbols - that share a common weight, width, and style. Select a font type from the drop down menu.

- You can also apply a font point size to the current selection by typing or picking a size value in points. (A point is equal to 1/72 of an inch in a 72-ppi image). To use an alternate unit of measurement, enter the unit (in, cm, pt, px, or pica) after the value in the Size text box.

- You can also select type style which is a variant version of an individual font in the font family. Select type style from Regular, Bold, Italic or Bold Italic. The range of available type styles varies with each font.

- Anti-aliasing lets you produce smooth-edged text by partially filling the edge pixels of the text. This filling of pixels blends the edges into background to produce smoothening effect. To select an anti-aliasing option, click on the drop-down menu and select from None, Crisp, Strong or smooth.

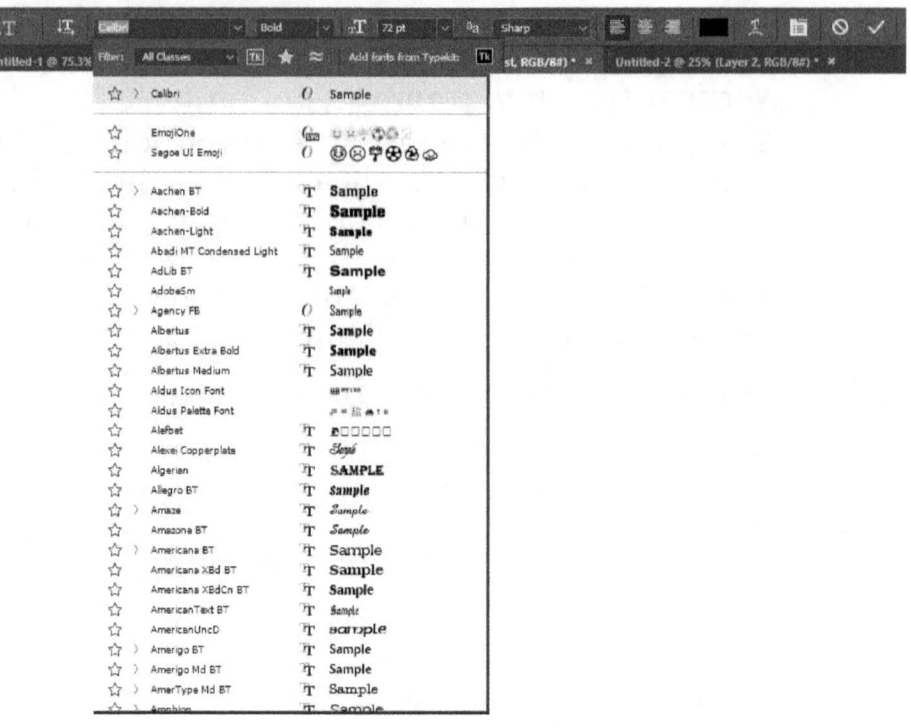

Fig 8.6 Selecting various Text options from Option Bar

- You can align type to one edge of a paragraph (left, center, or right for horizontal type; top, center, or bottom for vertical type) and justify type to both edges of a paragraph.

  To specify alignment select any one of the following option.

▦	Aligns type to the left.
▦	Aligns type to the center.
▦	Aligns type to right.
▥	Aligns type to the top.
▥	Aligns type to the center.
▥	Aligns type to bottom.

- To change the colour of the type, click the colour box, choose a colour as described in Using the Adobe Photoshop Colour Picker, and click OK.

FORMATTING ATTRIBUTES

USING CHARACTER PALETTE

Character palette provides all the basic formatting and advance formatting options for the characters. It also includes the option that are included in the option bar like fonts, size, colour etc. along with the advance formatting options like leading, kerning, baseline alignment etc.

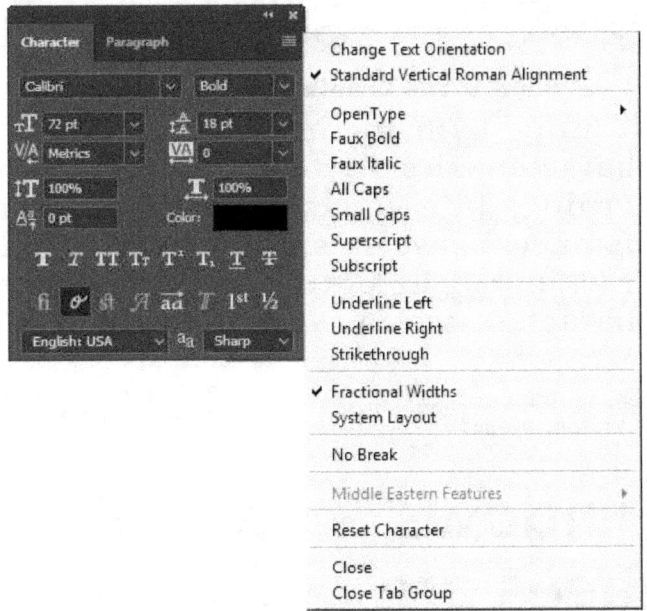

Fig 8.7 Using Character palette

To display the character palette, click on the palette button in the Option bar or select the option Windows ➢ Show Character.

The Character palette displays many options, out of which you will find four familiar options. These are - Selecting a font, font size, type style and colour of the font. Here, we will discuss the other options.

 Specify leading, which controls the space between lines. The leading is the distance of the baseline of one line from the baseline of other line. If the distance between two baseline is less than the font size then the lower line will overlap the upper one. Therefore, the leading should always be more that the font size.

- To select the leading, click on the drop-down menu to select it from the list or type in the box.

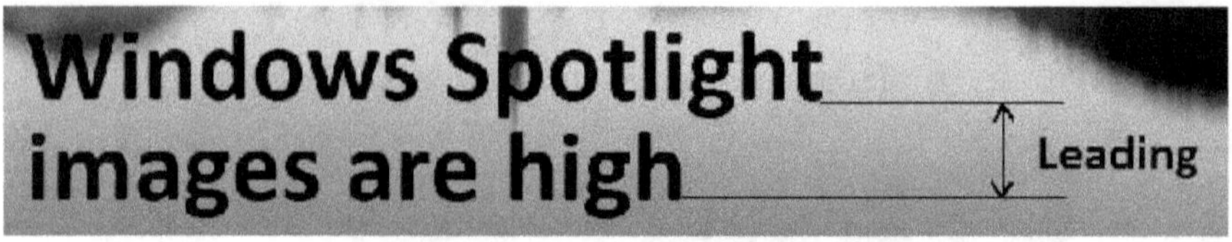
Windows Spotlight
images are high
Leading

Fig 8.8 The Leading between lines

Kerning ( )controls the distance between character pairs. By default, the font have specific kerning, but you can manually control the distance between specific pair of characters. Tracking ( ) is controlling the distance between characters over a range of characters.

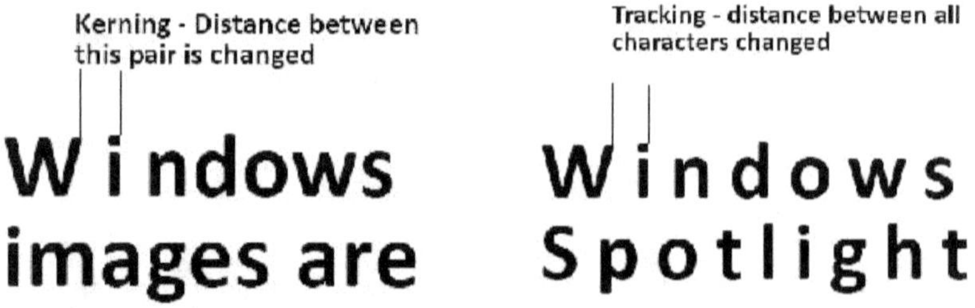
Kerning - Distance between this pair is changed
Tracking - distance between all characters changed
W indows
images are
W i n d o w s
S p o t l i g h t

Fig 8.9 Kerning and Tracking

The higher the value of Kerning or Tracking, the larger will be distance between characters. A negative value will bring the characters closer to each other. Both Kerning and Tracking are measured in units that are 1/1000 of an em space. (1 em space = font size). As kerning and tracking units are 1/1000 em, 100 units in a 10-point font are equivalent to 1 point.

- To specify Kerning between two characters, place the cursor between the two characters and select a value from the drop down menu. Metrics option sets the kerning to default.

- To specify Tracking, select the range of characters. This disables the Kerning option and activates the Tracking option. Select a value from the drop down menu.

↕T/↔T Vertical (↕T) and Horizontal (↔T) scale specify the proportion between height and width. The Vertical scale controls the width of the characters, whereas horizontal scale controls the height of the characters.

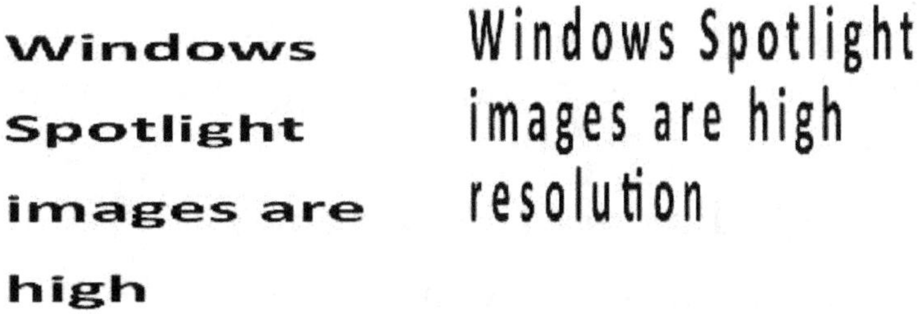

Windows

Spotlight

images are

high

Windows Spotlight images are high resolution

Fig 8.10 Scaling of Text

Specify the baseline shift. You can raise or lower the selected text above or below the baseline respectively.

Shift in Baseline

Windows Spotlight

Fig 8.11 Baseline Shift

Applying External Type Style

We have discussed that the type style is the variant version of an individual font in the font family. It may include Normal/Select Regular, Bold, Italic or Bold Italic. But there are font which don't have any variant version. You may , at times, require to use their Bold or Italic variant.

In such cases, you can apply faux styles, which are simulated versions of bold, italic styles of font. To apply the faux bold or faux Italic style, select the characters on which you want to apply the simulated variant. Now select the required variant from the Character palette.

Specifying the position of text

You can set the position of text relative to its normal position, making the text superscript or subscript. Superscript as well as Subscript characters are reduced in size and shifted above or below respectively, the type baseline. To make character as superscript or subscript, select the characters and select the option from Character palette.

Specify Underline or Strike through

To emphasize key words and phrases in the image, you can either underline the text or strike through it. To underline and strike through, you can select the characters and select the underline or strike through option from Character palette.

Changing Case

By default, the characters appear in the case in which they were entered. But Photoshop lets you change the case to Small Caps or All Caps. In Small Caps, all the characters are capitalized, but their size remains small as compared to Capital Letter. All caps converts all the characters to capital letters.

Windows SPOTLIGHT
IMAGES ARE HIGH

Fig 8.12 Normal, Small Caps and All Caps characters

Specifying Fractional Width

If the spacing between character varies, then the readability and appearance is improved so that the characters are placed at best spacing from each other. By default, the fractional width option is selected. You can deselect it by selecting the text and selecting this option from the Character palette menu. However, if the font size is small, fractional character widths can cause type to run together or have too much extra space, making it difficult to read.

Keeping the words together

Photoshop also provides the facility for controlling the line break. The No Break options in Character palette menu If you want that two words should not be broken in different line, select the text and turn on No break.

The No Break option is commonly used to keep dates from separating into two lines. e.g. with the date August 13, 1969, it is definitely not a good idea to have August at the end of one line and 13, 1969 at the beginning of next. By selecting the text and turning on No break, the date wouldn't be split.

Toggle Text Orientation

When you type vertical text, you are provided with two option to write the text as displayed in the following figure 8.13. Although, in both the figures, the text has been written using the Vertical orient tool, but the characters has been toggled by 90°.

By default, Toggle Text Orientation option 🎁 in option bar is selected and the characters appear in the upright fashion. If you select the Toggle Text Orientation option, the unrotated characters appear sideways (perpendicular to the type line).

Fig 8.13 Vertical character in Normal and Rotated mode

USING PARAGRAPH PALETTE

Similar to Character palette, Paragraph palette also provides all the basic formatting and advance formatting options for the paragraph. It also includes the option that are included in the option bar like justification etc. along with the advance formatting options like hyphenation, indentation etc.

To apply various paragraph formatting options, you can select single, multiple or all paragraphs. To apply formatting to single paragraph, click in that paragraph. To apply formatting to more than one paragraph, select range which is covers both paragraphs.

To select all paragraph, Press Ctrl+A, after clicking anywhere in the paragraph.

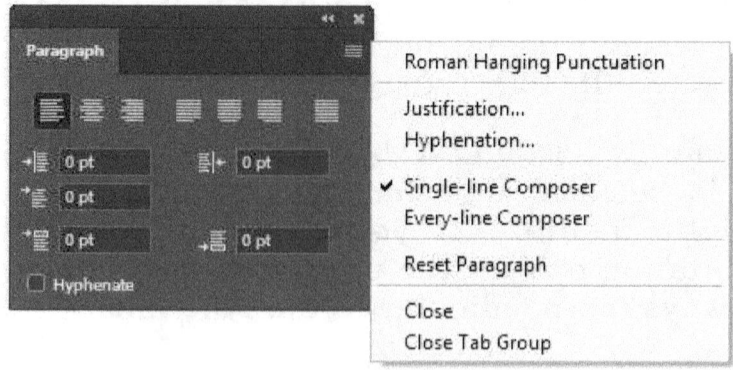

Fig 8.14 The Paragraph palette

Aligning and Justification

Using Photoshop, paragraphs can be aligned in seven ways - left, right, centered, justify last left, justify last centered, justify last right or justified. The default paragraph alignment is left.

The other options available centered & right can be applied to special text designed to stand out from rest.

Besides these standard option, there are four justification options, which makes the text to span the entire width of the text block. -

Justifies Last Left	All lines are justified except the last line which is left justified.
Justifies Last Right	All lines are justified except the last line which is right justified.
Justifies Last Right	Justifies all lines except the last, which is centered.
Justified	Justifies all lines including the last, which is force-justified.

When you select the Vertical orient tool for paragraph, the paragraph palette still shows the seven justification option as discussed above for Horizontal orient tool. the only difference is that left and right are replaced by top and bottom.

You can also precisely control various aspect of Justification. To do so, click on the Justification option on the Paragraph palette menu to bring the Justification dialog box.

The dialog box gives you option to control Word Spacing, Letter Spacing, and Glyph Spacing. Word spacing (0 to 1000%) refers to space between words that a spacebar would create. Letter spacing (-100 to 500%) controls the distance between letters and includes kerning or tracking values. Glyph spacing (50 to 200%) refers to the width of characters (a glyph is any font character).

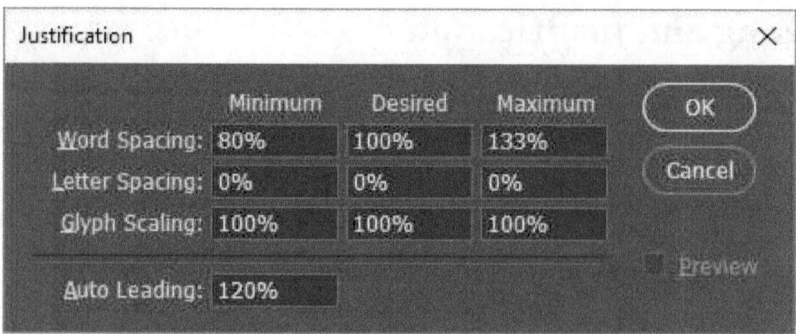

Fig 8.15 Specifying Justification Options

You can select Minimum, Desired and Maximum values of the three properties.

Indenting Paragraphs

An indent is extra space on the left or right side of the paragraph. The indents in Photoshop can be set by using the Paragraph palette. The Paragraph palette has the boxes to define left indent (▐▤), right indent (▤▐) and first line indent (▐▤) values as per requirement.

The left Indent controls the distance between the box border and the left edge of the paragraph. The right indent controls the distance between the box border and the right edge of the paragraph. The First Indent option specified the distance between the left edge of first line and left edge of paragraph.

If you select the vertical orient tool, the left and right indent is replaced by top and bottom indent and control the distance accordingly.

Controlling Distance between Paragraph

Photoshop lets you define the amount of white space before (▤◀) and after (▶▤) paragraphs. You can enter spacing settings in inches (in), centimeters (cm) or pixels(px). If you enter the distance in inch or centimeter, the Paragraph palette converts it into pixels.

Each paragraph can have a unique before and after spacing if you wish. One advantage to adding space this way is that the spacing before and after paragraphs does not change when you change the point size of your text. Another advantage is that you can use different spacing combinations for different purposes.

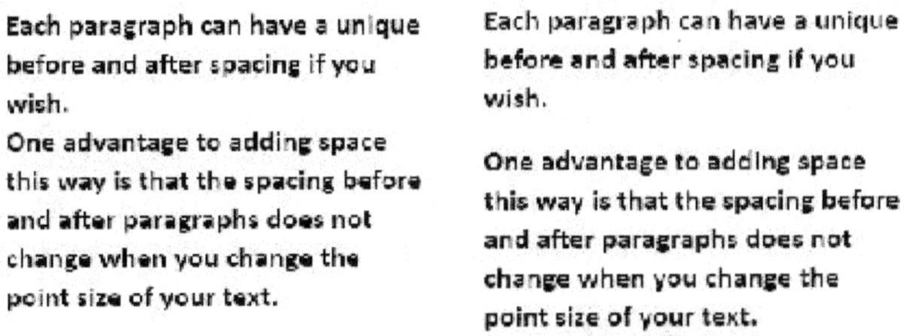

Each paragraph can have a unique before and after spacing if you wish.

One advantage to adding space this way is that the spacing before and after paragraphs does not change when you change the point size of your text.

Each paragraph can have a unique before and after spacing if you wish.

One advantage to adding space this way is that the spacing before and after paragraphs does not change when you change the point size of your text.

Fig 8.16 Specifying distance between paragraph

Hyphenation

Photoshop provides the facility to hyphenates the word. By default hyphenation is on for all paragraph. To change the hyphenation setting, deselect the Hyphenate option in the Paragraph palette. The hyphenation setting can be changed for selected text or for entire story by selecting Hyphenation option from the Paragraph's palette menu to bring the Hyphenation menu. (Fig 8.17)

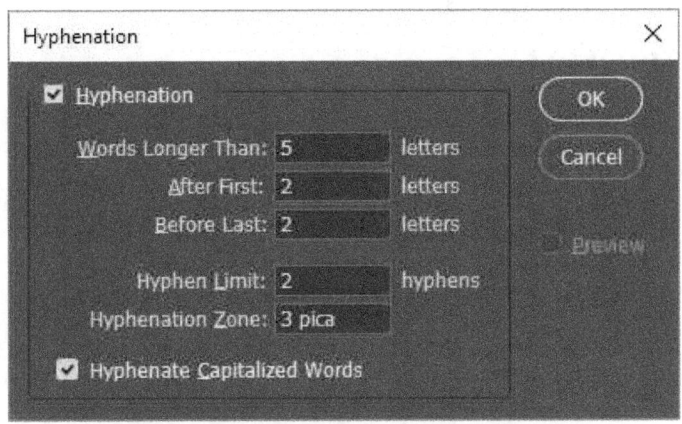

Fig 8.17 Hyphenation options

The hyphenation dialog box lets you select the length of the word which should be hyphenated. It gives you total control over hyphenation. You can also specify after how many words after and before, hyphen should come. Select the Hyphenate Capatalized word to hyphenate capital words also.

Hanging punctuation

You can also control the punctuations to fall outside the margin. In such case the punctuation is called Hanging Punctuation. To make the punctuation marks appear in the margin, select the Roman Hanging punctuation from the Paragraph palette menu.

EDITING TYPE LAYERS

Once you have created type, you can edit the contents, attributes, and orientation at any time by using its type layer. Type layers save with the image. You can move, restack, copy, and change the layer options of a type layer just as for a regular layer. You can also apply these commands to a type layer and still be able to edit the text:

- Transformation commands under the Edit menu, except for Perspective and Distort.
- Apply all the layers blending effect
- Fill shortcuts.

Rasterizing Text

To apply the full range of Photoshop effects (such as filters) to a type layer, you can convert the type layer to a regular layer. Converting a type layer makes its contents uneditable as text.

To convert a type layer to a regular layer:

- Select the type layer in the Layers palette.
- Choose Layer ➢ Raterize ➢ Type.

Wrapping Text

Wrapping text option lets you distort the text in such a way that it takes the shape of predefined Style. You could wrap the text of point type or paragraph type to a particular shape.

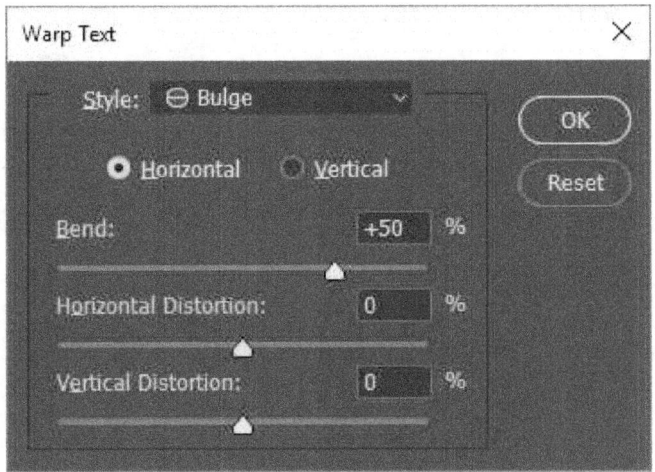

Fig 8.18 Wrapping Text

To wrap the text to a particular style, select the text layer and choose Layer ➤ Text ➤ Wrap Text (Fig 8.20) or Click on the Wrap Text button on the Option bar. This brings the Wrap Text dialog box shown in Fig 8.18.

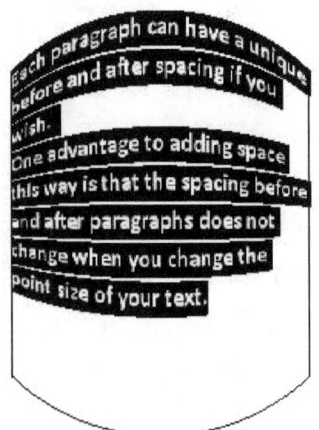

Fig 8.19 Text applied with Bulge shape and Vertical distortion

Now, select the shape from the Style drop down menu. As you select the shape, the text takes the form of the shape and dialog box displays various properties to control the shape. These include controls to change bend, horizontal distortion and vertical distortion. Experiment with different shapes and properties to create various effects.

Changing Anti-aliasing

You can also change the anti-aliasing of the text layer by selecting the required option in Character palette - None, Crisp, Strong or Smooth. You can also select Type ➤ Anti-Alias.

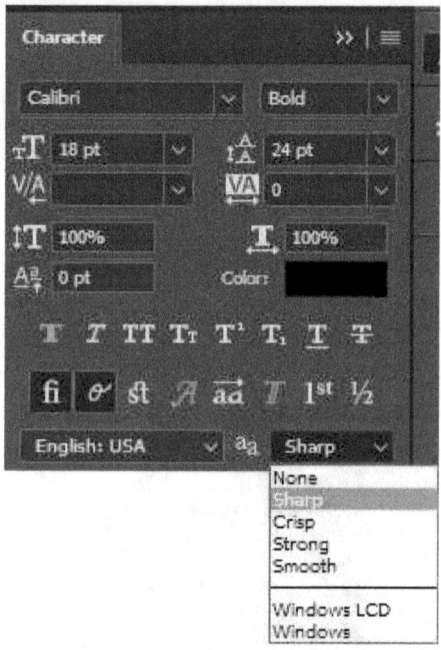

Fig 8.20 Specifying Anti-aliasing

Converting between Text type

Photoshop lets you convert the Point type text to paragraph type and paragraph type text to point type. To do so, select the text layer you want to convert and select Type ➤ Convert to Point Type (paragraph type).

Similarly you can also convert horizontal type text to vertical type or vice-versa. Select the text layer and choose Type ➤ Orientation ➤ Horizontal/Vertical.

Converting Text to Workpath or Shape

You can convert any text layer to a workpath or shape using the Type ➤ Convert to Workpath (shape). You can maipulate and save the workpath or shape like any other workpath or shape. You cannot edit characters in the path or shape as text. The original type layer is converted to shape layer if you create a shape from the text layer. However, the original type layer remains intact and editable if you create the workpath.

Fig 8.21 Original text and workpath created from text

WORKING WITH LAYERS

WORKING WITH LAYERS

Layers are series of transparent planes on which you can place images, add effects to images in the background without altering images. You can control how different images overlay one another by moving the layer and the elements they contain. You can also lock layers and make them invisible and nonprintable. You can use layers to help you organize different elements of a complex image.

The vertical order of these layers - the stacking order - helps determine the appearance of the final image. The stacking order is most evident when you have overlapping elements with contrasting properties. If the elements do not overlap, the stacking order may not be evident. In all cases, however, the stacking order is determined by the order in which you add elements to the image.

Every image in Photoshop has atleast one layer. When you start a new image, it starts with the lone layer termed as background layer. In stacking order, this layer always remains the lowest layer and its stacking order can't be changed.

You can imagine layers as stack of papers lying one over another. You can control the opacity of layers. These you can imagine as transparent paper in stack of papers. Through the transparent paper you can view the contents below that layer. Similarly, you can view the contents of the layer through the transparent layer.

THE LAYERS PALETTE

The Layers palette lists all layers in an image, starting with the topmost layer. A thumbnail of layer contents appears to the left of the layer name. It is updated as you edit. You can use the scroll bars or resize the palette to see additional layers.

You use the Layers palette to create, hide, display, copy, merge, and delete layers. Changes to an image affect only the highlighted or active layer. You select a layer to make it active, and only one layer can be active at a time. The active layer's name appears in the image window's title bar, and a paintbrush icon appears next to the layer in the Layers palette, indicating that the layer can be modified.

You can also create Layer Set using Layer palette. These Layer sets are like folders storing various contiguous layers. You can expand a layer set to display the layers it contains or collapse it to reduce clutter. However unlike folders, you can't create one layer set inside other Layer Set.

To display the Layers palette, choose Window ➤ Show Layers. Fig 9.1 displays the Layer palette with various options.

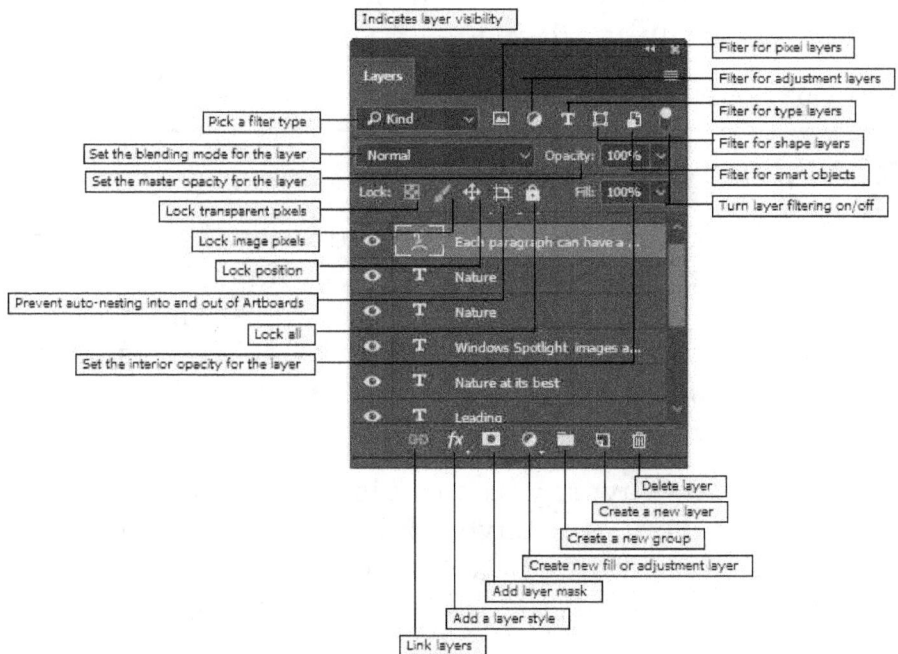

Fig 9.1 The Layers palette

To select a layer or to make any layer as active layer, do one of the following:

- In the Layers palette, click a layer to make it active.

- Select the move tool, right-click in the image, and choose the layer you want from the context menu. The context menu lists all the layers that contain pixels under the current pointer location.

You can also select layers interactively as you use the move tool.

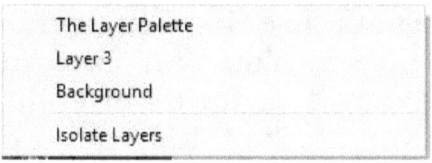

The Layer Palette
Layer 3
Background
Isolate Layers

Fig 9.2 Selecting a layer

To change the size of a Layers thumbnail or hide the thumbnail, select palette Options from the Layers palette menu. From the Layer palette option dialog box, select the size of the thumbnail or select none to hide the thumbnails.

ORGANIZING LAYERS

CREATING NEW LAYERS

In the Layer palette, you can add new layers to help you organize the elements in your image. To add a new layer, click on the New Layer button at the bottom of the Layer palette. (Fig 9.1) The new layer is created above the selected layer. The new layer also becomes the active layer.

To add a new layer, you can also select the New Layer command from the Layer palette menu. This brings the New Layer dialog box. In the dialog box, specify the layer name, colour, blending mode and opacity for the layer.

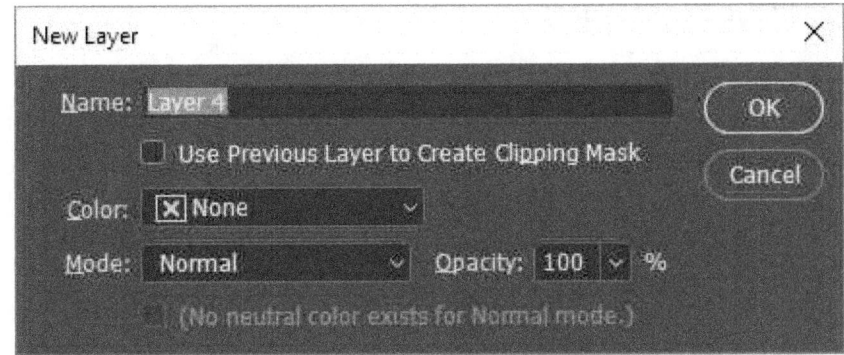

Fig 9.3 Adding New Layer

You can also create new layers by converting selections into layers, converting a background to a regular layer, pasting selections into the image or by creating type tool.

The last two options of creating layers has already been discussed.

• To convert selections into layers, make the selection which you want to be on the new layer. Now select Layer ➤ New option to bring the submenu. Select the option Layer via Copy or Layer via Cut option to create new layer by copying or cutting the selection.

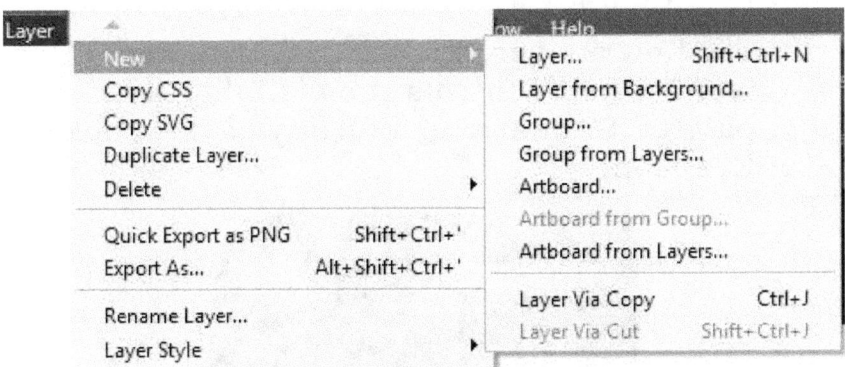

Fig 9.4 Using Layer Menu

• To convert the background into layer, select the option Layer from the Background from the Layer ➤ New submenu.

DELETING LAYERS

To delete a layer, either drag the layer into the Trash can at the bottom of the palette or select the Delete Layer command from the Layer palette menu option. This brings the confirmation dialog box (Fig 9.5), click OK to confirm that you want to delete the layer.

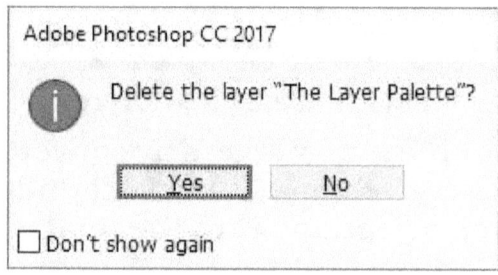

Fig 9.5 Deleting Layer

VIEWING LAYERS

With Layer palette, you can control the Layers visibility. By hiding certain layers, you make it easier to identify and edit the elements on other layers. You also reduce the time Photoshop needs to refresh your image when you edit it. This setting is particularly effective in images with many elements on multiple layers. To show or hide a layer, do one of the following:

● To show a layer, click the layer name or the Eye icon, which controls the visibility, in the Layer palette. Similarly to hide any Layer, click on the Eye icon.

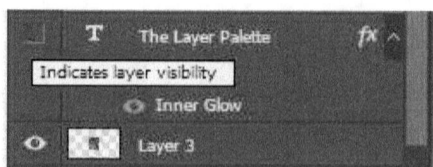

Fig 9.6 Hiding Layers - Land

● You can also drag through the eye column to hide multiple layers.

- Alt-click the eye icon for a layer to display just that layer. Alt-click in the eye column again to redisplay all the layers. Only visible layers are printed. Making layers temporarily invisible can speed performance.

THE STACKING ORDER

The Layer palette shows the order in which layers are stacked in the active image. The first layer in the list is the bottom layer - the background layer and the last layer is the top layer.

To change a layer's position in the stacking order,

- You can drag the layer's name tag to the desired position. As you drag, a position line indicates the layer's current position.

- You can also use the command defined in Layer ➤ Arrange submenu.

Fig 9.7 Arranging Layers

- To move a selected layer one level up in the Layers palette, select Bring Forward or press Ctrl+] without activating the menu.

- To move one level down select Send Backward or press Ctrl+[without activating the menu.

- To move to the topmost level select Bring to Front or press Ctrl+Shift+].

- To move to the bottommost level (above the background), select send to Back or press Ctrl+Shift+[.

RENAMING LAYERS

You can assign a new name to any layer you create. You might want a layer's name to indicate its contents, position in the stacking order, or relationship with the image's other layers.

- To rename a layer, In the Layer palette, double-click the layer name. Type a new name for the layer and press ENTER.

Fig 9.8 Renaming Layers

LINKING LAYERS

You can also link two or more layers to simultaneously apply various effects on the linked layers. After linking, you can together move their contents, apply transformations, align layer contents, merge layers or create clipping groups.

To link layers, select layers to be linked in the Layers palette. Now, click Link the Layer at the bottom of Layer palette. The link icon appears in right side column.

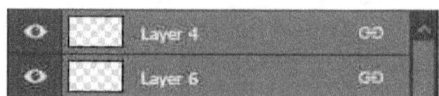

Fig 9.9 The Land layer is linked to Butterfly layer

To unlink layers, click the link icon to remove it.

MOVING, COPYING AND PASTING LAYERS

You can copy layers in an image by duplicating it. To copy layers to other images, you can use drag and drop option.

Moving Within an image

Using Move tool, you can drag a layer to a new location in the image. With the Info palette open, you can track the exact distance of the move. To move a layer, you must ensure that nothing is selected on the layer. Click on the move tool and drag the layer to the required place.

Copying Layers

To copy a layer to another image, drag the layer using move tool to the the other image. A border highlights the window. Now drop the layer into the windows.

DUPLICATING LAYERS

You can duplicate any layer (including the background) or layer set within the same image or to a different image. If you want to duplicate the layer into other image, ensure to open both the images - the source and the destination.

To duplicate a layer in an image, select the layer in the Layers palette. Now, select Layer ➢ Duplicate Layer or choose Duplicate Layer from the Layers palette menu to bring the Duplicate Layer dialog box.

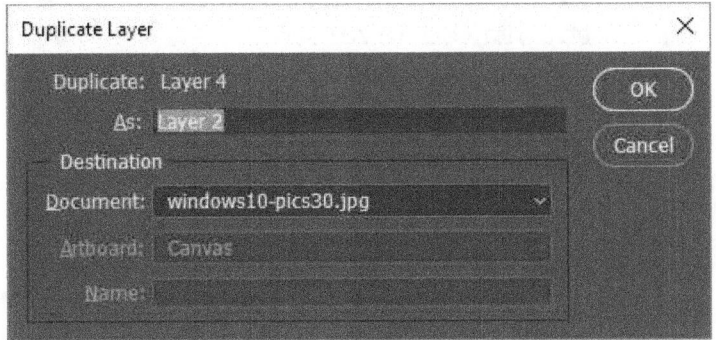

Fig 9.10 Duplicating Layers

Select the destination from the drop down menu, which displays all the documents open along with the option of opening New document. You can also specify the name of the new document.

ALIGNING LAYER CONTENTS

You can align the contents of layer one layer to the contents of the active layer or to a selection border within the image's boundaries. To align the contents of two different layers, the layers must be linked. You can also position the contents of linked layers at evenly spaced intervals using the distributed linked option.

To align or distribute align to a selection border, make a selection. You can also align or distribute align to the contents of the active layer.

- In the Layers palette, specify the layers you want to align or distribute.
    - To align a single layer to a selection, make the layer active.
    - To align multiple layers to a selection or to the active layer, link together two or more layers and select any one of them.
    - To distribute multiple layers, link together three or more layers and select any one of the linked layers.
- To align layers, choose Layer ➤ Align Linked (or Align To Selection if you made a selection), and choose an option from the submenu.

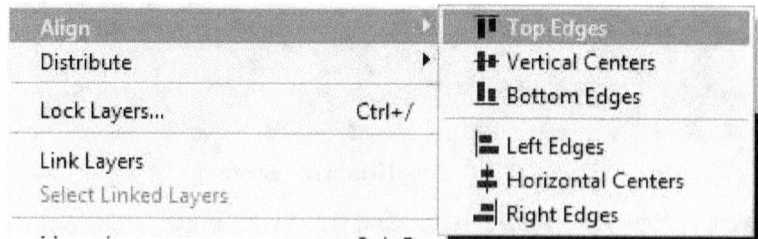

Fig 9.11 Aligning Linked Layers

- To distribute layers, choose Layer ➤ Distribute Linked, and choose an option from the submenu:

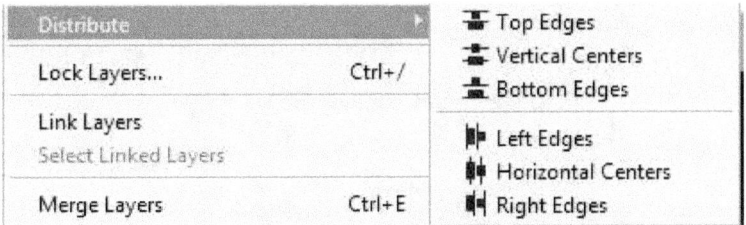

Fig 9.12 Distributing Linked Layers

MERGING LAYERS

You can merge layers, layer sets, layer clipping paths, clipping groups, linked layers, or adjustment layers so as to combine several layers into one. When you merge a layer into another layer, the transparent areas in the merged layers remains transparent.

● To merge a layer with the layer below it, select the layer to be merged and choose choose Layer ➢ Merge Down option or choose Merge Down from the Layers palette menu. If you want to merge the linked layers, the Merge Down command is replaced with Merged Linked.

● To merge all the visible layers in an image, hide any layers you do not want to merge. Now, select Layer ➢ Merge Visible or choose Merge Visible from the Layers palette menu.

● To merge all the layers in a Layer set, select the Layer set and choose Layer ➢ Merge Layer set or choose Merge Layer set from the Layers palette menu.

FLATTENING ALL LAYERS

When image is flattened, all the layers are merged into the background. This reduces the size of the file to a great extent. You should flatten the image when you have finished editing.

To flatten an image, make all the layers visible, when you want to include in the flattened image and choose Layer ➢ Flatten Image. If you hide any layer, Photoshop will ask you to discard the hidden layer.

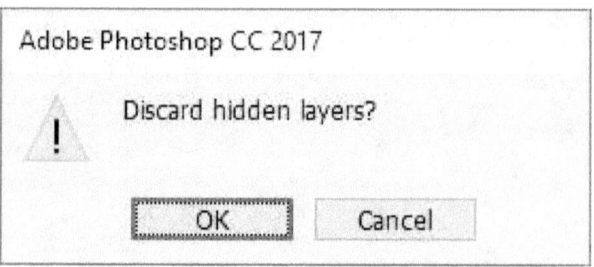

Fig 9.13 Flattening Image

EDITING LAYERS

When you create a new layer, it is transparent by default. You can use the layer as a clean transparent paper in the stack of papers where you can add as many colours and effects as you want.

SPECIFYING BLENDING MODES & OPACITY

You can use specify layer blending modes to determine how the pixels in a layer are blended with underlying pixels on other layers. By applying modes to individual layers, you can create a variety of special effects. To apply various blending mode, click on the blending mode drop down menu in the Layer palette.

You can also change the opacity of the layer by using the Opacity pop-up slider. A layer with 1% opacity appears nearly transparent, one with 100% opacity completely opaque. You cannot change the opacity of an image that has only a background.

CREATING CLIPPING GROUPS

In a clipping group, the bottommost layer covers the entire group as mask. For example, if you want to fill a shape or text with a image which is above the shape layer you can clipping group the image layer with the text layer so that the image appear only through the text layer.

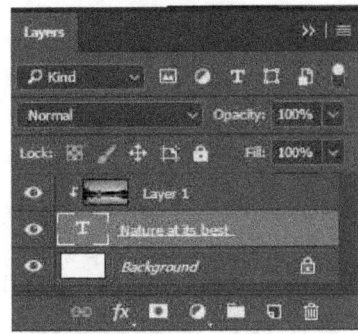

Nature at its best

Fig 9.14 Creating Clipping Group

To create a clipping group, do one of the following:

- Hold down Alt, position the pointer over the solid line dividing two layers in the Layers palette (the pointer changes to two overlapping circles, and click.

- Select a layer in the Layers palette and choose Layer ➤ Group with Previous.

- Link together the desired layers in the Layers palette, as described in Linking layers. Then choose Layer ➤ Group Linked.

To remove a layer from a clipping group, do one of the following:

- Hold down Alt, position the pointer over the dotted line separating two grouped layers in the Layers palette (the pointer changes to two overlapping circles), and click.

- In the Layers palette, select a layer in the clipping group and choose Layer ➤ Ungroup. This command removes the selected layer and any layers above it from the clipping group.

To ungroup all layers in a clipping group:

- In the Layers palette, select the base layer in the clipping group.

- Choose Layer ➤ Ungroup.

CREATING AN ADJUSTMENT LAYER

Adjustment layers works as a mask on the existing layers. These layers let you control the tones of overall image. Adjustment layers otherwise are similar to normal layer except that you also specify a colour adjustment type for an adjustment layer. Depending on your choice, the dialog box for the selected adjustment command may appear. This colour adjustmet type affects all the layers below the adjustment layer.

You can rearrange the adjustment layer in order, delete, hide, and duplicate in the same manner as you do for normal layer. well. However, you also specify a colour adjustment type for an adjustment layer. The adjustment layer takes the name of the adjustment type.

To create an adjustment layer:

- If you want to apply the adjustment layer to a limited area, make the selection first. Now click the New Fill or adjustment layer at the palette bottom or select Layer ➤ New Adjustment layer option from the menu. From the submenu that appears, select the type of the adjustment effects you want to select.

- In the New Adjustment Layer dialog box, type a name for the layer. Choose layer options as desired, and then click OK.

CREATING FILL LAYER

Similar to Adjustment layer, you can also create a fill layer from solid colour, gradient or pattern. If you want to apply the Fill layer to a limited area, make the selection first. Now click the New fill or adjustment layer at the palette bottom or select Layer ➤ New Fill layer option from the menu. From the submenu that appears, select the type of the adjustment effects you want to select.

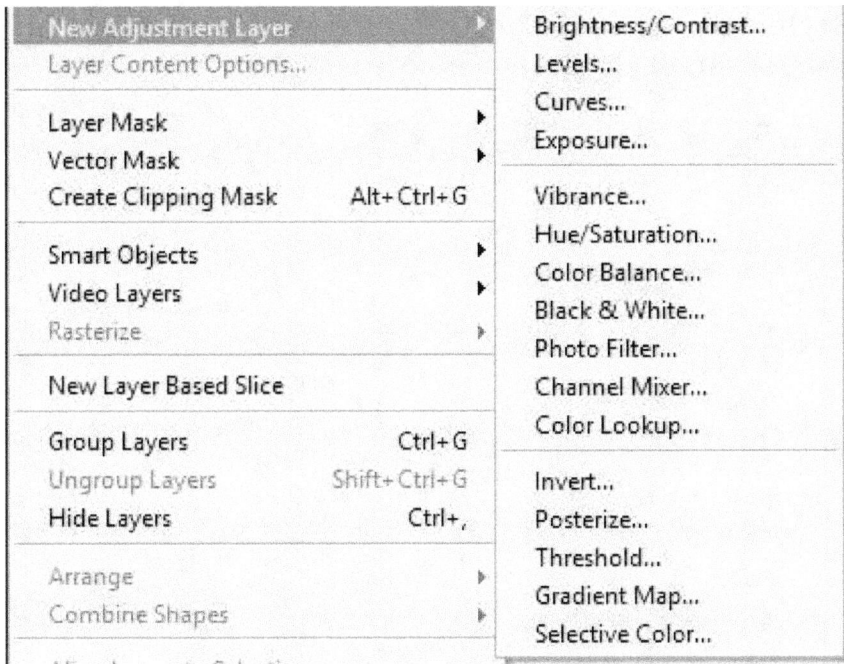

Fig 9.15 Adding adjustment layer

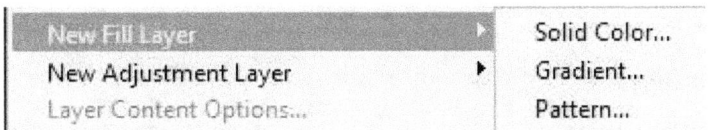

Fig 9.16 Creating a Fill Layer

ADDING LAYER STYLES

Photoshop has numerous different effects that you can apply in any combination to a layer. You can access the original effects by selecting the layer and selecting the style from Layer ➤ Layer style submenu (Fig 9.17). Photoshop also has predefined styles, which are combination of these original effects, which are stored as styles in Style palette. The style palette will be discussed in the next section.

You can also select the Blending option from the Layer ➤ Layer style submenu or from the Layer palette menu or from the right click menu that appears when you right click on the layer. You can also click at the Layer

Style button at he bottom of the palette. This brings the Layer Style dialog box (Fig 9.18).

Fig 9.17 Specifying Layer Style using menu options

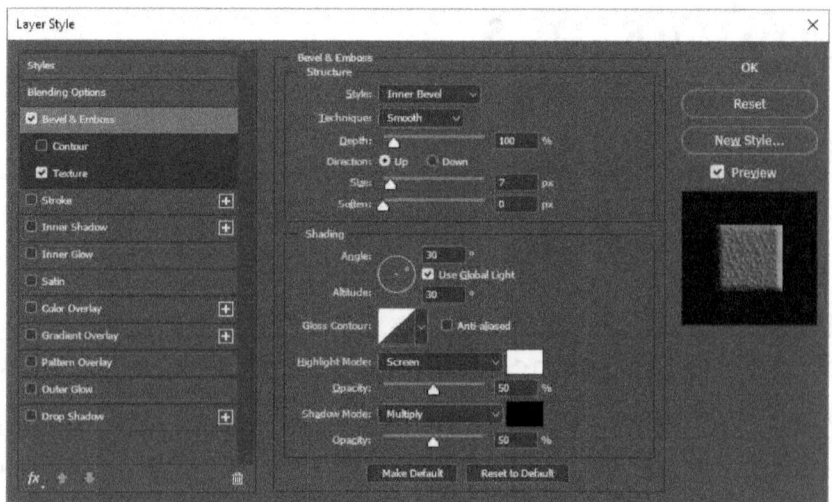

Fig 9.18 Specifying Layer Style using dialog box

- The Drop Shadow effect lets you add a shadow that falls behind the contents on the layer.

- The Inner Shadow effect lets you add a shadow that falls just inside the edges of the layer contents, giving the layer a recessed appearance.

- The Outer Glow and Inner Glow effects let you add glows that emanate from the outside or inside edges of the layer contents.

- The Bevel and Emboss effect lets you add various combinations of highlights and shadows to a layer.

- Satin effect lets you apply shading to the interior of a layer that reacts to the shape of the layer, typically creating a satiny finish.

- Colour, Gradient, and Pattern Overlay lets you overlay a colour, gradient, or pattern on a layer.

- Stroke is used outline the object on the current layer using colour, a gradient, or a pattern. It is particularly useful on hard-edged shapes such as type.

The default blending options lets you control the blending mode and opacity of the layer. You can also specify the advance blending options. In the Advance option area

- Select the Fill opacity of the layer by dragging the slider. Also select the channels you want to display.

- Select the knockout option from shallow, deep or none.

- Use the This Layer and Underlying sliders to set the brightness range of the blended pixels (you can also select the colour from the Blend If drop down menu) - measured on a scale from 0 (black) to 255 (white). Drag the white slider to set the high value of the range. Drag the black slider to set the low value of the range.

- To define a range of partially blended pixels, hold down Alt, and drag one half of a slider triangle. The two values that appear above the divided slider indicate the partial blending range.

- Select the preview check box to displays a preview of the layer effect in the image as you change the layer effect settings.

Select various other styles from the dialog box to display various options related to that style and experiment with different parameters.

Hiding Layer effects

You can hide all the effects that has been applied on the layer by selecting Layer ➢ Layer Style ➢ Hide All Layer Styles. To display them again, select Show All Layer Styles option.

To expand or collapse layer styles in the Layers palette, click the triangle next to the layer styles icon to expand the list of layer effects applied to that layer. Now, click the inverted triangle to collapse the layer effects.

Editing Layer Effects

To edit the layer effects applied to a layer, either you can expand all the layer effects and then double-click the required layer effects to bring the Blending option dialog box displaying parameters for that effect.

Fig 9.19 Displaying Layer styles in Layer palette

Copying Layer Effects

To copy effects between layers:

- In the Layers palette, select the source layer containing the effects you want to copy.

- Choose Layer ➤ Layer styles ➤ Copy layer style or right click on the layer and select Copy Layer style option from the menu that appears.

- To paste the effects into a single layer, select the destination layer in the palette and choose Layer ➤ Layer styles ➤ Paste layer style. To paste into multiple layers, link the destination layers and choose Layer ➤ Layer styles ➤ Paste Layer Style to Linked.

The pasted effects will replace any existing effects on the destination layer or layers.

Scaling Layer Effects

You can also scale the layer effects to improve your result. When you scale effects, the effect changes without scaling the image. To scale effects, select the layer containing effects and choose Layer ➤ Layer style ➤ Scale effects.

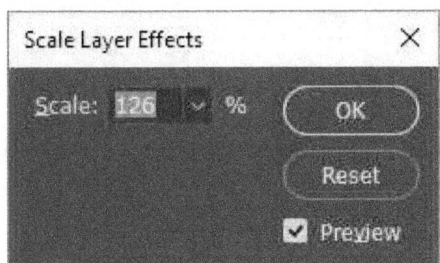

Fig 9.20 Scaling Layer effect

In the dialog box, specify the value for Scale which varies from 1 to 1000%.

Clearing Layer effects

You can clear all the effects that has been applied on the layer by selecting Layer ➤ Layer Style ➤ Clear

Layer Styles or selecting Clear Layer style option from the Layer palette menu.

To delete any particular layer style, expand all the layer styles and click and drag on the particular layer style to the Trash can. You can also deselect the style from the Blending option dialog box.

Converting Styles to Layers

To customize or fine-tune the appearance of layer styles, you can convert the layer styles to regular image layers. Once you convert then to layers, you can apply various commands to enhance and change the appearance. To convert a layer style to image layers, select the layer containing the layer style you want to convert and choose Layer ➢ Layer Style ➢ Create Layers.

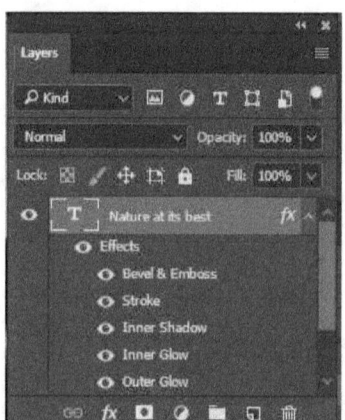 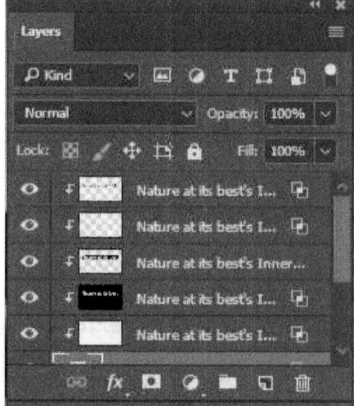

Fig 9.21 Layer styles and Layer styles converted to Layers

MANAGING LAYER STYLES

Photoshop also manages the libraries of styles besides the styles defined above in the Layer Style dialog box. These preset styles are displayed in the the Style palette. To display the Style palette, select the Windows ➢ Show style option.

Fig 9.22 Using Style palette

You can also display all the predefined style in the Layer Style dialog box. To do so, open the Layer Style dialog box and select the Style option at the top left corner of the dialog box. This brings the complete set of predefined styles (Basically, it is style palette fitted into the Layer Style dialog box) of Photoshop. You can also click on the small triangle to display all the options of Style palette pop-up menu. (Fig 9.23).

Creating New Styles

As you create the Layer styles defined in the Layer Style dialog box, you can also save them to use at a later stage with other images. These Styles can be combination of styles shown in Fig 9.18. To save these combination of styles for later use, double click on the layer, containing the combination of layer effects, to bring the Layer Style dialog box. Now click on the New

Style button (Fig 9.18) to save the present combination of styles.

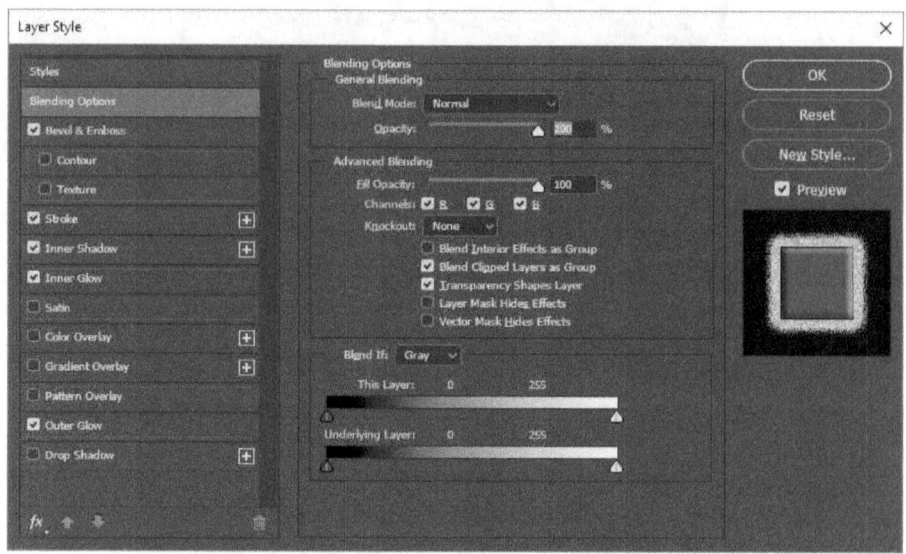

Fig 9.23 Using Style palette in Style dialog box

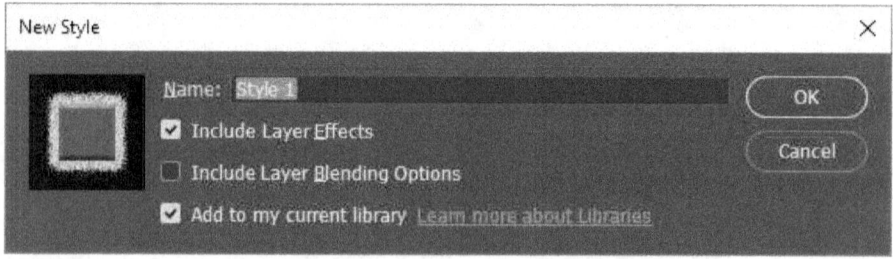

Fig 9.24 Creating New Style

You can also select the New Style option from the Style palette menu shown in Fig 9.22. Specify the name for the new style in the New Style dialog box. This style is appended in the default library of the Style palette.

APPLYING PREDEFINED STYLE

To apply any of the style, defined in Style palette, to a Layer or Layer set, select the layer in the Layer palette. Now, to apply any style from the style palette:

• Click on any style in Style palette, the style is applied to the selected Layer. If you wish to apply another style, click on the other style in the style palette. Hold down Shift key as you click in the Style palette to add the layer style while preserving layer effects on the destination layer that are not duplicated by the new layer style.

- Drag the style thumbnail from the Styles palette onto a layer in the Layers palette or a layer pixel in the image. Press Shift as you drag to add the layer style while preserving layer effects on the destination layer that are not duplicated by the new layer style.

USING LAYER MASK

You can use a layer mask to hide the unwanted areas in the image. To apply various effects, you can leave the layer untouched and apply all the effects to the mask. You can then apply the mask and make the changes permanent or remove the mask without applying the changes. You can also save all layer masks with a layered document.

You can also use layer clipping path to hide various areas of the image. The clipping path, basically acts as a sharp-edge mask. The basic difference between a layer mask and a clipping path is that, while layer mask is resolution-dependent and is mask is created with the painting or selection tools, whereas the clipping path is resolution-independent and is created with the pen or shape tools.

- To add a mask that shows or hides the entire layer, select the layer and do any of the following:
  - Click on the New Layer Mask button at the bottom of the Layers palette to reveal the layer. To create a mask that hides the entire layer, hold down Alt and click on the New Layer Mask button.

- Select Layer ➢ Add Layer Mask ➢ Reveal All or Hide All option as per requirement.

- To add a mask that shows or hides a selection, select the desired area, which you want to reveal or hide. Now select the layer on which you want to hide or reveal the selected area. This layer could be the same layer on which you make the selection or could be a different layer. Select any one of the following option:

  - Click on the New Layer Mask button at the bottom of the Layers palette to reveal the selected area and hide the rest of the area. To create a mask that hides the selected area, hold down Alt and click on the New Layer Mask button.

  - Select Layer ➢ Add Layer Mask ➢ Reveal Selection or Hide selection option as per requirement.

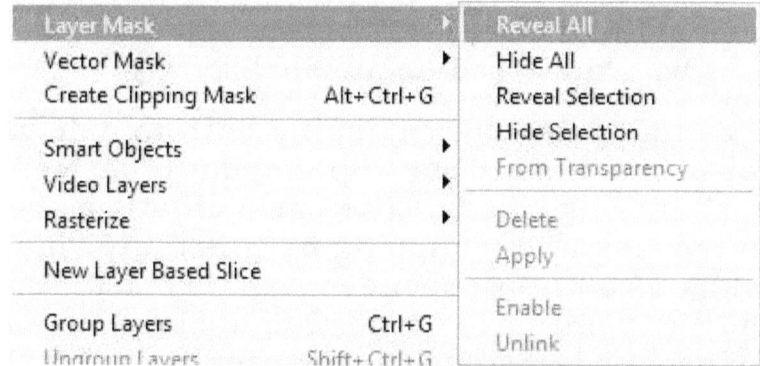

Layer Mask	▶	Reveal All
Vector Mask	▶	Hide All
Create Clipping Mask	Alt+Ctrl+G	Reveal Selection
		Hide Selection
Smart Objects	▶	From Transparency
Video Layers	▶	
Rasterize	▶	Delete
		Apply
New Layer Based Slice		
		Enable
Group Layers	Ctrl+G	Unlink
Ungroup Layers	Shift+Ctrl+G	

Fig 9.25 Adding Layer Mask

Fig 9.26 The portion was selected using Layer 1 and Text Layer was selected to hide the selected portion

- To add a layer clipping path that shows or hides the entire layer (Photoshop), select the layer to which you want to add a layer clipping path and choose Layer ➤ Add Layer Clipping Path ➤ Reveal All or Hide All to create a layer clipping path that reveal or hides the entire layer.

To turn off the Layer Clipping path temporarily, hold down the Shift key and Click on the mask. A red cross appears on the mask and the entire underlying layer appears without masking effects.

Deleting the Layer mask or Clipping Path

To apply or discard a layer mask, select the layer mask thumbnail in the Layers palette. To remove the layer mask, drag the layer mask to trash button or select the mask and click on the Trash can. This brings the confirmation box, which gives you option to apply or discard the mask before deleting.

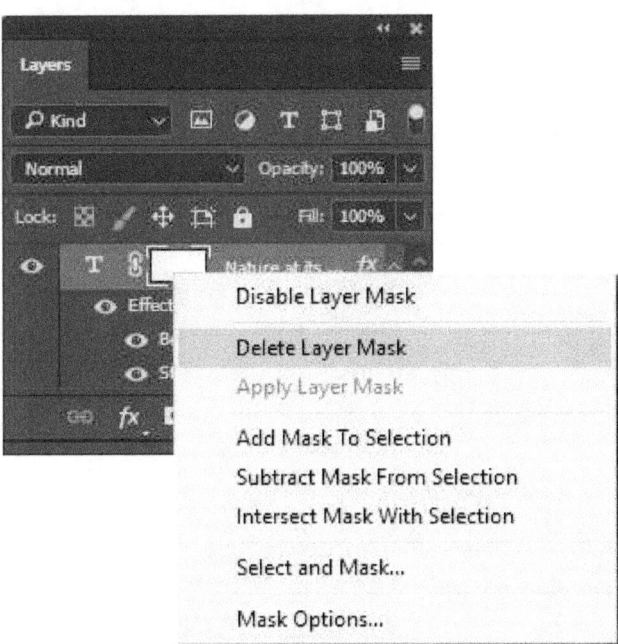

Fig 9.27 Deleting Mask

WORKING WITH CHANNELS AND MASKS

WORKING WITH CHANNELS AND MASKS

Colour information channels is a type of channel that represents one component of an image's colour model.

Colour information channels are automatically generated by Photoshop when you create or open a colour image file that has a 24-bit or 32-bit colour depth. These channels store an image's colour information. In addition, channels and masks store selections that let you manipulate and control specific parts of an image in sophisticated ways.

Individual channels include information about how much red, green, or blue is used in each image pixel, to produce the colours of the image. Combining all colour channels displays the entire range of colour present in the image.

Many of the features and commands that you can use to adjust the colour and quality of an image are applied directly to the colour channels that make up the image. Each image has one or more colour channels that hold information about the colour elements. The number of colour channels in an image depends on the number of elements in the colour model associated with the image. For example, an RGB image has three separate colour channels, one for each colour: red (R), green (G), and blue (B). The R, G, and B colour channels store information about how much red, green, or blue is used in each pixel to produce the colours of the image.

When you view the combined colour channels of an image, the resulting composite image displays the entire range of colours in the image. When you view colour channels individually, you see a grayscale representation of the colour information. A colour channel can be edited and manipulated in the same way that you edit or manipulate a grayscale image.

In addition, alpha channels and spot colour channels can be added to an image to let you specify additional plates temporary storage area of mask or for printing with spot colour inks respectively.

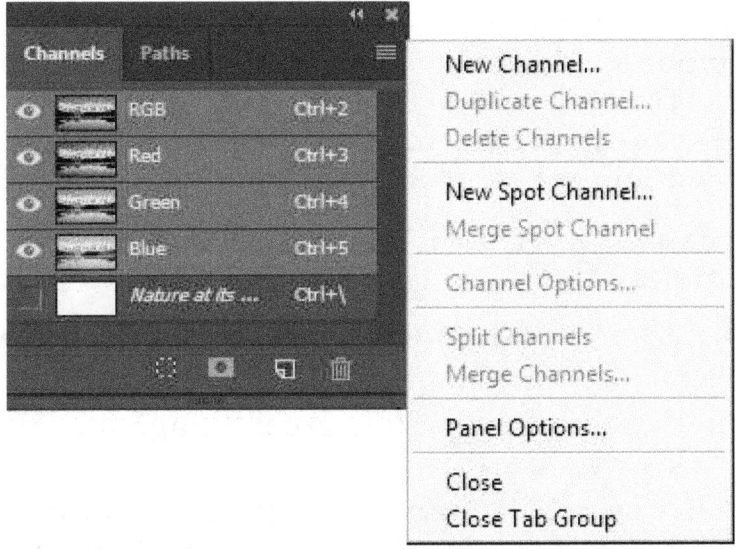

Fig 10.1 Image (RGB), and channels in Channels palette

THE CHANNEL PALETTE

The Channels palette provides you the details of existing channels and lets you create and manage channels. It also lets you monitor the effects of editing.

The palette displays the complete information about the channels which includes a composite channel, then individual colour channels, spot colour channels, and finally alpha channels. The thumbnail of the channel is also displayed in the left of channel name.

To display the channel palette, choose Windows ➢ Show Channels. This activates the channel palette.

VIEWING CHANNELS

You can use the Channel palette to view all the channels of the current image, in a series of 8-bit grayscale images. The palette contains one channel for each colour of the colour mode you choose. Photoshop automatically displays an image, that was created in one colour mode, into the channels associated with another colour mode, if you change the mode of the image. For example, if you have an oversaturated RGB image, you can reduce the saturation by converting the image into the HSB mode and reducing the saturation (S) channel.

You can convert an image into the following colour channels:

RGB   red (R), green (G), blue (B)

CMYK   cyan (C), magenta (M), yellow (Y), black (K)

Lab   luminosity (L), green/magenta (a), blue/yellow (b)

- To select a channel, click the channel name. Shift-click to select (or deselect) multiple channels. The names of all selected, or active, channels are highlighted. Editing changes apply to the active channels. When a channel is visible, an eye icon appears to its left.

- To show or hide a channel, click in the eye column next to the channel.

- To show or hide multiple channels, drag through the eye column in the Channels palette.

You can view any combination of individual channels. By default, individual channels are displayed in grayscale. But when you take the combination of two channels, they are displayed in colour. You can also set the options to view the individual channel in colour. To see individual channels in colour, choose File ➢ Preferences ➢ Display & Cursors and select Colour Channels in Colour, and click OK.

To change the size of a channels thumbnail or hide the thumbnail, select palette Options from the Channel palette menu. From the Channel palette option dialog box, select the size of the thumbnail or select none to hide the thumbnails.

ALPHA CHANNEL

Alpha channel is a temporary storage area for masks. You use alpha channels to create and store masks, which let you manipulate, isolate, and protect specific parts of an image. When you save a mask to an alpha channel, you can access and reuse it in the image as many times as you want. You can save an alpha channel to a file or load a previously saved channel in the active image.

Alpha channels store selections as 8-bit grayscale images and are added to the colour channels in an image. An image can have up to 24 channels, including all colour and alpha channels.

- If you display an alpha channel at the same time as colour channels, the alpha channel appears as a transparent colour overlay, analogous to a printer's rubylith or a sheet of acetate. To change the colour of this overlay or set other alpha channel options.

- To change the order of alpha channels, drag the channel up or down. When the heavy black line appears in the position you want, release the mouse button.

EDITING CHANNELS

Channels are 8-bit grayscale images that contain information about an image. You can edit channels the same way that you edit other grayscale images. For example, you can select areas, apply paints and fills, add special effects or enhancement filters, and cut and paste objects in the image channel.

To edit an individual colour channel in the Channel palette, click the channel that you want to edit. Now, edit the image using any tools or commands. You can use any painting or editing tool to paint in the image. You should paint with white to add to the channel; paint with black to remove from the channel; paint with a lower opacity or a colour to add to the channel with lower opacities.

DUPLICATING CHANNELS

You can duplicate any channel within or between images. Duplicating is required at various places. For example, you may require to duplicate an image's channels to make a backup before editing the channel. If duplicating between images, alpha channels must have identical pixel dimensions.

You can duplicate a channel using Duplicate Channel command from the Channel palette menu. But you must select a channel before duplicating it. The Duplicate Channel command brings the dialog box:

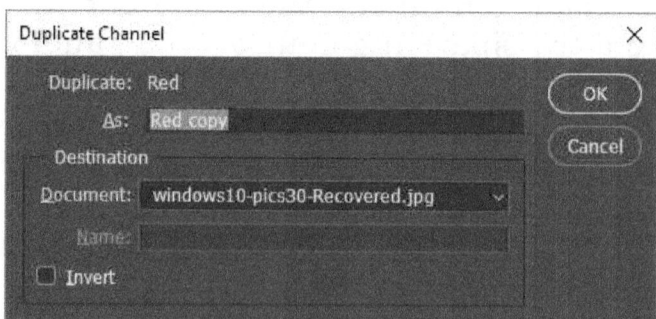

Fig 10.2 Duplicating Channels

- Type a name for the duplicate channel. Select the destination from the drop down menu, which displays all the documents open along with the option of opening New document. You can also specify the name of the new document.

- To reverse the selected and masked areas in the duplicate channel, select Invert. Click OK.

You can also duplicate a channel by dragging. To duplicate a channel by dragging, drag the channel into the image window or onto the New Channel button at the bottom of the palette. To duplicate the channel into another image, make sure that the destination image is open. Then drag the channel into the destination image window.

DELETING CHANNELS

You may want to delete channels from the image, such as alpha channel which you no longer may need before saving an image. Complex alpha channels can substantially increase the disk space required for an image.

To delete a channel, either drag the channel into the Trash can at the bottom of the palette or select the Delete Channel command from the Channel palette menu option. This brings the confirmation dialog box (Fig 9.5), click OK to confirm that you want to delete the channel.

If you delete a channel from a file with layers, PhotoShop asks you to to flatten the visible layers irrespective of the method used for deletion. This is necessary because removing a colour channel converts the image to Multichannel mode, which does not support layers.

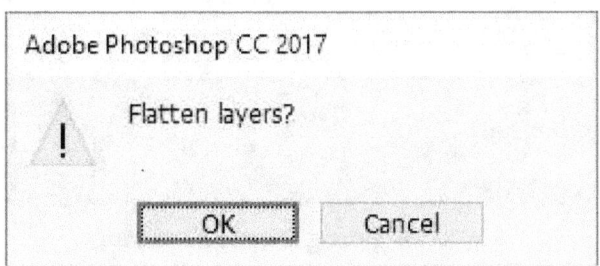

Fig 10.3 Flattening Layers before Deleting Channel

CHANNEL MIXER

The Channel Mixer option lets you modify a Colour channel using a mix of the current Colour channels.

This command is useful, when you want to make creative colour adjustments, which is not easily done with the other colour adjustment tools. You can also create high quality grayscale images by choosing the percentage contribution from each colour channel. It also helps you to convert images to and from some alternative colour spaces, such as YCrCb.

To modify a colour channel

- Click Image ➢ Adjust ➢ Channel Mixer to bring the Channel Mixer dialog box.

- Choose a Colour channel from the Output Channel list box.

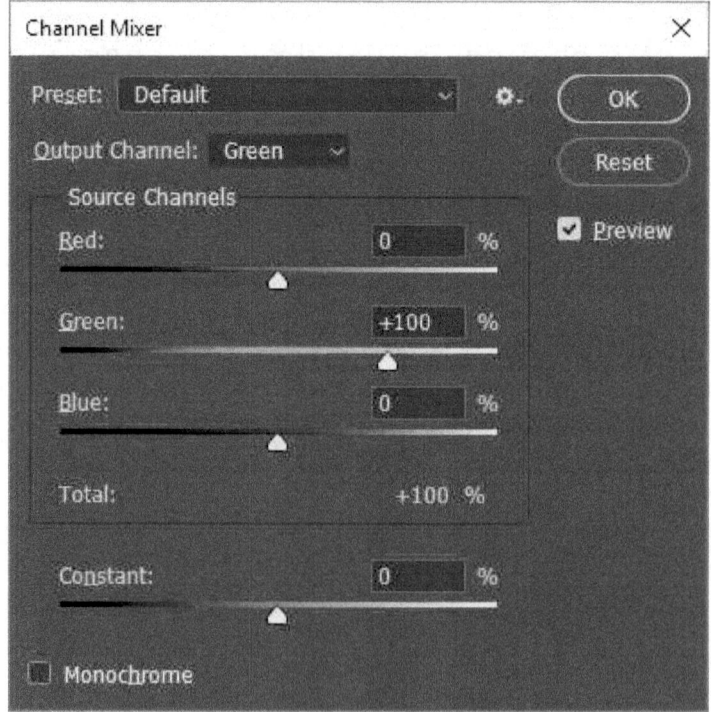

Fig 10.4 Using Channel Mixer

- Now drag the required source channel's slider to the left to decrease the channel's contribution to the output channel or to the right to increase it.

- Drag the slider or enter a value for the Constant option. Using this option, you can add a channel of varying opacity to the output channel. The more negative is the value, the more black the channel will be.

- Select Monochrome to apply the same settings to all the output channels. This will create a Colour image that contains only gray values.

MANAGING CHANNELS

SPLITTING CHANNELS INTO SEPARATE IMAGES

You can use the Split Channels command from the Channel palette menu, to create from the current image a series of 8-bit grayscale images - one for each colour channel of the colour mode you choose. You can split an image that was created in one colour mode into the channels associated with another colour mode after changing the mode of the image.

If your image contains layers, you must Flatten the image before Splitting the image. When you split an image into colour channels, the original file is closed and a file is created for each channel which is named according to the colour component it represents. For example, an RGB image, named as sample.psd, gives the following three files: sample_R.psd, sample_G.psd, and sample_B.psd.

Splitting an image into channels lets you edit one channel without affecting the others.

MERGING CHANNELS

After you split an image into its component colour channels, you can recombine the channels. The colour mode that you choose for merging the channels does not have to match the original colour mode of the image. For example, if you split an RGB image into red, green, and blue component channels, you can recombine the individual channel files into the Lab colour mode. The images you want to merge must be in grayscale mode, be flattened (have no layers), have the same pixel dimensions, and be open.

To merge images must be in Grayscale mode, have the same pixel dimensions, and be open. The number of grayscale images you have open determines the colour modes available when merging channels. The Merge Channels in the Channel palette menu associates each channel from the target colour mode with an existing component channel file of your choice. To recombine the above mentioned RGB channels into the Lab mode, you can associate any of the L, a, and b channels with any of the existing RED, BLUE, and GREEN component channel files.

To merge split channels

● Open the grayscale images containing the channels you want to merge and make one of the images active. Now, choose Merge Channel command from the Channel palette menu.

Fig 10.5 Merging Channels

● Select the Mode from the drop down menu that corresponds to the colour mode that you want to combine the channels into. If an image mode is unavailable, it is dimmed.

● In the Channel text box, type the number of channels appropriate for the selected colour mode.

● Click OK. This brings the Merge Channel dialog box. Specify the name of the Image files associated with each colour of the selected channel.

- When finished selecting channels, click OK. The selected channels are merged into a new image of the specified type, and the original images closed without any changes. The new image appears in an untitled window.

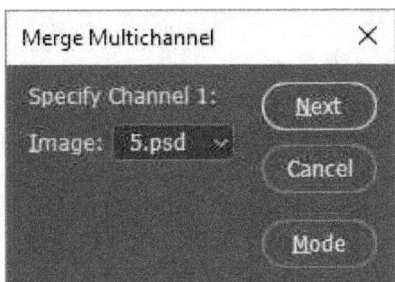

Fig 10.6 Specifying Image for Merging

SPOT CHANNELS

Spot colours are widely used in printing, when you use a particular ink to print a particular area. Each spot colour requires its own plate on the press on which special premixed inks are used.

Spot channels let you add and preview spot colours in an image. The following guidelines can help you in using spot channels:

- If you need spot colour graphics that have crisp edges and knock out the underlying image, consider creating the additional artwork in a page-layout or illustration application.

- You can create new spot channels or convert an existing alpha channel to a spot channel.

- Like alpha channels, spot channels can be edited or deleted at any time.

- Spot colours can't be applied to individual layers.

- Spot colours are overprinted on top of the fully composite image.

- If you print an image that includes spot colour channels to a composite printer, the spot colours print out as extra pages.

- You can merge spot channels with colour channels, splitting the spot colour into its colour channel components. Merging spot channels lets you print a single-page proof of your spot colour image on a desktop printer.

- The names of the spot colours print on the separations.

- You cannot move spot colours above a default channel in the Channels palette except in Multichannel mode. To move spot colour channels in the Channels palette so that they print before other plates, convert the image to Multichannel mode.

CREATING SPOT CHANNEL

To create a spot channel

- Select or load a selection, if you want to fill a selected area with a spot colour, make or load a selection. Now, Ctrl-click the New Channel button in the Channels palette or choose New Spot Channel from the Channels palette menu to bring the New Spot Channel dialog box.

Fig 10.7 Adding New Spot Channel

- If you made a selection, that area is filled with the currently specified spot colour. To fill a different colour, click on the colour box to bring the Colour Picker. By selecting a custom colour, your print service can more easily provide the proper ink to reproduce the image.

- For Solidity, enter a value between 0% and 100% and specify the name if required. Click OK.

EDITING SPOT CHANNEL

To edit a spot channel

- Select the spot channel in the Channels palette. You can use any painting or editing tool to paint in the image. Paint with black to add more spot colour at 100% opacity; paint with gray to add spot colour with lower opacity.

Changing Spot Channel Options

To change a spot channel options:

- Double-click the spot channel name in the Channels palette.

Fig 10.8 Changing Spot Channel Options

Merging Spot Channel

- To merge spot channels, select the spot channel you want to merge. Choose Merge Spot Channel from the palette menu. This merge the Spot channel to the colour channels.

Removing Underlying Spot Colour

To remove an underlying spot colour, select the spot channel whose colour you want to remove. Choose Select ➢ Load Selection.

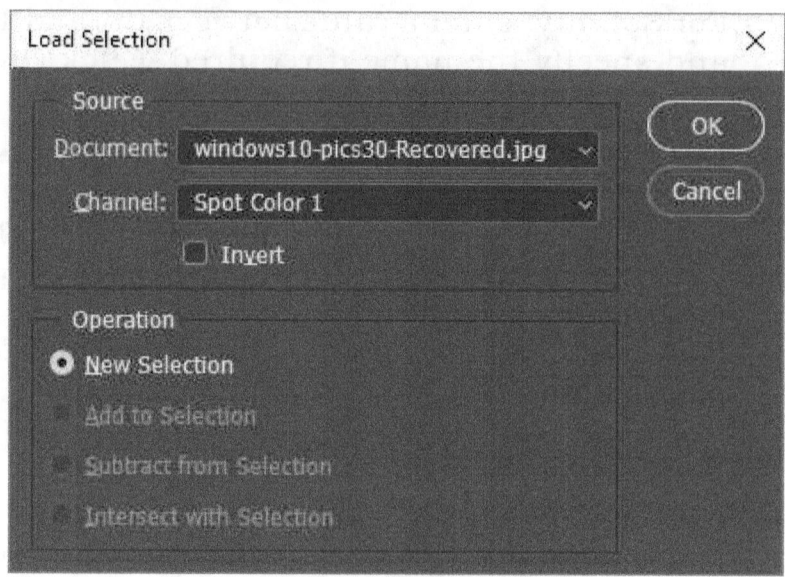

Fig 10.9 Loading Selection

- To quickly select an image in a channel, hold down Ctrl, and click the channel in the Channels palette.

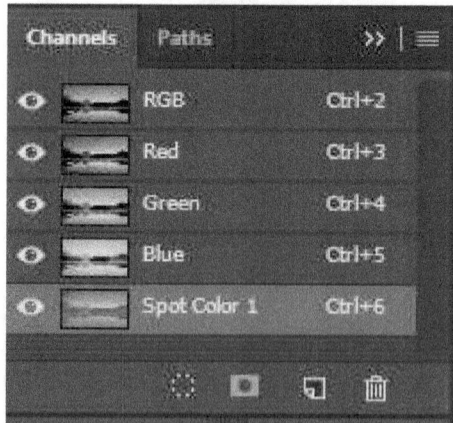

Fig 10.10 Image after adding the Spot Colour around Butterfly and Removing the Blue from the Butterfly

- To create trap when knocking out the underlying colour, choose Select ➤ Modify ➤ Expand or Contract.

- In the Channels palette, select the underlying channel that contains areas you want to knock out. Press Delete. This method can be used to knock out areas from any channels under a spot colour, such as the CMYK channels.

- If a spot colour in one channel overlaps more than one other spot colour, repeat this process for each channel that contains areas you want removed.

BLENDING CHANNELS

You can use the blending modes of layers to combine channels within and between images into new images using the Calculations command (on single channels only) and the Apply Image command (on single and composite channels). These commands offer two additional blending modes not available in the Layers palette: Add and Subtract.

The Add merge mode adds the values of the current paint and base colours whereas the Subtract merge mode adds the values of the current paint and base colours, and subtracts 255 from the result.

Although it's possible to combine channels into new combinations by copying channels into layers in the Layers palette, you may find it quicker to use the calculations commands to blend channel information.

The calculation commands perform mathematical operations on the corresponding pixels of two channels (the pixels with identical locations on the image) and then combine the results in a single channel. Two concepts are fundamental to understanding how the calculation commands work:

Each pixel in a channel has a brightness value from 0 (off or black) to 255 (on or white). The Calculations and Apply Image commands manipulate these values to produce the resulting composite pixels.

These commands overlay the pixels in two or more channels. Thus, the images used for calculations must have the same pixel dimensions.

USING THE CALCULATIONS COMMAND

You can use the Calculations command to modify an existing image or create a composite image by combining the channel data from one image with the channel data from another image. A merge mode calculation is performed on the pixels of the two source channels. The result of the calculation is then applied to one of the following: a channel in either of the source images, an image that is open in PhotoShop, or a new file. You can adjust the transparency level of the source images in relation to the destination image.

To use the Calculations command:

- Open the source image or images. The pixel dimensions of the images must match for image names to appear in the Calculations dialog box.

- Choose Image ➤ Calculations.

- To preview the calculation results in the image window, select Preview.

- In the Source 1 section, choose a filename from the Image list box. Select the layer from the Layer Drop down menu. Select Merged Layer to select all the Layers in the source image. In the Source 1 section, choose a channel type from the Channel list box.

- Choose the second source image, layer, and channel, specifying further options as described in the previous step.

- Select the blending option from Blending drop down menu, you want to apply.

- Enter an opacity for the effect's strength.

- Select Mask if you want to apply the blending through a mask. Then choose the image and layer containing the mask. For Channel, you can choose any colour or alpha channel to use as the mask.

- For Result, specify whether to place the blending results in a new image, or in a new channel or selection in the active image.

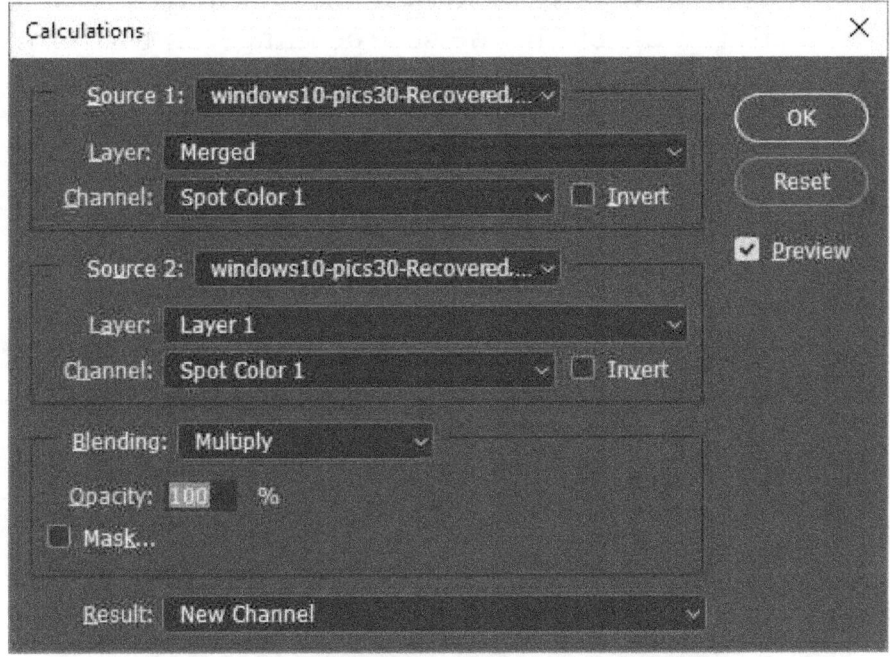

Fig 10.11 Using Calculation command

- Click OK to perform the calculation.

USING THE APPLY IMAGE COMMAND

The Apply Image command lets you blend one image's layer and channel (the source) with a layer and channel of the active image (the destination).

To use the Apply Image command:

- Open the source and destination images, and make active the desired layer and channel in the destination image. The pixel dimensions of the images must match for image names to appear in the Apply Image dialog box.

- Choose Image ➢ Apply Image. Select Preview to preview the results in the image window.

- In the Source section, choose a filename from the Image list box which you want to combine with destination. Select the layer from the Layer Drop down menu. Select Merged Layer to select all the Layers in the source image. In the Source section, choose a channel type from the Channel list box. Select Invert to use the negative of the channel contents in the calculation.

- Select the blending option from Blending drop down menu, you want to apply.

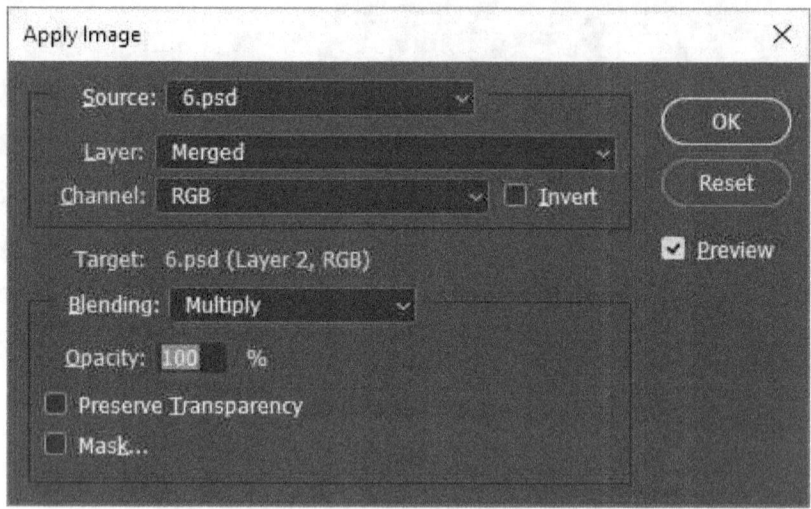

Fig 10.12 Using Apply Image command

- Enter an opacity for the effect's strength. Select Preserve Transparency to apply the results only to opaque areas in the result layer.

- Select Mask if you want to apply the blending through a mask. Then choose the image and layer containing the mask. For Channel, you can choose any colour or alpha channel to use as the mask.

- Click OK to apply the blending effect.

MASKS IN PHOTOSHOP

You can use Mask in Photoshop to protect the area against editing. When you select a part of image, you can do the editing only in the selected part. Thus, it is said that the area not selected is masked. You can also use masks for complex image editing such as gradually applying colour or filter effects to an image.

In Photoshop, you can create following type of mask. All these type of mask are stored temporarily as grayscale channels. When you create a mask, you can edit the mask, using the Photoshop tool to change the selected area.

• Quick Mask mode lets you create and view a temporary mask for an image.

• Alpha channels let you save and load a selection to be used as a mask.

• Layer masks let you create a mask for a specific layer.

USING QUICK MASK MODE

The Quick Mask mode is the quickest of any mask that can be created in PhotoShop. The advantage of Mask is that you can edit your selection using almost any Photoshop tool or filter to modify the selection. Thus if you make a selection, and want to apply a distort effect to the selected area, then you can create a mask, apply the distort effect to the mask, and then remove the mask to get the distort effect on the selected area. You can also use selection tools on the mask, because the quick mask is not a selection.

To create a Quick Mask,

• Make a selection, which you want to change, using any selection tool. If you don't select any area, entire layer is converted into Quick Mask.

• Now, click the Quick Mask mode button in the toolbox. This creates a mask on the unselected area, which you can recognize by colour differentiation in protected and unprotected areas. By default, Quick Mask mode colours the protected area using a red, 50% opaque overlay.

Fig 10.13 Selected area, and Quick Mask mode applied

- A temporary Quick Mask channel appears in the Channels palette, as shown in Fig 10.14, while you work in Quick Mask mode. However, you do all mask editing in the image window.

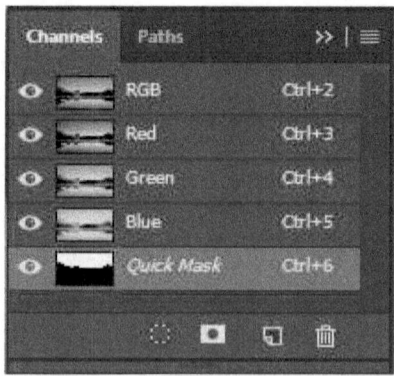

Fig 10.14 The Channel palette after adding Quick Mask

- The mask that appears is like any other layer, which can be edited using any tool from the toolbox. To edit the mask, select a painting or editing tool from the toolbox, or select a filter or adjustment command from the menu bar. Paint with black to add more spot colour at 100% opacity; paint with gray to add spot colour with lower opacity.

Fig 10.15 Smudge tool applied to the Mask and modified selection

- Once you're done with the dithering of mask, click the Standard mode button in the toolbox to turn off the quick mask and return to your original image. A modified selection border now surrounds the unprotected area of the quick mask.

Changing Quick Mask Option

To change the Quick Mask options:

- Double-click the Quick Mask mode button in the toolbox to bring the Quick Mask Option dialog box.

- In the Colour Indicates section, select Masked Areas (the default) to have masked (protected or unselected) areas appear opaque, and to have selected areas appear transparent. To have it otherwise, choose the Selected Area option.

- The protected area (or unprotected area if you choose the Selected Area option above) is filled with the currently specified spot colour. To fill a different colour, click on the colour box to bring the Colour Picker. For Opacity, enter a value between 0% and 100% and specify the name if required. Click OK. Changing these settings may make the mask more easily visible against the colours in the image. These settings don't effect the editing of mask.

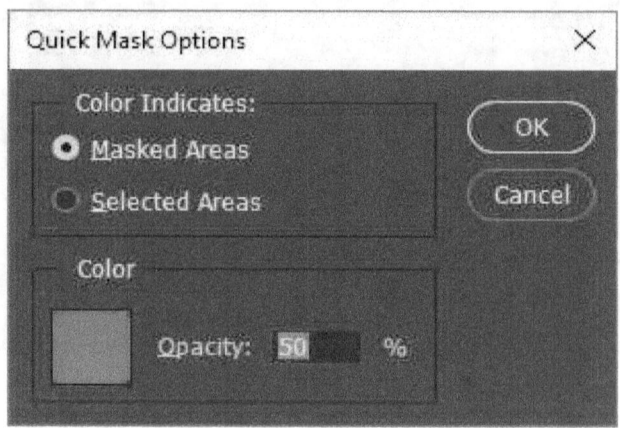

Fig 10.16 Quick Mask options

USING ALPHA CHANNELS

Quick Mask is a temporary mask. You can create more permanent masks by storing and editing selections in alpha channels. When you save a mask to an alpha channel, you can access and reuse it in the image as many times as you want. You can save an alpha channel to a file or load a previously saved channel in the active image.

You can add and delete alpha channels in the Channel palette. When you create a new alpha channel, it has same dimensions and number of pixels as the original image. Storing selections in alpha channels makes the selections permanent, so that they can be used again in the same image or in a different image.

CREATING ALPHA CHANNELS

You can create a new alpha channel as a mask. To create a new alpha channel using current options, click the New Channel button at the bottom of the Channels palette.

To create a new alpha channel and specify options:

- Alt-click the New Channel button at the bottom of the palette or choose New Channel from the Channels palette menu.

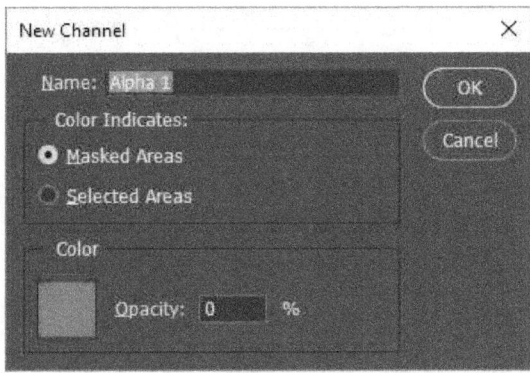

Fig 10.17 Adding New Channel

- Type a name for the channel. In the Colour Indicates section, select Masked Areas (the default) to have masked (protected or unselected) areas appear opaque, and to have selected areas appear transparent. To have it otherwise, choose the Selected Area option.

- The protected area (or unprotected area if you choose the Selected Area option above) is displayed with the currently specified colour.

- Click OK. This creates a new channel as alpha channel which appears at the bottom of the Channels palette and is the only channel visible in the image window.

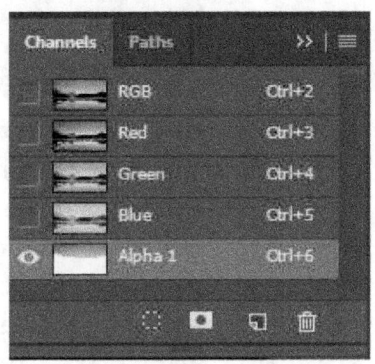

Fig 10.18 Adding Alpha Channel

Editing Alpha Channel

To edit an alpha channel, use a painting or editing tool to paint in the image. Paint with black to add more spot colour at 100% opacity; paint with gray to add spot colour with lower opacity.

Saving Alpha Channel

To save any alpha channel, you can save it while creating it by selecting the Save Alpha Channel given at the bottom of the Channel palette.

To save a selection to a new or existing channel, select the area or areas of the image that you want to isolate. Now choose the option Select ➢ Save Selection to bring the Save Selection dialog box.

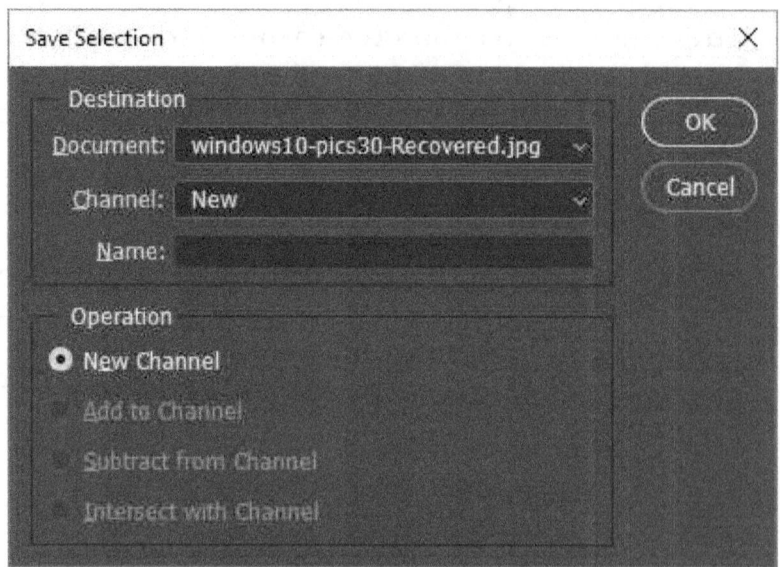

Fig 10.19 Saving Selections

- In the dialog box, select the name of the destination document. By default, the selection is saved in alpha channel in your active image. To save into another image, the image must be opened with the same pixel dimensions. If no image is opened, you can also save to a new image.

- The Channel option lets you select a channel from the existing channels or the new channel.

- Select the method to combine the new selection with the existing selection. You could Replace Channel, Add to the existing channel, Subtract from the existing channel or Intersect with the Channel.

- Click OK.

APPLYING SPECIAL EFFECTS

APPLYING SPECIAL EFFECTS

PhotoShop has a wide range of professional-quality effects filters you can use to enhance or customize layers or images. These filters can completely change the look and feel of your bitmaps.

Effects filters are small programs that execute a predefined series of commands to produce a specific effect when applied to a layer or image. They automatically calculate the values and characteristics of every pixel in your bitmap and then alter the pixels according to new values. For example, if you apply the Motion Blur effect to a layer or image, the effect analyzes all pixel values, then "smears" the values in a specified direction, creating the illusion of motion.

Photoshop divides the filter effects in various groups. These Include:

Artistic Effects   Give your images an organic, hand-painted look. (Available in Filter ➤ Filter Gallery)

Blur Effects   Change the pixels of your image to soften them, smooth their edges, blend them, or create motion effects.

Brush Stroke   Give a painterly or fine-arts look using different brush and ink stroke effects.

Distort Filter   Transform the appearance of your images without adding depth.

Noise Filter   Create, control, or eliminate noise.

Pixelate   Define a selection by clumping pixels of similar colour values in cells.

Render Filters   Let you simulate lighting, photographic realism, and the appearance of three-dimensional depth in your images.

Sharpen Filters   Improve the focus and enhance edges.

Sketch Filters   Add texture to images, often for a 3D effect

Styles Filters   Produce a painted or impressionistic effect on a selection

Texture Filters   Add texture to your image using a variety of shapes and surfaces.

Video Filter   Include the NTSC (National Television Standards Committee) Colour filter

APPLYING ARTISTIC EFFECTS

PhotoShop provides various Artistic effects that give images an organic, hand-painted look. You can use these effects to turn your images into pastel drawings, sponge paintings, watercolours, or to knife painting for your artwork.

Fig. 11.1 Adding art strokes

The Art Strokes effects are:

Coloured Pencil   Draws an image using coloured pencils on a solid background. The dialog box lets you control the Pencil width, Stroke Pressure and

283

Paper Brightness. Experiment with various values and view the result in Preview box. Fig 11.1 displays the impact of Coloured Pencil on the image shown in Fig 10.1.

Fig 11.2 Adding Coloured Pencil

Cutout	Converts the image as if it has been made from roughly cut-out pieces of coloured paper. It also has three parameters to control - No. of Levels, Edge Simplicity and Edge Fidelity.
Dry Brush	Paints the edges of the image using a dry brush technique. The resultant output has less number of colours. You can change the Brush size, Brush Details and Texture to give the required effect.
Film Grain	Changes the shadow tones and midtones of an image. It adds a smooth, saturated pattern to the image's lighter areas. You can control the Grain size, highlight area and Intensity by moving the sliders.

Fresco Paints an image in a coarse style. It uses short, rounded, and hastily applied strokes. You can vary the Brush size and Brush details and add or remove texture from the image.

Neon Glow Adds various types of glows to the objects similar to the Neon Glow sign. It softens the look of the image. You can choose Glow Size and Glow brightness and to select a glow colour, click the glow box and select a colour from the colour picker.

Paint Daubs Paints the image using a various brush types. You can select the brush size and control its sharpness. You can also select the brush type from the predefined types, which include simple, light rough, light dark, wide sharp, wide blurry, and sparkle.

palette Knife Gives the impact as the painting has been done using the knife strokes. It reduces the details of the image. You can control the Stroke size, Stroke details and softness.

Plastic Wrap Gives the illusion as if the image has been wrapped in shiny plastic. You can control Highlight Strength, Details and Smoothness.

Poster Edges Lets you posterize the image by reducing the number of colours. Converts the edges in the image to black line. Large broad areas of the image have simple shading while fine dark detail is distributed throughout the image. You can select the Edge thickness and Edge Intensity and control the number of colours from Posterization.

Rough Pastels   Gives the impact as if the image is stroked with coloured pastel chalk on a textured background. You can control the Stroke length and Stroke details and select a texture from the texture drop down menu. You can also define the various options for the texture in texture area.

Smudge Stick   It softens an image using short diagonal strokes to smudge or smear the darker areas of the images. Lighter areas become brighter and lose detail, whereas the darker area becomes more prominent on the image.

Sponge   Converts the image with highly textured areas of contrasting colour, giving an impression as if it has been painted with a sponge.

Underpainting   Underpainting paints the image on a textured background, similar to Rough pastel. You can control the Brush Size and Texture Coverage and select a texture from the texture drop down menu. You can also define the various options for the texture in texture area.

Watercolour   Transforms your image into a watercolour painting, using a medium brush loaded with water and colour. You can specify the values for Brush detail, Shadow Intensity and Texture.

APPLYING BLUR EFFECTS

Blur filters change the pixels of your image to soften them, smooth their edges, blend them, or create motion effects. You can blur the entire image or select a part of image to apply the Blur effect..

Blur

Mutes the differences between adjacent pixels to smooth the image or image area without losing detail. It is especially useful for removing the dithering that is created when you convert a paletted image to the RGB colour model. The Blur More filter produces a more pronounced effect (about three to four times) than the Blur filter.

Motion Blur

The Motion Blur filter blurs your image so that it looks like a photograph of a moving object. You can specify the direction of movement using the Angle (from -360° to +360°) and intensity (from 1 to 999).

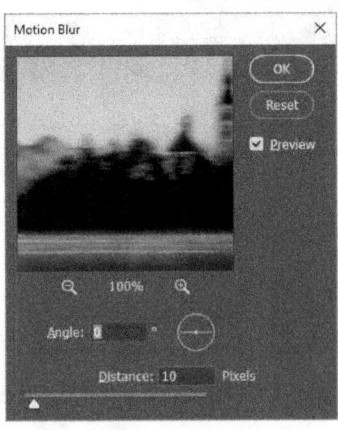

Fig 11.3 Blur Motion effect

Gaussian Blur	The Gaussian Blur filter produces a hazy effect, blurring the image according to a Gaussian distribution (a bell-shaped curve), which spreads the pixel information outward using bell-shaped curves.
Radial Blur	The Radial Blur filter gives your image a blurred effect that radiates out from the center point that you select. You can reposition a center point by clicking in Blur Centre box, set the intensity of the effect, choose a blur method , and set the quality of the output. In Blur Method, choose Spin, to blur along concentric circular lines, and then specify a degree of rotation; or Zoom, to blur along radial lines, as if zooming in or out of the image, and specify an amount from 1 to 100.

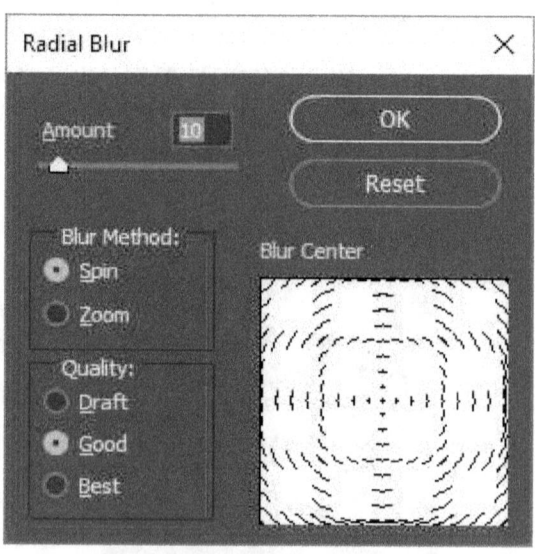

Fig 11.4 Radial Blur Effect

Smart Blur   It lets you specify a radius to precisely blurs an image. The radius value determines how far the filter searches for dissimilar pixels to blur and threshold determines how different the pixels' values should be before they are eliminated. You can also specify blur quality and mode for blur.

APPLYING BRUSH EFFECT

Similar to Artistic effects, Brush Strokes also applies various fine-art effects to the image. These filters can add grain, paint, noise, edge detail, or texture to an image for a pointillist effect.

Accented Edges   Emphasize the edges of an image. You can control the Edge width, Edge brightness and the Smoothness.

Angled Strokes   Quite similar to Coloured Pencil. Paints the image using diagonal strokes. The lighter areas and darker areas of the image are distinguished by painted strokes in different direction.

Crosshatch   Paints the image using coloured pencil hatching which adds texture and roughening the edges of the coloured areas. Provides the control in form of Stroke length, sharpness and Strength.

Dark Strokes   Converts the darker area to black using small tight strokes and lighter areas to white using the long strokes. You can control the White and Black areas by selecting the White Intensity and Black

Intensity respectively. Balance option lets you control the pixels to be included in darker area.

Ink Outlines   Redraws an image as if it has been drawn using the fine narrow ink lines. You can control Stroke Length, and Dark and Light Intensity.

Spatter   Gives the impact as if painting has been done using a spatter airbrush. Control the Spray Radius and Smoothness to vary the effect.

Fig 11.5 Spatter effect

Sprayed   It gives the combined effect of strokes and spray. You can specify the value for Stroke length and Spray Radius. You can also select the stroke direction from the drop down menu.

Sumi-e   It gives an impact as if painting has been done on bon rice paper with a wet brush full of black ink. It is a Japanese style, which gives lot of black with soft edges.

APPLYING DISTORT EFFECTS

PhotoShop provides twelve Distort effects that transform the appearance of an image without adding depth.

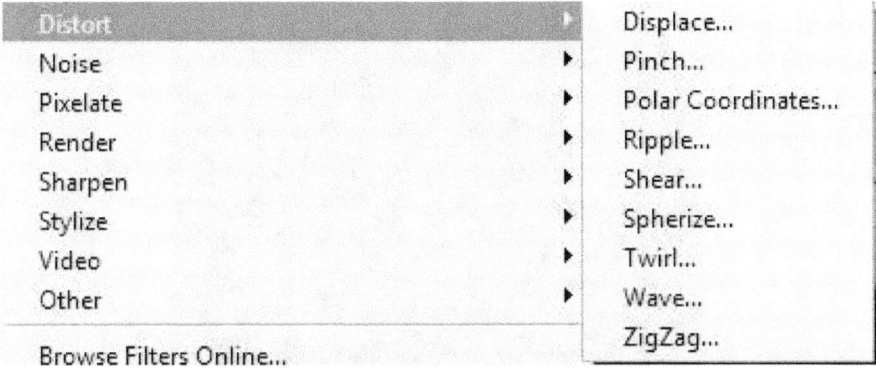

Fig 11.6 Distort options

The Distort effects are:

Diffuse Glow	Converts the image as though it were viewed through a soft diffusion filter. It add a white noise having fading glow from the centre.
Displace	The Displace filter evaluates the colour value of pixels in both images and then shifts the active image according to the values of

the displacement map. Values from the displacement map appear as forms, colours, and warp patterns in your image.

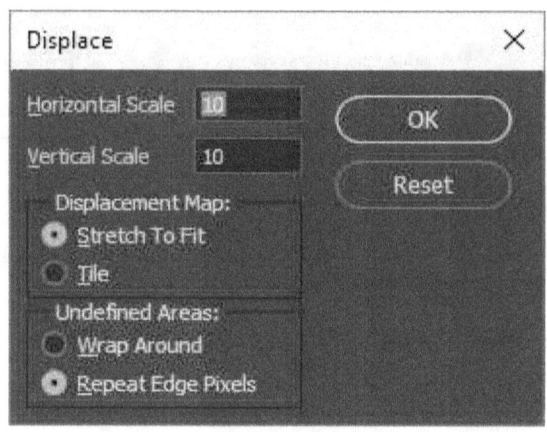

Fig 11.7 Displace dialog box

Glass	You can use the Glass filter to make your image look like it is being viewed through different types of glass. You can choose a glass effect or create your own glass surface as a Photoshop file and apply it. You can also select Distortion and Smoothness.
Ocean Ripple	Adds randomly spaced ripples to the image's surface, making the image look as if it were under water.
Pinch	This filter squeezes a selection or image either towards the centre (+ve value)or away from the centre (-ve value).
Polar Coordinates	This effect can be used to converts a selection from its rectangular to polar coordinates, and vice versa. It creates cylinder anamorphosis of the image - art popular in the 18th century. Such image, when

viewed through a cylindrical mirror, appears normal.

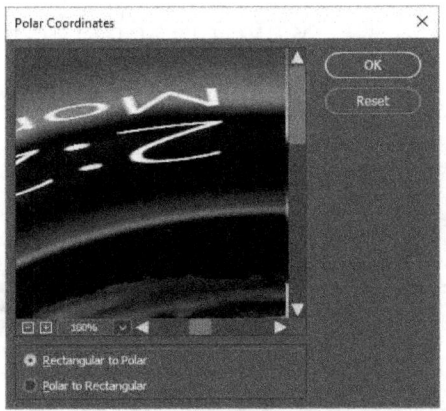

Fig 11.8 Converting from Rectangular to Polar

Ripple	The Ripple filter lets you distort your image by adding wave in the image.
Shear	This filter distorts an image along a curve. You can specify the curve using the flexible line in the box. Click on the curve to create more control points on the curve. Specify the curve by dragging the line in the box to form a curve for the distortion. You can adjust any point along the curve.
Spherize	Similar to Pinch effect but gives a 3D effect to the image by wrapping it around a spherical shape. You could either wrap outside the sphere (+ve value)or inside the sphere (-ve value).
Twirl	The Twirl filter creates a spiraling twirl across your image. You can set the direction and the degree of rotation of the Twirl.
Wave	It works in a similar way to the Ripple filter, but with greater

control. You can control the number of wave generators, the wavelength (distance from one wave crest to the next), the height of the wave, and the wave type.

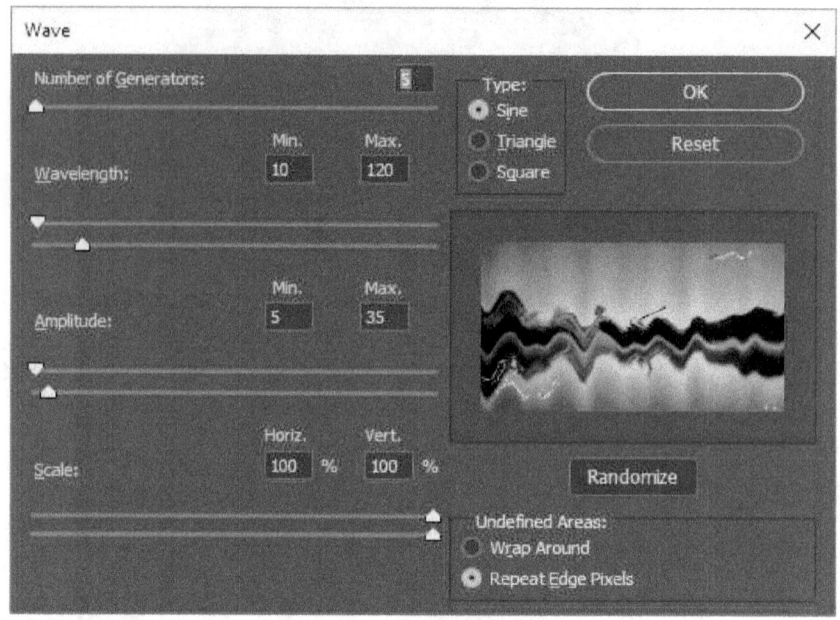

Fig 11.9 Wave Effect

ZigZag
It distorts the image radially. You can specify the Radius of the pixel and Ridges. You also choose how to displace the pixels, from the drop down menu - Pond Ripples, Out From Center or Around Center.

APPLYING NOISE EFFECTS

PhotoShop comes with different noise effects that create, control, and eliminate noise. Noise refers to the graininess of a bitmap, when random pixels on the surface of a bitmap resemble static on a television screen. These noise effects are:

Add Noise	Creates a granular effect that adds texture to a flat or overly blended bitmap
Despeckle	It blurs all of the image except the edges. This blur-ring removes noise while preserving detail.
Dust and Scratch	Reduces image noise by averaging pixel values
Median	Removes noise and detail by averaging the colour values of the pixels in an image.

APPLYING PIXELATE EFFECT

The Pixelate filters clump pixels of similar colour values in cells. It includes filters like Colour Halftone, Crystallize, Facet, Fragment, Mezzotint, Mosaic and Pointillize.

Colour Halftone	Use the Halftone filter to give your image the appearance of a colour halftone. A colour halftone is an image that has been converted from a continuous tone image to a series of dots of various sizes that represent different tones. You can adjust the screen angles to produce a wider range of colours.

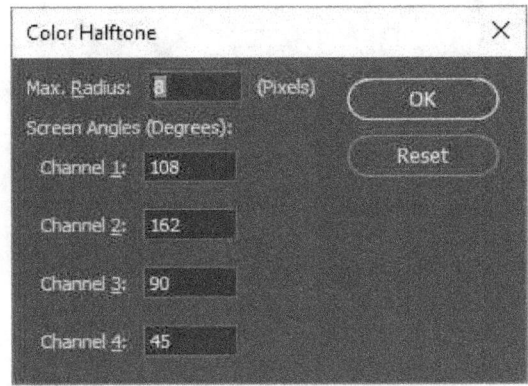

Fig 11.10 Applying Colour Halftone

Crystallize   You can crystallize your image using the Crystallize filter. Use the Cell Size slider to control the dimensions of the crystals. Higher values produce larger crystals and create a more abstract effect. Lower values produce smaller crystals, causing less distortion.

Facet   Clumps pixels of solid or similar colours into blocks of like-coloured pixels.

Fragment   Creates four copies of the pixels in the image, averages them, and offsets them from each other.

Mezzotint   Add random pattern of black, white or fully saturated colours in a colour image. Lets you select various type of Mezzotint from the drop down menu.

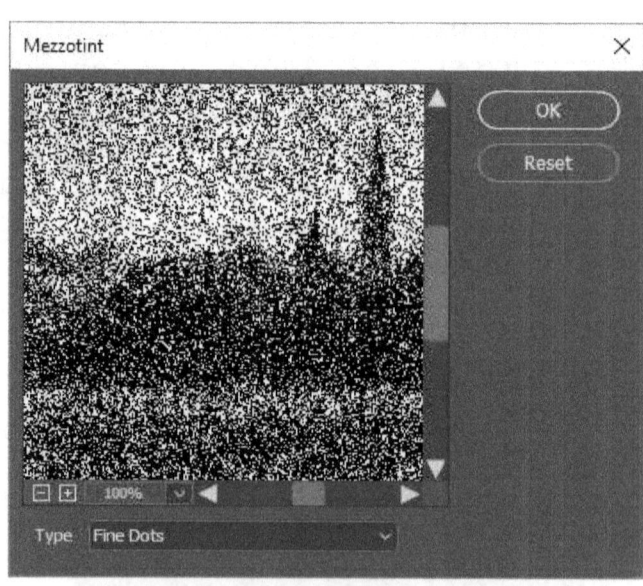

Fig 11.11 Mezzopoint effect

Mosaic   Use the Mosaic filter to divide your image into coloured pieces to form a mosaic artwork. You can

	select the Cell size of the pieces by moving the slider. Higher values produce larger size and create a more abstract effect. Lower values produce smaller size mosaic, causing less distortion.
Pointillize	Converts the image into randomly placed dots, as in a pointillist painting. The gap between the dots is filled with background colour.

APPLYING SHARPEN EFFECTS

Sharpen filters increase the contrast between the pixels in your image to improve the focus and enhance edges.

Sharpen	It improves the clarity of the image or the selection. The Sharpen More filter applies a stronger sharpening effect than does the Sharpen filter.
Unsharp Mask	It emphasize edge detail and focuses blurred areas in the image but does not remove low-frequency areas.

APPLYING SKETCH EFFECTS

PhotoShop provides 14 sketch effects. These effects transform images into a variety of textures. The filters also are useful for creating a fine-arts or hand-drawn look. Many of the Sketch filters use the foreground and background colour as they redraw the image.

Bas Relief	This filter transforms the image to appear carved out of background colour. The dark area on the image is carved out and appears in foreground colour, irrespective of colour of the image.

Chalk & Charcoal You can convert your image to a charcoal drawing using the this filter. Shadow areas are replaced with black diagonal charcoal lines. When you use this, coloured images are desaturated.

Chrome Converts the image as if it were a polished chrome surface. You can control the Details and smoothness of the converted Image.

Conté Crayon The Conté Crayon filter lets you texture your image using a conté crayon. The Dark are uses the foreground colour, whereas the light area uses the background colour. You can also control the crayon foreground level and background level to customize the granularity.

Graphic Pen This filter uses the fine graphic pen strokes to capture the details in the original image. The filter uses the foreground colour for the dark areas and background colours for the light areas.

Halftone Pattern Simulates the effect of a halftone screen while maintaining the continuous range of tones.

Note Paper Converts the image so as to look like made of handmade paper. The filter uses the foreground colour for the dark areas and background colours for the light areas. Select Image Balance for specifying dark areas and light areas.

Photocopy It gives the effect of photocopying an image in foreground colour.

Plaster
Converts the image as if it has been created using the plaster moulds. The image gives a 3D plaster look in foreground colour. The filter uses the foreground colour for the dark areas and background colours for the light areas. Select Image Balance for specifying dark areas and light areas.

Reticulation
This makes the image to look clumped in shadow areas and lightly grained in highlights.

Stamp
Simply converts the image to look as if it has been stamped with a rubber or wood stamp. The filter uses the foreground colour for the dark areas and background colours for the light areas. Select Light/Dark Balance for specifying dark areas and light areas.

Torn Edges
The filter reconstructs the image as ragged, torn pieces of paper, and then colourizes the image using the foreground and background colours. The filter uses the foreground colour for the dark areas and background colours for the light areas. Select Image Balance for specifying dark areas and light areas.

Water Paper
This filter uses blotchy daubs that appear painted onto fibrous, damp paper, causing the colours to flow and blend.

Fig 11.12 Water Paper effect

APPLYING STYLEZ EFFECT

The Stylize filters displaces the pixels and heightens the contrast in the image.

Diffuse

Diffuses the image to look less focused. Gives you the option to select Normal, Darken only and Lighten only mode.

Emboss

The Emboss filter transforms your image into a relief, making the details appear as ridges and crevices on a flat surface. You can control the embossing colour and depth as well as the direction of the light source. The Emboss filter works best on images with medium to high contrast.

Extrude

Gives a 3D texture to a selection or layer. Specify the options for Type, size and depth in the Extrude dialog box.

Find Edges

Finds the edges by identifying the areas of the image with significant transitions and emphasizes the edges.

Glowing Edges   Find the edges of colour and adds a neon-like glow to them.

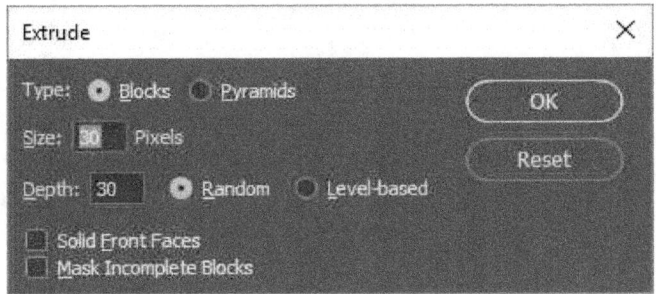

Fig 11.13 Extruding effect

Solarize   The Solarize filter makes your image look like a negative photographic image. You can apply the Solarize filter to the entire image or to part of it using a lens.

Tiles   The Tile filter reproduces your image as a series of tiles. The horizontal and vertical values that you set represent the number of images duplicated on each axis.

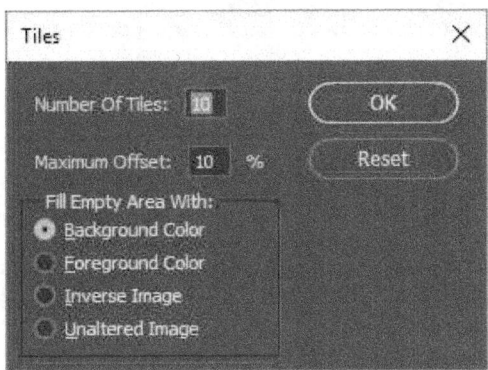

Fig 11.14 Tiles effect

Trace Contour   You can highlight the edges of the objects in an image using the Trace Contour filter. You can specify which pixels are highlighted by setting a threshold level. The threshold level is a brightness value that determines which pixels are affected by the Trace Contour filter.

Wind   The Wind filter blurs your image, creating the effect of wind blowing across your image. You can control the strength and direction of the wind.

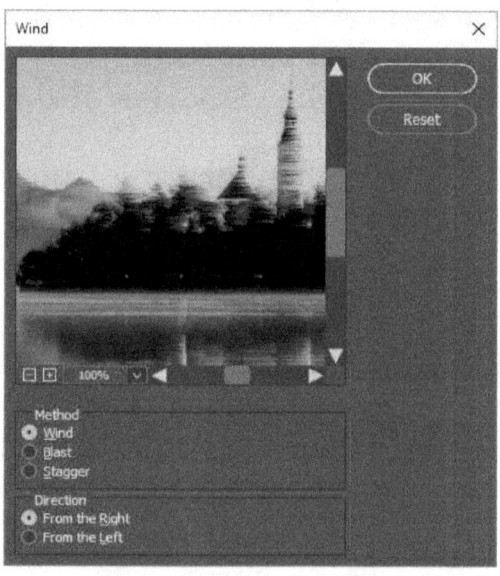

Fig 11.15 Wind effect

Applying Texture Effects

Texture special effects filters let you add texture to your image using a variety of shapes and surfaces.

Craquelure   Gives the impact as if the image has been painted on the wall and cracks has developed in the image. You can control the Crack spacing, depth and brightness.

Grain   Adds different type of grains - regular, soft, sprinkles, clumped, contrasty, enlarged, stippled, horizontal, vertical, and speckle to give the textured effect to the image.

Mosaic Tiles   Use the Mosaic filter to divide your image into coloured Chips and Tile pieces to form a mosaic artwork. You can select the size and grout width of the pieces. It also adds grout between the tiles.

Patchwork   It breaks up an image into squares filled with the predominant colour in that area of the image. It lets you control the square size and Relief.

Stained Glass   The Stained Glass filter breaks up your image into ornate polygonal pieces that resemble stained glass. You can create border between the glass pieces and control the thickness and colour of these edges.

Texturizer   Applies a texture you select or create to an image.

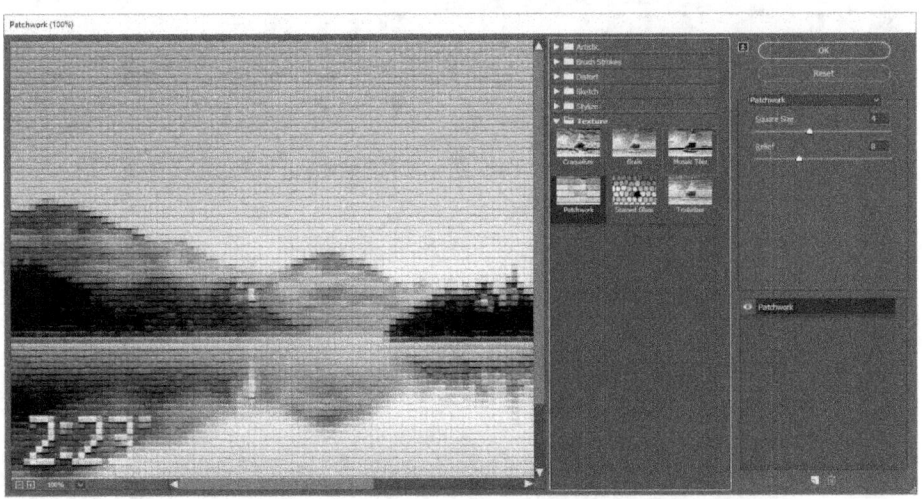

Fig 11.16 Patchwork effect

VIDEO EFFECTS

The Video submenu contains the De-Interlace and NTSC Colours filters. The De-Interlace filter smoothens the moving images captured on video by removing either the odd or even interlaced lines in a video image. The NTSC Colours filter removes those colours which are not acceptable for television reproduction.

OTHER FILTERS

The option defined in the submenu lets you define your own filters beside offering filters to modify masks, offset a selection within an image, and make quick colour adjustments.

Creating Custom Filter

To design your own filter, select the Filter ➤ Other ➤ Custom option to bring the Custom Filter dialog box.

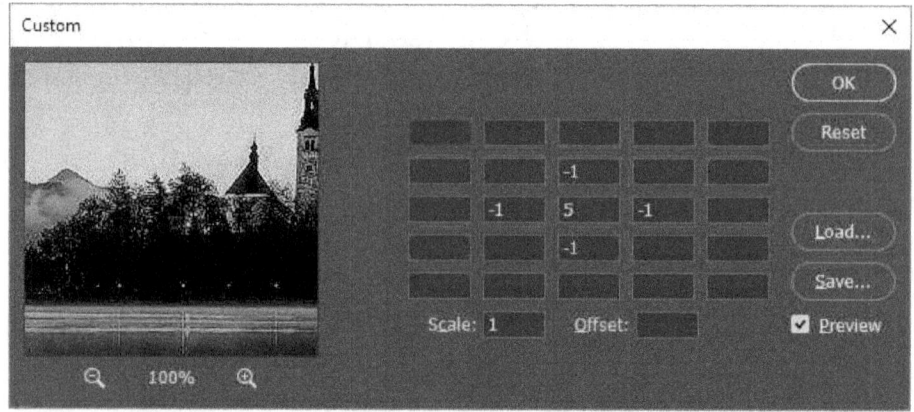

Fig 11.17 Creating Custom Filter

- In the dialog box, the centre box in the matrix represents the pixel being evaluated. Enter the value by which you want to multiply that pixel's brightness value, from -999 to +999.

- Now select the adjacent text box which represent an adjacent pixel. Enter the value by which you want the pixel in this position multiplied. Repeat the above steps to include more and more pixels in the operation.

- Enter the value for Scale and Offset. The scale value divides the sum of all the pixels included in the operation. The Offset value is added into the result to give the final value. Click Ok to apply the Filter.

OPTIMIZING & AUTOMATING TASK
SAVING FOR WEB
SLICES
SAVING IMAGES
AUTOMATING TASK - APPLYING ACTION
THE ACTION PALETTE

OPTIMIZING & AUTOMATING TASK

Optimization is the process of fine- tuning the display quality and file size of an image for use on the Web or other online media. Photoshop offers various formats, in which you can save the image. If you want a higher quality of image to be stored, you can't compromise on space. And if you have to reduce the size of the file, you have to compromise with the quality. In Web, the later option holds good as we can't afford a bigger size, but at the same time, we have to have a good quality also. Thus, you have to make a fine balance between quality and size.

The dimensions of the image plays a crucial role in such a case. If you save the image in bigger dimension, whereas your requirement is of a smaller dimensions, then you can reduce the dimensions of the image in the web page, but that will not reduce the image size. On the other hand, if you store the image in smaller dimensions, then the size will remain small, but in increasing the dimension, you will lose the clarity in the picture.

SAVING FOR WEB

As we discussed above that you have to make a fine balance between the image size and dimension. Photoshop offers Save for Web option to optimize the file in such a way that it neither looses the clarity nor is heavy in size.

But before we move ahead, you must understand the concept of slicing.

SLICES

If you image size is quite big, you can't save the image as a whole, as it's size will be big, which will take more time in downloading on web. In such situations, you can cut the image into slices and save each slice as an independent file that contains its own settings, colour palette, links, rollover effects, and animation effects.

This will help you achieving faster download speed. Another advantage of slicing is that you can work with different type of data in the same image i.e., if you want a little animation in you whole image, you needn't to save the whole image in GIF format. You can save only a small slice in GIF format and rest of the image can be stored in JPEG format. This will save you lot of space and downloading will also be faster.

Defining Slices

To create a slice with the slice tool, select the slice tool. Any existing slices automatically display in the document window. Now select a slice option in the Option bar from the drop down menu. The options offered are - Normal, Constrained Aspect Ratio and Fixed size.

Fig 12.1 Crop flyout with Slice options

- Now drag over the area in the image, where you want to have a slice. Hold down Shift key to slice a square.

- You can also add the Layer based Slice by selecting the layer and choosing the option Layer ➢ New Layer Based Slice.

- To resize the slices, select the Slice select tool and click on the slice to resize. This brings the handles on the slice. If you click on the Layer Based Slice, no handles will appear. To resize the Layer based slice, you must convert the slice into User Slice. To do so, you can click on the Promote to user slice button or select the same option from the right click menu of slice. Now, the handles will appear on the layer based slice also.

- To resize, move your pointer to any one of the handle to convert it into double headed arrow and drag it in required direction.

SAVING IMAGES

Once all the image is divided into slices, you are ready to save the slices of the Image as a whole. To save any image for Web, select Layer ➢ Export ➢ Save for Web to bring the dialog box.

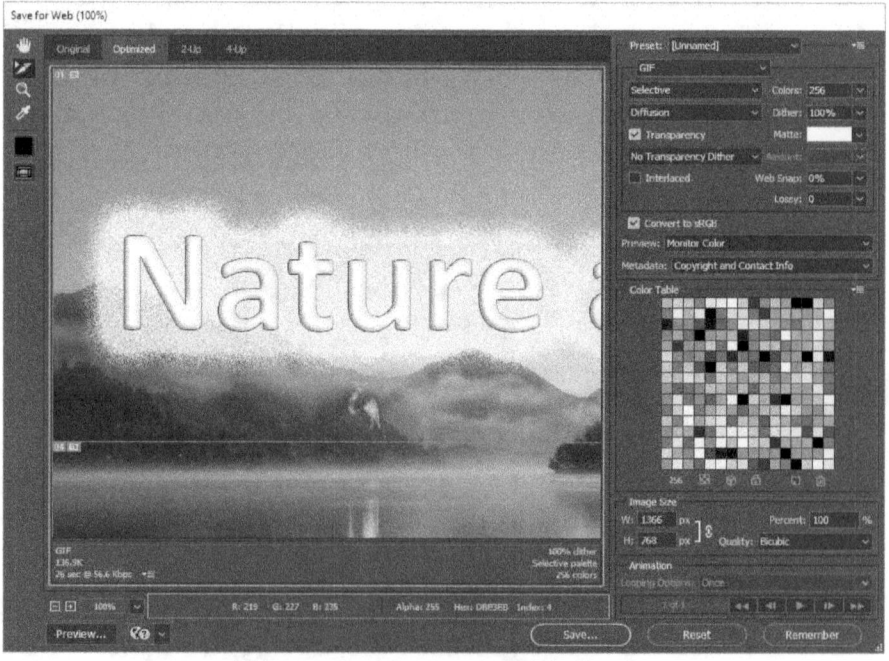

Fig 12.2 Saving for Web

The dialog box lets you select various options that are considered good for Web. It not only offers you many predefined options, but also lets you define your own settings and save them for future use.

Also these setting could be same for all the slice or different for different slice as per your requirement. To select any one slice, click on the Slice Select tool in the

Save for Web dialog box and click on the slice to be selected. To select more than one slice, hold down the shift key and click on the slices you want to select. The selected slices becomes a bit darker as compared to unselected slices.

You must remember that if you have specified slices before saving, the images will be saved in sliced form only i.e. all the slices will be saved in different files which will have a common name followed by slice number.

To view the various optimized form of your image, you can select Optimized, 2-up or 4-up tab. These tabs displays you the original image, and the optimized image at different parameters. The Optimized forms displays the file format, dither value, size of the file, type of colour palette used, time taken by modem to download at specified internet speed and number of colours used.

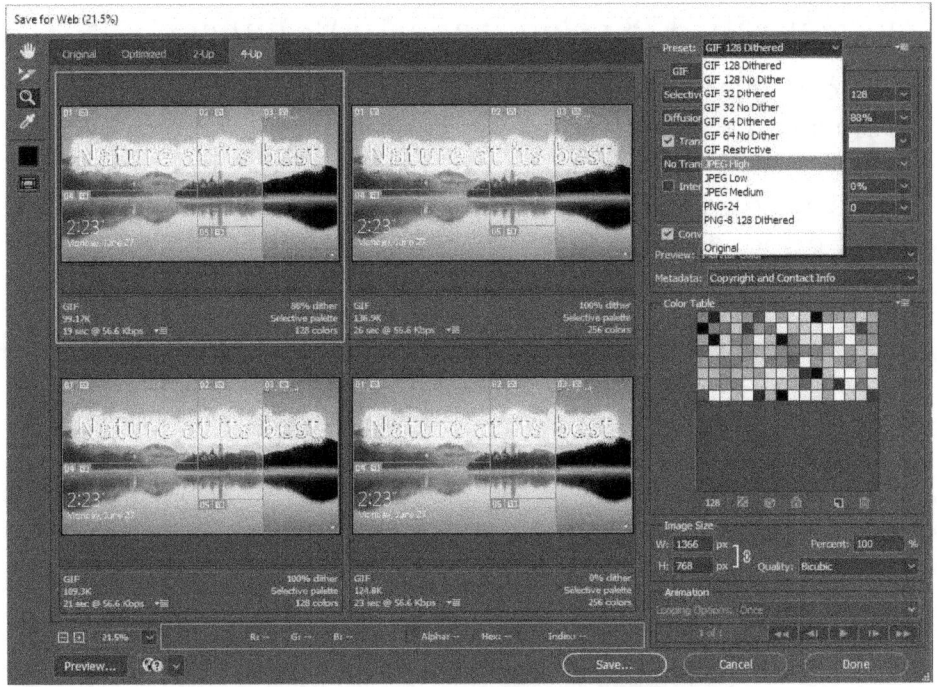

Fig 12.3 Various options for web saving

To have the views with different setting in 4-up tab, select the Repopulate views option from the Setting palette menu.

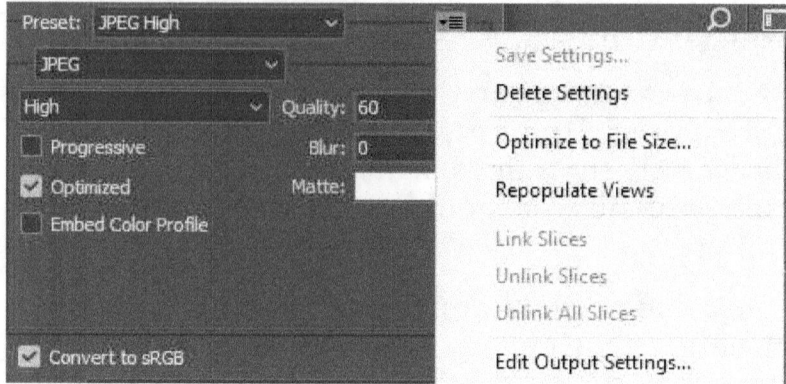

Fig 12.4 Setting palette

You can select any of the options displayed in the dialog box or select any other option available in Setting drop down menu. These option specifies the format name, number of colours used, and dither / No dither option i.e. GIF128 dither option refers to GIF format with 128 colours and 100% dither.

If you select any option from the Setting menu, the related data is displayed in the various boxes in the setting palette. You can customize the selected option to suit you need. These options in Setting palettes lets you choose the following parameters :

- File format
- Reduction Algorithm
- Dithering Algorithm
- Amount of Lossiness in GIF compression
- Maximum number of Colours in Colour table
- Dither pattern to reduce banding
- Tranparency based on colour opacity
- Colour to blend transparent pixel against
- Colours to Web palette based on tolerance

Below the setting palette, the dialog box displays two other palettes, Colour table palette and Image size palette.

Colour Table palette

The Colour Table palette displays the selected colours for saving the Image. It gives the option to view the colours according to various properties of colours. It also lets you add new colours and delete the existing colours.

Image Size palette

The Image size palette displays the width and height of the original image and gives the option to increase or decrease the size as per requirement. Select the Constrain Proportions option to have the constant width to height ratio.

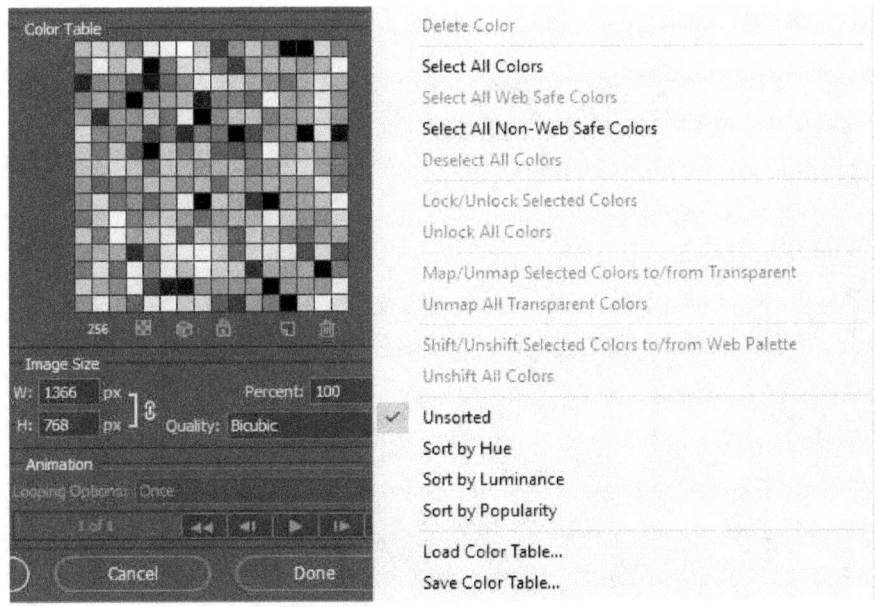

Fig 12.5 Colour Table option

You can also select the Quality from the quality drop down menu.

After satisfying yourself with the size and the file format properties, you can click OK.

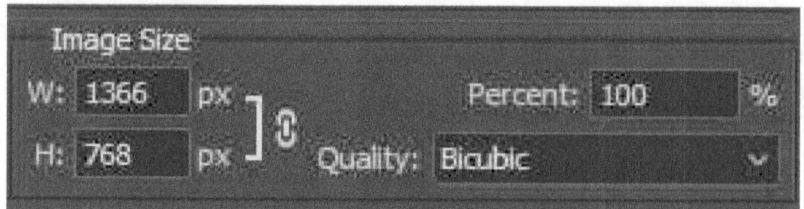

Fig 12.6 Image size option

Photoshop asks you to define the name of the file. Specify the name of the file in the Save As dialog box and your file is saved. If you have defined slices, the file is saved in parts and various slice portions of the file are automatically named. Fig 12.7 displays the thumbnails of files saved using slice. The file was named as Slice and its various slice portions with extension _01, _02, _3, _04, _05 and _06 were created automatically.

Fig 12.7 various parts of the sliced image

AUTOMATING TASK - APPLYING ACTION

PhotoShop lets you use recordings to automate a series of actions that you want to repeat on the same image or on several images. In Photoshop, it is called action. An action is a series of commands that you record using the controls in the Actions palette. You can also save the actions for future use and play them on any image. Photoshop also offers predefined actions which you can load through the action palette and run them on your applications.

Actions can save time when you are performing many standard operations, including resampling images, selecting image areas, and making global adjustments. For example, if you scan a series of photographs into Photoshop and discover that they are all too small and underexposed, you can resample and adjust the images to increase their size and brightness. If you record the resampling and adjustment operations as you apply them to the first photograph, you can then replay the actions on all the other photographs to repair their problems simultaneously.

You can create, edit, and play actions using the controls in the Action palette.

THE ACTION PALETTE

You use the Actions palette to record, play, edit, and delete individual actions. This palette also lets you save and load action files.

To display the Actions palette, select Window ➤ Show Actions, or click the Actions palette tab if the palette is visible but not active.

The Action palette displays various predefined actions, which gives wonderful effects to your image. The Fig 12.8 displays the actions of Image effects.atn file and one of the action "Obsidian" has been applied to the image. To display all the operations included in the action, click on the expand button to convert it into button. All the operation included in the action are displayed.

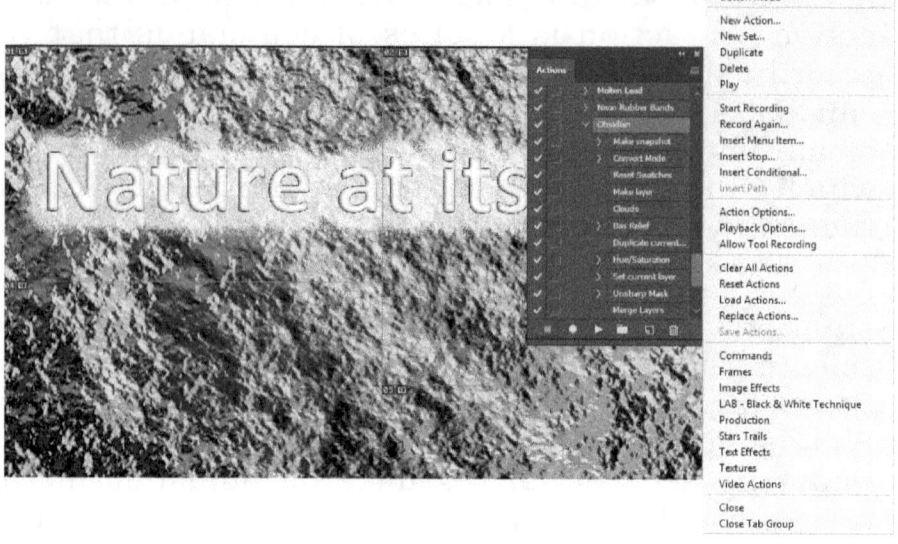

Fig 12.8 Action palette

Creating an Action

You can record most of your keyboard, toolbar, Toolbox, menu, and mouse operations. As you record the action, the operations are translated into command statements that appear one below the other in order of their occurrence. These command statements are displayed in the same format as those found in the History palette. These commands also displays the main parameters used by them. You can view the parameters by clicking on the expand button to convert it into button. All the parameters of the command are displayed.

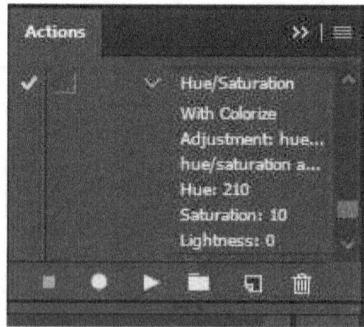

Fig 12.9 The Action palette displaying parameters

To create a new action, you must select a set in which you want to create an action. You can also create a new set in which you will create the actions. To create a new set, click on the Create new set button on the Action palette to bring the New Set dialog box.

Fig 12.10 Creating New Set

Now, select this newly created set and click on the New action button to bring the New Action dialog box.

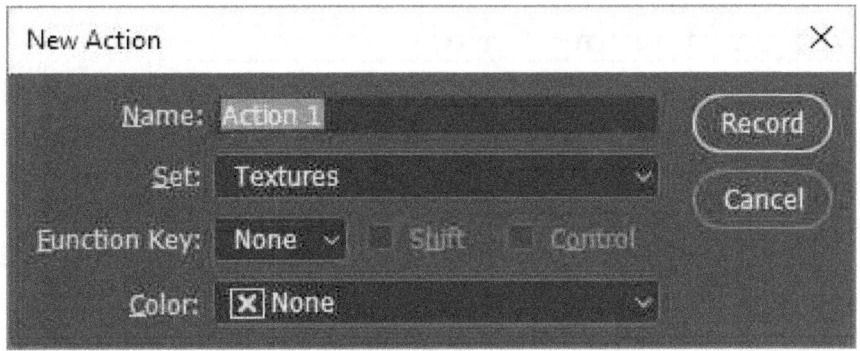

Fig 12.11 Creating New action

Specify the set and Function key for the action. The new action is created with recording button in On mode. Now, perform the operations you want to record. Every operation is recorded under the action. When you are done, click on the Stop recording button.

Playing Action

To play an action on a file, open the file and click on the Play action button at the bottom of the palette or choose Play from the palette menu. To play part of an action, select the command from which you want to start playing, and click the Play button in the Actions palette, or choose Play from the palette menu. To play a single command in an action, select the command you want to play and Ctrl-click in Actions palette.

Rearranging Actions

You can also rearrange the actions or operations in the action. To rearrange the actions or operations, select the action or operation you want to rearrange and drag it to the new position. You can also move the actions or operations to another set but you can't move the operation to another action.

Deleting Actions

To delete an action or command, select the action or command you want to delete and click on the trash button.

Loading and Saving Actions

You can append as many actions as you want in the Action palette. Photoshop also provides various action libraries as shown in Fig 12.8. You can also define your own set of libraries which you can load into Action palette.

To load a predefined action set into Action palette,

- Select the library from the list in Action palette menu or select the option Load Action from the menu to select *.ATN files.

- As you select the file, Photoshop appends the selected library into Action palette.

To save the action, select the Action set you want to save and click Save Action option to save the new set of actions as a library.

Select the other options from the Action palette menu, shown in Fig 12.8), as described below:

- Select Reset Actions option to load the default actions.

- Select Replace Actions option to replace the current action set with actions stored in a file.

- Select Rename Action option to change the name of the selected action set.

- Select the option from Text only, Thumbnails or list to change the view of the brush palette.

- Select the button mode option to convert all the actions as buttons in the Action palette. In button mode, click on the required action button to play it.

www.ingramcontent.com/pod-product-compliance
Lightning Source LLC
Chambersburg PA
CBHW051759170526
45167CB00005B/1806